GROUNDED DESIGNS FOR
ONLINE AND HYBRID LEARNING

ONLINE AND HYBRID LEARNING DESIGNS IN ACTION

EDITED BY ATSUSI "2C" HIRUMI

International Society for Technology in Education

EUGENE, OREGON • WASHINGTON, DC

Grounded Designs for Online and Hybrid Learning Series
Online and Hybrid Learning Designs in Action
Edited by Atsusi "2C" Hirumi

© 2014 International Society for Technology in Education

Production Editor: *Lynda Gansel*
Production Coordinator: *Emily Reed*
Copy Editor: *Kathy Hamman*
Proofreader: *Ann Skaugset*
Indexer: *Wendy Allex*
Cover Design: *Tamra Holmes*
Book Design and Production: *Kim McGovern*

Library of Congress Cataloging-in-Publication Data

Online and hybrid learning designs in action / edited by Atsusi "2C" Hirumi.
    pages cm. — (Grounded designs for online and hybrid learning series)
    Includes bibliographical references and index.
    ISBN 978-1-56484-336-4 (pbk. : alk. paper)
    1. Blended learning. 2. Computer-assisted instruction. 3. Educational technology.
    4. Distance education.   I. Hirumi, Atsusi editor of compilation.
    LB1028.3.O5515 2014
    371.3—dc23

                                                                2013039903

First Edition
ISBN: 978-1-56484-336-4 (paperback)
ISBN: 978-1-56484-486-6 (e-book)

Printed in the United States of America

Cover Art: © fotolia.com/radoma

ISTE® is a registered trademark of the International Society for Technology in Education.

About ISTE

The International Society for Technology in Education is the premier membership association for educators and education leaders committed to empowering connected learners in a connected world. Home to the ISTE Conference and Expo and the widely adopted ISTE Standards for learning, teaching, and leading in the digital age, the association represents more than 100,000 professionals worldwide.

We support our members with professional development, networking opportunities, advocacy, and ed tech resources to help advance the transformation of education. To find out more about these and other ISTE initiatives, visit iste.org.

As part of our mission, ISTE works with experienced educators to develop and publish practical resources for classroom teachers, teacher educators and technology leaders. Every manuscript we select for publication is carefully peer reviewed and professionally edited.

About the Editor and Authors

Editor and contributor **Atsusi "2c" Hirumi** is an associate professor in the Instructional Design and Technology program at the University of Central Florida (UCF). Born in New York, Hirumi spent most of his formative years growing up in Nairobi, Kenya, where he went to middle school and high school at the International School of Kenya. He earned a bachelor's degree in science education at Purdue University, a master's degree in educational technology at San Diego State University, and a doctorate in instructional systems at Florida State University. He earned tenure and promotion to associate professor at the University of Houston–Clear Lake before moving to the University of Central Florida in 2003.

Since 1995, Hirumi has centered his teaching, research, and service on the design of online and hybrid learning environments. At UHCL and UCF, Hirumi led efforts to transform entire certificate and master's degree programs in Instructional Design & Technology for totally online and hybrid course delivery. He has also worked with universities, community colleges, K–12 school districts, medical centers, and the military across North America, South America, and the Middle East to establish online and hybrid training programs, courses, and degree programs. For the past five years, Hirumi has focused his research and development on using story, play, and games to evoke emotions and spark the imagination to enhance experiential learning. He is currently working with colleagues to examine the neurobiological foundations for experiential learning and to develop, test, and refine the Inter*PLAY* instructional theory to guide the design of experiential learning landscapes.

Based on his work, Hirumi has published 28 refereed journal articles, 16 book chapters, and has made more than 100 presentations at international, national, and state conferences on related topics. He also recently edited the book *Playing Games in Schools: Video Games and Simulations for Primary and Secondary Education* published by ISTE. Awards include the Army Training dL Maverick Award for leadership in distance learning, the Texas Distance Learning Association award for Commitment to Excellence and Innovation, the WebCT Exemplary Online Course Award, the University of Houston-Clear Lake Star Faculty Award, the Phi Delta Kappa Outstanding Practitioner Award, the ENRON Award for Innovation, and a second place Award for Excellence for an electronic performance support system designed to help faculty develop and deliver interactive television courses.

Dedication

This book is dedicated to my best friend and love—Karen Bloom. Thank you for bringing true love, meaning, and joy into my life. Your caring and kindness to all those around you inspire me every day. I hope I make you as happy as you make me. Your Guy J.

Chapter Authors

Leanna Archambault is an assistant professor of educational technology at Arizona State University. Her areas of research include K–12 teacher preparation and development for online, hybrid, and blended settings; virtual gaming environments; the use of innovative technologies in education; and the nature of technological pedagogical content knowledge (TPACK).

Kent J. Crippen is an associate professor of STEM education at the University of Florida. His research includes the design, development, and evaluation of cyberlearning environments for STEM education as well as in-service teacher professional development.

Janet Daugherty earned a bachelor of arts degree from Smith College and earned an MBA in marketing and finance from Columbia University. She served as an assistant professor of marketing at Seton Hall; adjunct at American University's management and marketing departments; visiting instructor and researcher at Hong Kong University; and visiting instructor in management at the University of Central Florida's College of Business Administration. Daugherty is pursuing a doctorate in education; her research interests include global teaching and training with 21st-century skills and higher education policy.

Natalie Dopson is an assistant professor in foundations and social advocacy at the State University of New York in Cortland. She teaches principles of inclusive education, assessment and instruction of learners with special needs, and perspectives on disabilities: child, family, school, and community. She worked as a bilingual school psychologist for Seminole County Public Schools in Florida for three years. Dopson has experience serving and collaborating with parents, teachers, and children in preschool through high school. She is also a consultant, providing professional development workshops for teachers and parents in Head Start preschools. Her research interests include best practices for children with disabilities, collaboration with families from culturally and linguistically diverse backgrounds, family literacy, and infusing technology to enhance community building and learning environments.

Abigail Hawkins is a senior manager for instructional design at TD Ameritrade's Investools. She designs and develops investor education for face-to-face, virtual, and hybrid learning experiences. She was previously a senior instructional designer with Adobe Systems. Her research interests include blended learning, K–12 online learning, and learning analytics. In 2011, she completed a doctorate in instructional psychology and technology from Brigham Young University (Dissertation title: "We're Definitely on Our Own": Interaction and Disconnection in a Virtual High School). Hawkins also earned a master's degree in the same field from Indiana University. She has written several articles and book chapters on K–12 online learning.

Cindy Kern is an assistant professor of science education in the Department of Education at the University of New Haven, Connecticut, where she teaches secondary science strategies and elementary science strategies. Kern is a former science teacher and a graduate of the College of Education at the University of Nevada, Las Vegas. In 2010, she was recognized with the Presidential Award for Excellence in Mathematics and Science Teaching.

Yana Keyzerman earned a bachelor of arts degree in English literature and a master's degree in technical communication from the University of Central Florida. She is working as an instructional designer and taking classes toward a certificate in instructional design for simulations. Keyzerman has also taught English composition and worked as a writer and editor in various disciplines, including educational publishing, advertising, fiction, and professional and academic writing.

Matthew Laurence is a game economy designer at CrowdStar, where, in addition to developing gameplay mechanics, characters, story, and scripts, he designs and balances digital economies. He served as lead designer at 360Ed, an Orlando-based studio focused on educational games, social networks, and simulations. Dedicated to creating truly compelling games, Laurence believes that the ultimate goal of a product, whether for education or entertainment, has no bearing on how much "fun" it can be and that the key to success lies in kindling a spark of engagement in the user. He holds a bachelor of arts degree in psychology from New College of Florida and a master's degree in interactive entertainment from Florida Interactive Entertainment Academy, a division of the University of Central Florida.

Naomi Malone is a doctoral student at the University of Central Florida in the College of Education's Department of Educational and Human Science. She works as research assistant at UCF's Institute for Simulation & Training RAPTER (Research in Advanced Performance Technology and Educational Readiness) Labs to identify strategies that can train military personnel efficiently. Recent projects include a large-scale multidisciplinary review of literature that identified and organized instructional strategies for utilization in a variety of domains. Her current project involves researching instructional strategies that can be applied in adaptive learning systems. Malone's area of research interest is the design of virtual problem-based learning environments and simulations for ill-structured problem solving.

Kendra Minor is a doctoral candidate in instructional technology, College of Education at the University of Central Florida. She has experience designing interactive multimedia instruction, simulations, instructor-led training, self-paced e-learning courses, and virtual classrooms/seminars. She works at UCF's Center for Research in Education, Arts, Technology and Entertainment, where she helps facilitate professional development for K–12 teachers, focusing on the integration of digital media and educational technology into teaching and learning. Minor's research interests include instructional design and development, technology integration, virtual learning communities, K–12 virtual schooling, service learning in urban communities, and digital storytelling.

Kelley K. Rogers is an English teacher at Colonial High School in Orlando, Florida, and a graduate student in the College of Education at the University of Central Florida. In addition to teaching, she has spent the past three years writing curriculum, instruction, and assessment plans for Orange County Public Schools, as well as co-authoring two writing resource guides for middle school teachers.

Christopher Stapleton has applied his expertise and experience in design for entertainment toward developing transformative, lifelong learning experiences for the next generation. As a principal creator for global entertainment firms, such as Universal Studios, Nickelodeon, Paramount, MGM, Disney, and Sanrio, he has created major projects that entertain a great number of people from around the world. As a leading pioneer of mixed and augmented reality, Stapleton has invented several models and theories of providing viable innovative experiential media solutions for academic, civic, and commercial applications. As a creative venture catalyst at Simiosys Real World Collaboratory, he has launched commercial solutions that span educational, training, and entertainment sectors. He received a master's degree and a bachelor of fine arts degree from New York University's Tisch School of the Arts for design of theater and cinematic arts.

Scott M. Waring is an associate professor and program coordinator for the Social Science Education Program at the University of Central Florida. He teaches courses at the undergraduate and graduate levels in elementary and secondary social science education methodology, research, and theory, and is the director of the Library of Congress's Teaching with Primary Sources program at the University of Central Florida. Waring has written or co-written funded grants, including a Teaching with Primary Sources grant from the Library of Congress and three Teaching American History (TAH) grants. He earned a bachelor's degree and a master's degree in education from the University of South Florida and a doctorate from the University of Virginia in social studies education, with a minor in instructional technology. He has published a book and numerous journal articles and book chapters focusing on the teaching and learning of history and the utilization of technology in social studies education.

Shelly Wyatt is a doctoral candidate at the University of Central Florida in Orlando, Florida, and is professor of humanities at DeVry University. She teaches art history, ethics, and history; serves as national humanities curriculum co-chair; and develops online instructional materials for DeVry University. She worked as a project editor at the American Psychological Association, managing the reference series *Law and Mental Health Professionals* and developing single book titles. Wyatt's research interests include mobile learning and the use of social networks to enhance and supplement course content.

Contents

Chapter 8
Applying Game and Brain-Based Learning Principles to Enhance e-Learning and Education

Appendix
ISTE's National Educational Technology Standards

Index

Introduction

Atsusi "2c" Hirumi

Designing innovative, student-centered online or hybrid learning environments can be difficult, particularly if you haven't experienced one yourself. Many of you may have taken (or designed your own) online or hybrid courses or training programs. But have you ever taken a course or module that was truly learner-centered? Have you experienced online or hybrid environments that were based on a variety of learning theories and instructional strategies?

Over the past 10 to 15 years, I've had the privilege of working with hundreds of students, educators, and designers from across the United States and abroad to design e-learning programs for K–12 and higher education, as well as for business and industry. During these experiences, I've found that fewer than 10% of the people I've worked with have taken a problem-, case-, or inquiry-based online course, and even fewer have designed or delivered a totally online or hybrid course based on different learning theories or instructional strategies. If educators and instructional designers would like to or are expected to create innovative e-learning environments, they need concrete examples to facilitate their efforts. Of all the tools and techniques that I've prepared for class and used in presentations and workshops on designing online and hybrid learning environments, participants ask for examples of innovative, online, student-centered coursework more than any other resource. This book, *Online and Hybrid Learning Designs in Action,* compiles such examples.

Grounded Designs for Online and Hybrid Learning Series

The book you're holding is the second in a three-book series. The first book in the series, *Online and Hybrid Learning Design Fundamentals,* covers basic tasks associated with the systematic design of online and hybrid learning environments. It emphasizes the importance of and illustrates methods for aligning learner assessments to learning objectives, and it presents a framework for designing and sequencing meaningful e-learning interactions. The first book also provides tactics for searching vast repositories of existing, sharable content objects and compares Web 2.0 to prior technologies to facilitate the delivery of your course. In addition, the book discusses practical tools for preparing students for successful online learning and interprets laws and provides examples of how online instruction should be universally designed for children with special needs. The series' first book concludes by discussing how e-learning may be designed and delivered to meet ISTE's NETS for teachers and students and to follow quality guidelines for distance learning.

This second book in the series, *Online and Hybrid Learning Designs in Action,* presents examples of how to apply a range of instructional strategies that are grounded in cognitive information processing, as well as inquiry, experiential, and game-based theories of human learning. This book begins with two instructional strategies that may be relatively familiar to you. In Chapter 1, Abigail Hawkins shows us how to apply Gagné's nine events of instruction to design a totally online and a hybrid lesson. In Chapter 2, Kelley Rogers illustrates how WebQuests utilize existing web resources to implement inquiry-based learning. Continuing with inquiry-based pedagogies, Shelly Wyatt, Natalie Dopson, Yana Keyzerman, and Janet Daugherty exemplify the application of the 5E Instructional Model to develop e-learning in Chapter 3. Then, in Chapter 4, Kent Crippen, Leanna Archambault, and Cindy Kern depict the use of VeeMaps to scaffold e-learning, based on the processes and products of scientific investigations. For Chapter 5, Scott Waring proposes the use of authentic historical investigations that combine inquiry-based and experiential theories of learning to teach students how to search for and interpret primary sources of evidence to explain historical events from multiple perspectives. The next two chapters then focus on two different applications of experiential learning theory. In Chapter 6, Naomi Malone and Kendra Minor illustrate how guided experiential learning uses expert demonstrations to help students learn from authentic experiences. In Chapter 7, Christopher Stapleton and I explain how the Inter*PLAY* instructional strategy integrates key conventions of interactive entertainment (i.e., stories, play, and games) with experiential learning principles to engage learners and promote e-learning. To conclude this book, Matthew Laurence, in Chapter 8, continues with the notion of using concepts from the entertainment industry to design game-like environments that are grounded in brain-based learning principles.

The third and final book in the series, *Online and Hybrid Learning Trends and Technologies,* looks further into several key areas that I've found of interest and value for designing online or hybrid learning environments. Like the first two books, the chapters in this volume also focus on instructional components of an e-learning system; however, these authors look at overarching e-learning trends and technologies, such as managing large classes, creating podcasts, using virtual worlds in education, and developing virtual schools in North America and around the world.

All three books are written for K–12 educators, including teachers, education coaches, and administrators, as well as instructional designers who may be creating educational materials for K–12 online and hybrid courses. However, if you teach in a college or university setting or design educational and training materials for higher education or business and industry, I think you'll find that the fundamental principles, processes, and examples covered in these books offer insights and apply to design of e-learning environments across settings.

The three books in the series are based on three basic premises. To increase quality (reduce variance) and design effective, efficient, and engaging online and hybrid courses, we should (1) ground the designs of our coursework on research and theory; (2) follow a systematic design process to align basic elements of instruction (namely, objectives, assessments, and instructional strategy); and (3) think and, whenever possible, act systemically to ensure that all necessary components of the educational system are aligned and work together to facilitate e-learning.

This volume, *Online and Hybrid Learning Designs in Action,* serves as the heart of the three-book series, Grounded Designs for Online and Hybrid Learning. It illustrates how you can apply an assortment of instructional strategies, grounded in research and theory, to create an effective array of online and hybrid learning environments. While most strategies in this book depict learner-centered approaches to teaching and learning, teacher-directed strategies are also included so that you can compare methods and determine which approach is more appropriate for you to use, depending on your students and your desired learning outcomes (as discussed in the first book in the series, *Online and Hybrid Learning Design Fundamentals*).

Grounded Design

Grounded design is defined as "the systematic implementation of processes and procedures that are rooted in established theory and research in human learning" (Hannafin, Hannafin, & Land, 1997, p. 102). Grounded design articulates and aligns theory with practice for the purpose of optimizing learning. Regardless of your underlying educational values and beliefs, grounded design provides a procedure that you can use in a variety of settings.

To facilitate the process of aligning theory with practice, Hannafin et al. (1997) posit four criteria for grounded design:

1. The application of a defensible theoretical framework clearly distinguishable from other perspectives,

2. The use of methods that are consistent with the outcomes of the research conducted,

3. The ability to generalize beyond one particular instructional setting or problem, and

4. Iterative validation through successive implementations.

Using these criteria gives you a solid foundation for designing coursework, as well as for improving your methods and materials over time. However, grounding the design of your lessons and courses does not necessarily guarantee that your students will achieve targeted outcomes in an effective and efficient manner. A number of tasks must be completed before and after you design your course to facilitate e-learning.

Systematic Design

To create an online or hybrid course, you may or may not follow a systematic design process. Those who use a systematic process utilize the results of one task as input for subsequent tasks to link them sequentially. For instance, an educator or instructional designer following a systematic process may use (1) analyses to identify essential skills and knowledge; (2) the skills and knowledge to generate, cluster, and sequence objectives; (3) the objectives to define and align learner assessments; (4) the objectives and assessments to formulate an instructional strategy; and (5) the strategy to select tools and technologies for facilitating achievement of the objectives.

Systematic design is vital for a number of reasons:

- ▶ **It provides clear linkages between design tasks.** The resulting alignment of instructional objectives, strategies, and assessments is essential for facilitating learning in online, hybrid, and conventional classroom learning environments.

- ▶ **It begins with an analysis of the target learners and desired learning outcomes.** Such analyses are necessary for proper planning and decision making. Without it, key instructional components may be missing or misaligned.

- ▶ **It is based on a combination of practical experience, theory, and research.** Key design decisions are informed by what is known about human learning, instruction, and emerging technologies to avoid haphazard investments in unsubstantiated fads or opinions.

- ▶ **It is empirical and replicable.** To increase return on investment, instruction is designed to be used more than once with as many learners as possible. The costs associated with systematic design are worth the investment because the resulting materials are reusable.

- ▶ **It is generalizable across delivery systems.** The resulting materials may be used to support the delivery of instruction in conventional, hybrid, and totally online learning environments.

A number of limitations are also associated with systematic design. For instance, systematic design takes time and expertise—vital resources that may be spent on other projects. Educators and instructional designers are rarely given enough time and support to adhere to a systematic design process. Interim products (e.g., paper-based design documents) are not very flashy and may not capture the attention of key stakeholders, whose support is essential if your efforts are to be effective.

Many also associate systematic design with ADDIE (Analysis, Design, Development, Implementation, and Evaluation), a well-known model for producing training and educational programs. ADDIE has been used successfully by the military and corporations across the United States and around the world for decades. Variations of ADDIE (e.g., Dick, Carey, & Carey, 2009; Smith & Ragan, 1999) continue to be adopted by educators and instructional designers to produce training and education in a systematic fashion for the reasons mentioned earlier. Critics of ADDIE, however, argue that it is too linear, too time consuming, too resource intensive, and too inflexible—that it fails to accommodate changes in learner needs and instructional materials during development and delivery. Critics also point to poorly designed instructional materials, said to be based on the ADDIE process, that are not effective, efficient, or engaging. Yet, experienced instructional designers realize that more often than not, ineffective, inefficient, and unappealing instruction results from inappropriate or inadequate applications of ADDIE (e.g., people cutting corners due to lack of time, training, or resources), rather than inherent problems with the model itself. ADDIE also does not have to be applied in a linear fashion, which is a common myth; spiral and other iterative models of ADDIE are widespread.

Experts now advocate what are referred to as agile approaches to design, such as the Successive Approximation Model (SAM) that further accentuates the iterative and collaborative nature of design (Allen, 2012). Figure I.1 depicts what Allen has named the Extended Successive

Approximation Model (SAM2) for projects that require significant content or e-learning development and more advanced programming.

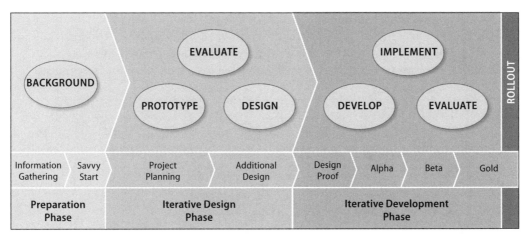

FIGURE I.1 ▶ The three-phase extended successive approximation model or SAM2 *(This figure is reprinted from Allen, 2012, with permission from ASTD Press.)*

Whether you use ADDIE, SAM2, or other processes you have tried, combined, or devised, it is important to remember that a focus on tangible results without sufficient planning or testing may result in a false sense of economy. The impact of poorly designed instruction may not be evident until would-be learners are asked to perform key tasks for which they are not prepared. Dissatisfied learners may also drop out and warn others to avoid your program. The bottom line is that you should use a process that ensures the alignment of objectives, assessments, and instructional strategies and leads to the development of instructional materials that consistently result in desired learning outcomes on time and in budget. Systematic design helps ensure alignment between fundamental instructional elements and reduces variance without inhibiting creativity if applied in an appropriate manner. Nevertheless, grounded and systematic design may not be sufficient for ensuring your students achieve targeted learning outcomes.

Systemic Thinking and Action

Well-designed instructional materials and coursework are essential but not necessarily sufficient for facilitating e-learning. In an online environment, an instructor may not be readily available to fill in gaps and make up for inadequacies in the instructional materials. Students may not be able to just drop what they are doing and see an advisor to address logistical issues. If students cannot readily register for and access coursework, acquire materials, submit assignments, obtain feedback, receive advice, access technical support, and otherwise navigate the training or educational system, it doesn't matter how good the instruction is—learning may not occur. Students may actually prefer an online program with high-quality student services and mediocre course materials rather than a program with mediocre student services and high-quality online coursework.

Systematic design is not sufficient for establishing effective and efficient online and hybrid programs. You must also think systemically; in other words, you must view e-learning as part of a larger system that consists of a set of interrelated components that must all be aligned to achieve a common goal. Figure I.2 depicts nine functional components of an e-learning system that must work together to facilitate student achievement (Hirumi, 2000, 2010). Figure I.2 also highlights the focus of this book series, instruction that is designed to facilitate achievement of specified outcomes, along with two very closely interrelated components—curriculum and assessment.

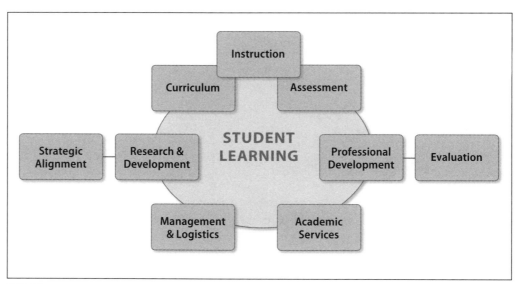

FIGURE I.2 ▶ e-learning system components

The nine functional e-learning components are the following: (1) strategic alignment, which aligns the mission and plans of the e-learning system with the mission and plans of the larger educational institution, organization, or system; (2) research and development, which facilitate the integration as well as the dissemination of new knowledge and information generated outside and within the system; (3) curriculum, which specifies and organizes learning outcomes; (4) instruction, which involves the deliberate arrangement of events, including tools and techniques, for facilitating achievement of specified learning outcomes; (5) assessment, which defines the methods and criteria for determining to what extent students have achieved the curriculum outcomes; (6) management and logistics, which bring together the human and physical resources necessary to support the system, including strategic plans, policies, procedures, and budgets; (7) academic services, which cover a wide range of support for students, such as, but not limited to, admissions, registration, fee payment, financial aid, academic advising, and so on; (8) professional development, which ensures all system stakeholders have the skills and knowledge necessary to fulfill their roles and responsibilities; and (9) evaluation, which serves to improve the effectiveness and efficiency of all system components. Addressing each system component in detail is well beyond the scope of this book series. Rather, these three books focus on the instructional components of the system, covering different instructional strategies, tools, and techniques for facilitating e-learning, which, in turn, necessitate some discussion of curriculum and assessment.

Taken together, the books in this series are written to provide valuable insights for educators and instructional designers tasked with designing online and hybrid e-learning environments. These insights are based on 15-plus years of experience designing and developing my own online and hybrid courses, as well as helping others in K–12 and higher education, and in business and industry across North America, South America, and the Middle East to establish and improve e-learning programs. The contents of the books in this series are also based on the skills, knowledge, and insights of my colleagues, who also have many years of experience in teaching and learning online. If you think that a systematic and systemic approach, grounded in research and theory, may help you in your efforts to create high-quality online and hybrid courses, I encourage you to use this book to design rich, engaging, and memorable learning experiences for your students. In addition, if you do use one of the strategies included in this book or if you know of and use other strategies grounded in research and theory to design an online or hybrid learning environment, please let me know; I'd love to hear about it. The more we can bring grounded practice and systematic design to light, the more we can do to increase the quality of e-learning environments and improve education for our children.

References

Allen, Michael. (2012). *Leaving ADDIE for SAM: An agile model for developing the best learning experiences.* Alexandria, VA: ASTD Press.

Christensen, C., Johnson, C., & Horn, M. (2011). *Disrupting class, expanded edition: How disruptive innovation will change the way the world learns.* New York, NY: McGraw-Hill.

Dick, W., Carey, L., & Carey, J. O. (2009). *The systematic design of instruction* (7th ed.). Upper Saddle River, NJ: Pearson.

Hannafin, M., Hannafin, K., & Land, S. (1997). Grounded practice and the design of constructivist learning environments. *Educational Technology Research and Development, 45*(2), 101–17.

Hirumi, A. (2000). Chronicling the challenges of web-basing a degree program: A systems perspective. *The Quarterly Review of Distance Education, 1*(2), 89–108.

Hirumi, A. (2010). Twenty-first century e-learning systems: The need for systemic thinking and change. Keynote presentation at the second Annual International Conference on e-Learning and Teaching, hosted by Iran University for Science and Technology, Tehran, Iran, November 30–December 2.

International Association for K–12 Online Learning (iNACOL). (2013). Fast facts about online learning. Retrieved from wwwl.inacol.org/cms/wp-content/uploads/2013/04/iNACOL_FastFacts_Feb2013.pdf

Smith, P. L., & Ragan, T. J. (1999). *Instructional design* (2nd ed.). Upper Saddle River, NJ: Prentice-Hall.

Watson, J., Murin, A., Vashaw, L., Gemin, B., & Rapp, C. (2010). *Keeping pace with K–12 online learning: An annual review of policy and practice.* Evergreen, CO: Evergreen Education Group. Retrieved from www.kpk12.com/cms/wpcontent/uploads/KeepingPaceK12_2010.pdf

Applying Gagné's Nine Events of Instruction to Facilitate Online and Hybrid Learning

Abigail Hawkins

IN 1974, ROBERT GAGNÉ PUBLISHED his seminal work, *Principles of Instructional Design,* where he outlined an instructional strategy that remains relevant today: the nine events of instruction. Four decades later, teachers still apply his instructional strategy in face-to-face, online, and hybrid learning environments. In this chapter, I provide an overview of Gagné's nine events of instruction and examples of each event in face-to-face and online settings. Two courses are explored in detail with explanations of how Gagné's nine events of instruction create a structure and instructional flow for the courses and related lessons. The chapter concludes with an examination of design and delivery issues and a discussion of the implications of several criticisms leveled at Gagné's instructional strategy.

I n 1974, Robert Gagné published *Principles of Instructional Design,* outlining nine events of instruction for facilitating learning. Now, almost 40 years later, teachers still apply his instructional strategy to planning their lessons. Its practicality, simplicity, and timeless principles have led to its long-standing use and widespread implementation (Ertmer, Driscoll, & Wager, 2003). Teachers have adopted and adapted Gagné's events of instruction throughout K–12 and higher education, as well as in business and industry training. In this chapter, Gagné's instructional strategy and its application in K–12 online and hybrid learning environments are examined. To begin, an overview of Gagné's nine events of instruction are given along with examples of each event in face-to-face and online contexts. Second, detailed explorations of how teachers in two programs use Gagné's nine events of instruction to structure their online lessons or class units are provided. I conclude by examining design and delivery issues and discussing the implications of several criticisms leveled at Gagné's instructional strategy.

Overview of Gagné's Nine Events of Instruction

Gagné believed that for learning to occur, certain external conditions had to be met during instruction to facilitate internal learning conditions within each student. Drawing on the cognitive, information-processing model of learning (e.g., Atkinson & Shiffrin, 1968), Gagné argued that information undergoes a series of transformations as it is processed in learners' minds. Like a computer that takes input in from the environment, stores it in memory, and retrieves it for use, learners sense new information, move it from their short-term to long-term memories, solidify it to memory through rehearsal, and retrieve it for later use (Driscoll, 2000). To facilitate information being effectively stored in the long-term memory and to make it retrievable, Gagné believed that new knowledge needed to be connected to existing knowledge, that learning needed to be situated in the larger context, and that instructors played a critical role in guiding attention, providing opportunities for practice, and reinforcing the learning through corrective feedback (Gagné, Briggs, & Wager, 1992).

The nine events of instruction reflect these stages of mental processing and teacher actions that support learning. Table 1.1 provides high-level descriptions of the nine events of instruction and corresponding teachers' actions. While the sequence and provider of each event may vary, Gagné posits that effective lessons include all nine events (McCown, Driscoll, & Roop, 1996).

TABLE 1.1 ▶ Gagné's nine events of instruction illustrated through corresponding teachers' actions

INSTRUCTIONAL EVENT	TEACHERS' ACTIONS
Gain learners' attention.	Orient the learners to the new information.
Inform learners of the learning objectives (describe the goal/s).	State what you expect the learners to know and do by the end of the lesson.
Stimulate recall of prior knowledge.	Ask students to recall previously learned knowledge or skills related to the current lesson.
Present the material to be learned.	Communicate new information.
Provide guidance for learning.	Guide learners to a better understanding through content organization and cuing.
Elicit performance "practice."	Ask the learners to do something with the new knowledge or skills.
Provide informative feedback.	Give corrective feedback.
Assess performance.	Evaluate learners' abilities to perform the task independently and provide feedback.
Enhance retention and transfer.	Provide additional practice in a variety of contexts and over time.

Gain Attention

To facilitate learning, first teachers need to gain and then maintain the students' attention. The elements of surprise, novelty, and provocation can help capture students' attention. Teachers maintain and redirect attention throughout a lesson by creating a change in stimulus any time students appear to stray off the task (Driscoll, 2000). Though this is a first step, it is a reoccurring one in the teacher's instructional process.

Common ways to gain attention in an online environment include using statements to direct students' attention, asking provocative questions, presenting a dilemma, using an analogy, showing a short video or audio clip, presenting something controversial, sharing an image or comic strip, or conducting an activity or demonstration to capture interest. In terms of which technique to use and what content to leverage, the best attention getters appeal to the learners' interests. As learners' interests vary, teachers ideally need to have a variety of creative ideas to draw from. Table 1.2 provides examples of what gaining attention might look like in a synchronous (face-to-face) setting and how these actions would translate into an online environment. The examples presented in Tables 1.2 through 1.10 draw from a U.S. history teacher's unit on the Vietnam War and a lesson about the Tet Offensive, a major turning point in the war. These tables illustrate how the lesson could be taught synchronously (face-to-face) or online. Note that some of the examples' content remains essentially the same, but the vehicles for delivering attention getters and engaging with learners are adapted appropriately to live (face-to-face) or online environments.

TABLE 1.2 ▶ Comparisons of face-to-face and online examples of gaining attention

HOW THEY COULD BE DONE FACE-TO-FACE	HOW THEY COULD BE DONE ONLINE
In class, ask student groups to chart the U.S., South Vietnamese, and Vietcong casualties from the start of U.S. involvement in the war from 1964 (Gulf of Tonkin) through 1969—one year after the Tet Offensive.	Post a 15-minute video clip narrated by Walter Cronkite on CBS News: The Vietnam War with Walter Cronkite—Tet Offensive part 1. (www.youtube.com/watch?v=S3mfXnFtwQc)
Discuss patterns that emerge. Ask whether students' charts reflect that the war was ending or on the rise by 1969. State that the Tet Offensive had a huge psychological impact on U.S. morale and was a turning point in the war because Americans realized that the war was not going as well as the U.S. government indicated.	Use an online discussion forum to have students answer the following question: Why was the Tet Offensive considered a turning point when, as Walter Cronkite said, "The Vietcong did not win by a knockout, but neither did we."?

Inform the Learners of the Learning Objectives

The second event communicates to learners what you expect them to know and do as a result of the lesson. This primes the students' filtering processes regarding what to pay particular attention to as they complete the lesson. It is critical that teachers explain these learning objectives in a language that the learners understand (Gagné, Briggs, & Wager, 1985). Too often, teachers write objectives for the wrong audience—instructional designers and other teachers. Instead, the learners themselves should readily understand objectives. Understanding the goals of the instruction helps prevent the students from getting off track, and, simultaneously, helps teachers stay on track (Gagné, Briggs, & Wager, 1992).

Common methods for explaining learning objectives in an online environment include listing the objectives verbally or in writing, and providing guidelines, rubrics, and checklists. Table 1.3 illustrates how communicating learning objectives might look like in a face-to-face setting or online environment.

TABLE 1.3 ▶ Comparisons of face-to-face and online examples of communicating learning objectives

HOW THEY COULD BE DONE FACE-TO-FACE	HOW THEY COULD BE DONE ONLINE
In class, specify on a presentation slide and/or state orally, "In this unit you will be asked to…"	In online course materials, post on a website and/or communicate via an email distribution list or online discussion forum, "In this module, you will be asked to…"
Describe the social and political factors that created an international and domestic crisis in 1968, and	Describe the social and political factors that created an international and domestic crisis in 1968, and
Work with primary source documents, paying attention to bias and balancing multiple perspectives.	Work with primary source documents, paying attention to bias and balancing multiple perspectives.

Stimulate Recall of Prior Knowledge

The third event reminds learners of related material they have already been exposed to. Associating new knowledge with existing knowledge already stored in the long-term memory helps learners know how and where to process, encode, and store the new, related concepts.

Common methods for stimulating recall of prior knowledge include asking recognition or recall questions, providing relevant examples or problems for students to work through again, or using a quiz followed by discussion to tie new concepts to old. Table 1.4 gives examples of what recalling prior knowledge might look like in a face-to-face setting and how this would translate into an online environment.

TABLE 1.4 ▶ Comparisons of face-to-face and online examples of stimulating prior knowledge

HOW THEY COULD BE DONE FACE-TO-FACE	HOW THEY COULD BE DONE ONLINE
Ask students to recall from previous lessons the major events that led up to the Tet Offensive and U.S. sentiments toward the war up to this point.	Have students review key events that led up to the Tet Offensive by exploring PBS's interactive timeline (www.pbs.org/wgbh/amex/vietnam/timeline) and map of the Vietnam War (www.pbs.org/wgbh/amex/vietnam/maps/map_pop_intro.html). Note key events that would have been familiar to students from previous lessons.

Present the Material to Be Learned

In this event, the teacher communicates new information to the students. *How* teachers present the new information depends on what is being learned. For example, if you want students to answer questions orally in French, you would present questions to them orally in French—not have them written out in English for students to respond to in French. If you want students to learn factual or procedural (i.e., knowing how) knowledge, communicate the distinguishing features and show examples illustrating these features to them. If you want students to learn a motor skill, then demonstrate the skill and give verbal directions. The learning should be presented in multiple learning modalities, including text, graphics, audio narration, and video, among others.

In all contexts, the material should be presented in a clear, focused, and organized manner. Common strategies for presenting information effectively in an online environment include the use of chunking, cuing, and examples (Gagné, Briggs, & Wager, 1992). In chunking, information is broken down into small blocks of content to prevent overwhelming the learner. Chunking facilitates the encoding of information into long-term memory. Cuing is another strategy to help students determine what to focus on and process internally. To cue students in written text, use color, italics, or bold print judiciously to draw attention to what is important. To give verbal cues, make statements such as, "Now, this is the important part…." Or, "Look what happens when we…." Additionally, teachers can cue students by providing a variety of examples and different visual forms (words, diagrams, images, etc.). The use of multiple and varied examples is important so that learners are able to recognize and transfer the learned concept to a variety of settings

(Gagné, Briggs, & Wager, 1992). Learners often recognize a concept in the abstract but fail to recognize the concept when it is situated in a real-world context. For example, students may be able to conduct a simple statistical test in class but struggle to apply the same statistical test when presented with a real-world example. The difficulty in transferring learning from one context to another justifies and makes critical the use of varied examples.

Table 1.5 illustrates how communicating the material may be presented in a face-to-face setting and how it might look in an online environment.

TABLE 1.5 ▶ Comparisons of face-to-face and online examples of presenting the material

HOW THEY COULD BE DONE FACE-TO-FACE	HOW THEY COULD BE DONE ONLINE
Lecture about the Tet Offensive. Show a map of the Tet Offensive and the major cities attacked. Project images from the Tet Offensive and discuss the effects the event had on public sentiment. Discuss the role of reporting and how this was the first war where Americans saw firsthand accounts of the war without censorship. Show images of the war that appeared on magazine covers. Ask what impact seeing these uncensored images would have had on U.S. opinion.	Provide a summary web page describing the Tet Offensive. Display a dynamic, interactive map illustrating U.S. troop movements throughout Vietnam. Describe the new role of reporting without censorship in the Vietnam War. Have students explore online images and film archives of the Vietnam War from Life and Time magazines (e.g., http://life.time.com/vietnam-war/) and the Tet Offensive (www.history.com/topics/tet-offensive/videos#tet-offensive). In an online forum, ask students to describe how the images on these magazine covers changed (http://life.time.com/history/vietnam-war-life-magazine-covers-from-the-era-defining-conflict/#1) as the war progressed and what impact these uncensored images would have had on U.S. opinion. Ask students to post a provocative image from the Iraq War in the discussion forum and tell how this impacted their personal opinion on the Iraq War.

Provide Guidance for Learning

In Gagné's fifth event, the teacher provides guidance to learners on their performances. The teacher provides scaffolds, feedback, and tools to facilitate learning while being careful not to give away any answers. The goal of this event is to help learners accurately focus on the important information and to help them organize and encode it from short-term to long-term memory.

Common strategies for providing guidance in an online environment include teacher or computer-generated hints, cues, mnemonics, advanced organizers, analogies, mind maps and other graphical representations, examples, elaborations, and guiding questions to lead learners to an understanding of the material. The frequency and form of guidance depends on the abilities of the learners, instructional time, and the learning goals (Driscoll, 2000).

TABLE 1.6 ▶ Comparisons of face-to-face and online examples of providing guidance

HOW THEY COULD BE DONE FACE-TO-FACE	HOW THEY COULD BE DONE ONLINE
Provide verbal cues, such as, "Now this is important…," or "Let's take some time to focus on this for a moment."	Post checklists and/or rubrics for papers or projects that students can download and examine.
Ask questions to elicit performance, such as, "What is another interpretation?" or "What else would impact public opinion besides what you mentioned?"	Post exemplars (e.g., quality projects, quality discussion posts, quality discussion replies) to model and elicit desired performance.
Present checklists and/or rubrics for papers or projects.	Provide teacher feedback on student posts in online discussion forums to provoke deeper understanding and learning.
	Have students post drafts of their work throughout the course to receive feedback from peers in the form of online comments and peer critiques.
	Create roll-over hints, timed cues, and supplemental materials.

Elicit Performance

Teachers elicit performance by asking learners to show that they know the information or are able to do the desired behavior. This step confirms to the teacher and the learners that they are mastering the material. Demonstrating their abilities for the teacher is important for learners' self-confidence as well. According to Gagné, Briggs, and Wager (1992), "We want them not only to convince us, but to convince themselves as well" (p. 196). Practice can build confidence. When practice is coupled with prompt, meaningful feedback, it can improve performance dramatically (Hattie & Timperley, 2007). It is important that learners be able to practice what they are learning without penalty for making mistakes. At this stage, learners are still trying to figure things out and, with the help of corrective feedback, improve their performances. This step is central to helping teachers detect misunderstandings and re-teach material if necessary. It is also critical to provide students with ample, varied practice to help them master the material over time.

Methods that students would use to practice are dependent on the nature of what it is to be learned. However, some examples to allow for practice in an online environment include group collaboration projects, practice quizzes, drafts, discussions, simulations, games, audio or video recordings of performances, virtual role plays, case studies, and problem sets, to name a few. Additionally, one of the benefits of online learning is the ability to provide *adaptive* practice and assessments. This is when the computer adjusts the presented content based on the students' performances. Thus, the practice or assessment items become progressively more difficult or easier, depending on the accuracy of the students' responses. This allows for more individualized instruction and pushes students to perform within their zones of proximal development.

TABLE 1.7 ▶ Comparisons of face-to-face and online examples of giving practice

HOW THEY COULD BE DONE FACE-TO-FACE	HOW THEY COULD BE DONE ONLINE
Conduct an in-class debate dividing the class into Hawks (pro-war) versus Doves (anti-war).	Use discussion forums to conduct an online, synchronous debate dividing the class into Hawks (pro-war) versus Doves (anti-war).
Have students write one-page summaries of their personal positions. Ask two or three to read theirs in front of the rest of the class.	Use a blog prompt where students post a two-paragraph summary of their personal positions and why they hold them. Require that students comment on postings of at least two peers.
Conduct a quiz about the Tet Offensive with an in-class discussion of the answers.	Offer an online quiz covering the Tet Offensive that gives automatic feedback.

Provide Informative Feedback

According to Colvin (2008), practice without corrective feedback is futile. Learners need feedback that both reinforces correctness and remediates misunderstanding. Without feedback that helps them know what they did incorrectly and how to improve their performances, learners may struggle to improve without their practice having any positive effects. Therefore, it is critical that teachers provide ongoing informative feedback regarding student performance and even re-teach material as a form of feedback.

Common methods for providing informative feedback in an online environment include peer collaboration, practice quizzes, remarks on papers/projects, responses in discussion forums, peer reviews, responses to blog posts, and annotations to video or audio posts.

Additionally, computerized feedback like that found in computerized simulations, games, or drills can also provide information on lower-order cognitive skills. Feedback generated for the student can be visual, auditory, or haptic (e.g., sensory) or a combination of the three.

TABLE 1.8 ▶ Comparisons of face-to-face and online examples of giving feedback

HOW THEY COULD BE DONE FACE-TO-FACE	HOW THEY COULD BE DONE ONLINE
Comment orally and in writing on students' work.	Comment on student responses in the online discussion forums.
	Provide automatic feedback for correct and incorrect answers in multiple-choice quizzes.
	Provide and post written, audio, or video feedback on students' work.

Assess Performance

The next event is to confirm whether students have actually learned the material and met the desired learning objectives. During this stage, students should receive no help from the teacher. This event typically occurs at the end of a unit or chapter.

Common methods for assessing performance in an online environment include end of unit/chapter tests, projects, portfolios, simulated demonstrations, adaptive testing, or traditional papers.

TABLE 1.9 ▶ Comparisons of face-to-face and online examples of assessing performance

HOW THEY COULD BE DONE FACE-TO-FACE	HOW THEY COULD BE DONE ONLINE
Present unit test with fixed- and open-response items in class.	Post unit test with fixed- and open-response items online.
Ask students to interview someone who lived during the Vietnam War era to understand the person's feelings toward the war and how these feelings evolved.	Ask students to conduct a film or audio interview of someone who lived during the Vietnam War era to understand his/her feelings toward the war at the time—was the person a Hawk or a Dove? Did this viewpoint change? Why or why not?
Have students summarize their interviews in a paper, and ask them to assess peers' papers using a specified performance checklist or rubric.	Have students post their films or audio recordings to a secure site for all students to view and comment on.
Teacher assesses papers using a specified performance checklist or rubric.	Teacher assesses recordings using a specified performance checklist or rubric.

Enhance Retention and Transfer

For the new learning to be retained and retrieved at appropriate times, learners need frequent opportunities to access and apply the learned material in a variety of contexts. Students often struggle with transferring what was learned in the classroom to contexts beyond the classroom walls. Using varied examples and giving learners a variety of new tasks forces them to apply the learning in different contexts.

Common methods for enhancing retention and transfer in an online environment include scheduling reviews of the material spaced out over time, using examples to illustrate the learning in other contexts, and applying the learning to new tasks in new environments.

TABLE 1.10 ▶ Comparisons of face-to-face and online examples of extending the learning

HOW THEY COULD BE DONE FACE-TO-FACE	HOW THEY COULD BE DONE ONLINE
Discuss ways in which the Vietnam War and Iraq War are similar and different.	Using a blog prompt, ask students to post one similarity and one difference between the Vietnam and Iraq wars. Ask students to comment on the posts of two peers. Each comment post must be unique.
Explore through an in-class discussion how U.S. opinion on the Iraq War shifted over time.	
Present verbal probes about opinions on the Iraq War, such as the role(s) of media, public sentiment, and strategy.	Post written probes about opinions on the Iraq War, such as the role(s) of media, public sentiment, and strategy.

Online Examples of the Nine Events of Instruction

This section highlights examples of how two virtual schools, Connections Academy and the Center for Distance Learning and Innovation, use elements of Gagné's nine events of instruction in their curriculum design.

Connections Academy

Connections Academy is a for-profit company offering an accredited online program that serves approximately 30,000 full-time equivalent K–12 students in 24 states. A common curriculum is used across all Connections Academy schools, and asynchronous, online instructional methods are employed. "Connections Academy virtual school teachers modify lessons and assignments to ensure that each student receives the right degree of challenge, or extra assistance, required to foster academic success and love of learning" (www.connectionsacademy.com/our-program/online-teaching.aspx).

I examined a Grade 2 language arts lesson titled "Cowboys." The type of lesson is an example of independent, online learning combined with active coaching from another adult (i.e., a parent). This sample online lesson is available for free review (www.connectionsacademy.com/curriculum/elementary-school/educational-materials.aspx). Go to this URL; under the heading, Sample Online Lessons, select Grade 2, Language Arts–Cowboys.

Center for Distance Learning and Innovation

The Center for Distance Learning and Innovation (CDLI) is a province-wide, supplemental virtual high school that serves the Province of Newfoundland and Labrador in Canada. CDLI is a program for high school students only, which for Canada means Grades 10–12. This virtual school focuses on delivering academic and advanced courses but no basic or credit recovery courses, using both synchronous and asynchronous online instructional methods. There are approximately 1,000 students, with many of those students enrolled in more than one course.

I examined a Grade 11–12 mathematics and physics lesson titled "Vector Kinematics." This lesson features both asynchronous and synchronous instruction.

It is important to note how the CDLI courses are designed. CDLI's course formats differ structurally from other online courses' designs. Typically, "hybrid" courses refer to a blend of face-to-face, synchronous instruction with virtual, asynchronous instruction. However, some online courses, such as those offered at the CDLI, define "hybrid" courses as those that offer both synchronous and asynchronous instruction—all within a virtual setting. Synchronous instruction time in CDLI courses can range from a low of 30% to 40% in elective courses to a high of 80% in French as a second language courses. In science and mathematics courses, the synchronous instruction usually ranges between 50% and 60% of the students' scheduled time. Using web-conferencing software, instructors teach a class in real-time, leveraging technologies such as virtual chat, whiteboards, video, and screen sharing for teaching and learning. Asynchronous instruction takes the form of reading and interacting with content, peers, and instructors in online discussion forums and with written feedback from instructors.

Lesson Plan A
Cowboys *(Online Lesson)*

This lesson from Connections Academy is designed for Grade 2 language arts. The lesson type is independent, online learning combined with active coaching from an adult. Connections Academy uses Gagné's nine events of instruction as the structuring framework for the lesson. Figures 1.A.1 through 1.A.7 illustrate the parts of the lesson.

1. Gain attention

In the Connections Academy sample lesson, students are prompted to write in their journals about their favorite piece of cowboy clothing (Figure 1.A.1).

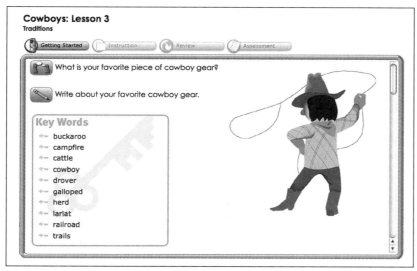

FIGURE 1.A.1 ▶ Mechanism for gaining attention

This activity uses personal experience, a writing prompt, and an image to gain learners' attention. The learners' attention is maintained throughout the lesson by ongoing interactions with the instructor and changes in instructional modalities (i.e., multiple, varied activities). Note that the tabs for the top menu items (Getting Started, Instruction, Review, and Assessment) follow a similar sequence and instructional flow to Gagné's nine events.

2. Inform the learners of the learning objectives

Immediately following the writing prompt, students click to see the objectives for the lesson (Figure 1.A.2).

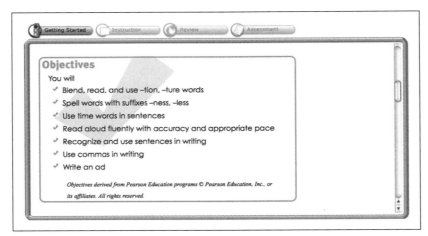

FIGURE 1.A.2   ▶   Mechanism for informing learners of lesson objectives

Note that the objectives for this lesson are not written at a language level that is appropriate for most Grade 2 learners; instead, the language of the objectives appears to be directed toward the teacher—something Gagné opposed.

3. Stimulate recall of prior knowledge

In this lesson, no overt attempts to recall prior knowledge were included. A simple way this could be done would be to reference a common nursery rhyme or song that uses "–tion" and "–ture" blends that students would be familiar with and then use that rhyme or song to lead into the subsequent learning activities.

4. Present the material to be learned

Students were prompted to read, play a drag-and-drop letters game, write sentences using the new vocabulary, watch a tutorial on becoming a good writer, and read out loud from a separate reading book (Figure 1.A.3).

Connections Academy designs its instruction to include live support from a "learning coach" (i.e., parent or other adult) to facilitate and expand on the learning experience (Figure 1.A.4).

The learning coach provides direct instruction in the form of modeling, asking questions, and defining keywords (e.g., buckaroo and drover).

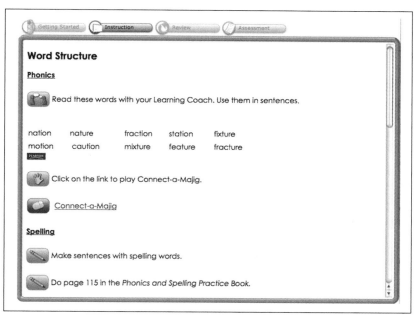

FIGURE 1.A.3 ▶ Presentation of materials to be learned

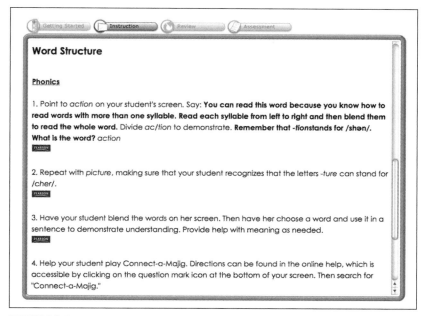

FIGURE 1.A.4 ▶ Instructions for the learning coach on how to present the material

5. Provide guidance for learning

As noted in Figure 1.A.4, several instances prompt instructor guidance. These include strategies for reading blends and asking questions to guide student responses. Additionally, there were several indications of how instructors could guide learning by modeling specific behaviors, such as circle diagramming, pronunciation, and taking turns when reading key passages.

6. Elicit performance

The presentation and practice of material are intertwined as expected. This is evidenced by the fact that both the material presented and practice activities are located under the Instruction tab. Figure 1.A.5 provides a sample of types of practice found in the lesson.

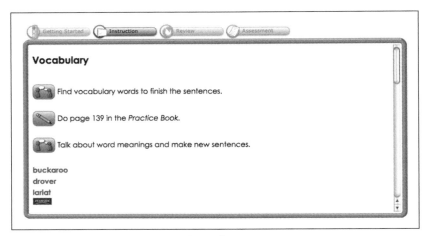

FIGURE 1.A.5 ▶ Sample activities to elicit performance

The practice for learners is varied, including writing sentences with the spelling words, completing exercises in a separate practice workbook, fill-in-the-blank exercises, read-along activities with the learning coach, responding to questions from the learning coach, and writing a job ad for a cowboy.

7. Provide informative feedback

With the exception of feedback as to correctness on the drag-and-drop letters game, much of the feedback for this lesson relies on the learning coach. Figure 1.A.6 provides a sample of the type of feedback learning coaches are prompted to provide.

Learning coaches are specifically prompted on the kinds of feedback to provide for each of the practice exercises. For example, the second writing activity prompts the instructor to review the student's job ad and encourage different sentence types. Instructors are told to guide students to use the model found on page 406 of the online support guide to see examples of desired performance.

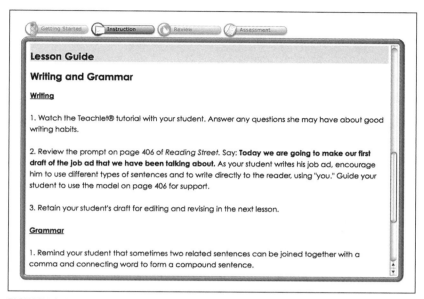

FIGURE 1.A.6 ▶ Sample mechanisms for providing informative feedback

8. Assess performance

To assess student learning for this lesson, the learning coach asks students to read a written word and indicate whether the student pronounced the word correctly. For example, the learning coach writes the word "campfire," asks the student to read it out loud, and indicates whether the student pronounced it correctly or incorrectly. Formal assessments by the learning coach were minimal and included only two questions. Additionally, students are asked to complete the quick check assessment.

9. Enhance retention and transfer

There were several practice activities that provided opportunities for long-term retention and transfer (Figure 1.A.7). However, it is difficult to distinguish short-term practice from long-term retention in this lesson, though it is likely that subsequent lessons build on concepts learned in this unit to solidify the learning over time.

Writing and grammar practice are varied, as students are asked to watch a video tutorial, read a story, write a job ad, and discuss compound sentences with their learning coach. This variation supports encoding for long-term retention and transferring the skill to different contexts.

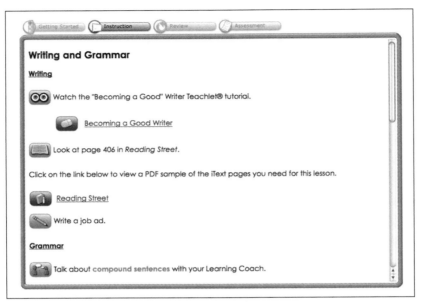

FIGURE 1.A.7 ▶ Sample practice to reinforce long-term retention and transfer

Lesson Plan B
Vector Kinematics *(Hybrid Lesson)*

This lesson from the Center for Distance Learning and Innovation (CDLI) is for Grade 11–12 students in mathematics and physics. This lesson uses synchronous and asynchronous online instruction. Figures 1.B.1 through 1.B.6 illustrate the details of this lesson.

1. Gain attention

CDLI courses are divided into major units, which are further subdivided into Get Ready and Go to Work tabs. Students are first directed to the Get Ready tab (Figure 1.B.1), where they learn the intended learning outcomes, prior knowledge they should have mastered, and an overview of the significance of the unit ahead. As the courses have a consistent look and design, students know what to expect, how to navigate courses, and where to find information. CDLI's consistent design elements are important factors that support and cue student learning (Barbour, 2007).

Beyond the Get Ready tab, other methods used early in the lesson to gain attention were asking students to draw graphs, respond to a provoking question, watch an animation, and read a story problem.

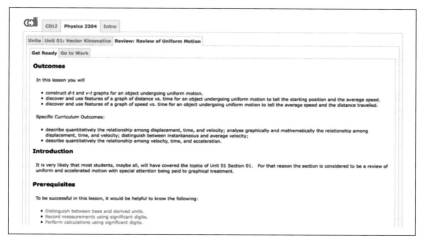

FIGURE 1.B.1 ▶ Mechanism for gaining attention

2. Inform the learners of the learning objectives

At the start of every lesson, learners are cued to get ready for the learning by reading the outcomes (objectives)—written in student-friendly language—that are expected of them for the lesson. Language from the printed curriculum guide is also provided. Figure 1.B.1 displays the outcomes for the vector unit and is a standard page that students view when they click into any unit or sub-unit. This type of page is what they view before seeing any instructional content.

Though clearly stated, the objectives here are rather abstract, with little or no explanation as to why students are learning said objectives (i.e., "in order to…"). This is contrary to what Gagné advocated in terms of learning objectives being communicated in a language that students understand and in terms of explaining why learning the elements of this lesson will be necessary for or useful to students.

3. Stimulate recall of prior knowledge

Students are able to review any prerequisite knowledge that the lesson builds on by clicking the hyperlinks in the Get Ready section. The links in this section encourage students to review relevant content taught in previous lessons and ensure that they review prerequisite knowledge from prior lessons. Additionally, throughout the written lessons, there are references to prior learning, as students are prompted to "remember…," "think back to…," "consider from the last lesson…," or "recall…" previous content learned. This format helps students see how the new material relates to and builds on prior knowledge and facilitates their abilities to encode the material into long-term memory, as students associate new information with existing schemas.

During synchronous instruction, the instructor frequently asks students to think back to previous lessons and recall the content learned. This guidance encourages students to make connections and assimilate new knowledge in relation to the old.

4. Present the material to be learned

CDLI students are presented with the content information through text, graphics, guiding questions, examples, and multimedia objects, including animations, that they can manipulate. Students also listen to the teacher's recorded presentations that accompany the slides' content; slides are also supplemented by synchronized, animated graphs. Figure 1.B.2 displays the animation that students can manipulate to show the relationship between speed/velocity of a cart and its slope on a curve.

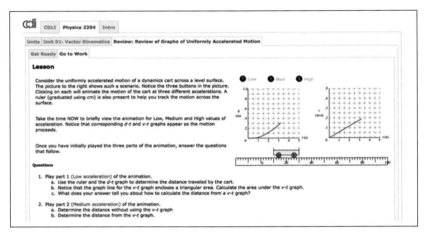

FIGURE 1.B.2 ▶ Example of animation used to present new information

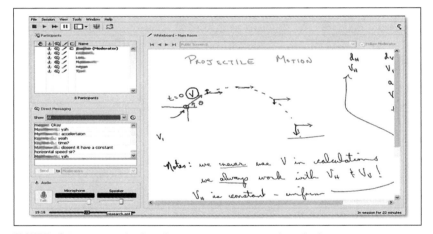

FIGURE 1.B.3 ▶ Sample of synchronous instruction in a 12th grade physics course

While Figure 1.B.2 illustrates portions of the asynchronous instruction, Figure 1.B.3 is a screen shot of the synchronous portion of a 12th grade physics course. Leveraging virtual tools, the instructor is able to write on a virtual whiteboard, write directly on top of slides or content images, and engage students in dialogue either through writing in the chat panel or one-way audio generated by the instructor. Students communicate back to the teacher and their peers via chat and by sharing their computer screens remotely. Note that all of these synchronous forms of interaction in CDLI courses could happen in a face-to-face setting as well, which is the more common model of hybrid online courses.

5. Provide guidance for learning

This lesson also illustrates several different ways that cuing can occur to provide learning guidance. Strategies to guide learning include the use of color to highlight key words or points, checklists of key points to keep in mind when solving a problem, multiple examples, and guiding questions that prompt learners to look for or consider particular points when solving a problem. Figure 1.B.4 provides examples of the use of questions to guide student thinking.

FIGURE 1.B.4 ▶ Example of questioning strategies used to guide learning

Note how related questions are used to build upon each other to guide students' thinking. Also, parts of the text are colored to highlight areas of emphasis.

During the synchronous sessions, students are guided through the learning process in a number of ways. Teachers use cuing techniques, such as annotation tools, to mark, highlight, and underline visual text and images to add emphasis and to direct students' attention to the content that is important. During a synchronous mathematics session that had students manipulating graphing calculators to conduct regression analysis, the instructor frequently displayed students' screens and had them complete the task "in front" of the rest of the class. Throughout the process, the teacher was skillfully leading the students' learning by using guiding questions and providing hints as to what to do next in the sequence of tasks.

6. Elicit performance

Throughout the lesson, students complete multiple activities that allow them to practice the material and reinforce the learning (Figure 1.B.5). In most instances, the correct solutions are displayed to allow students to check their understanding.

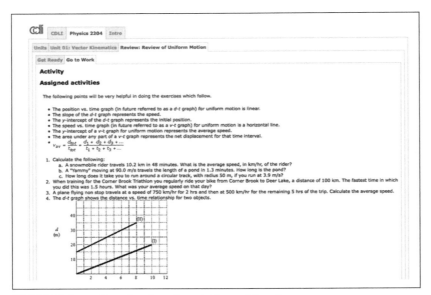

FIGURE 1.B.5 ▶ Examples of practice activities to elicit performance

The practice activities are highly varied, situated in a real-world context, and require the direct application and synthesis of what students have learned from the content information presented in the fourth part of the lesson (presentation of the material to be learned). Built into the synchronous sessions are multiple examples and practice activities. Additionally, the teacher has the ability to display a student's screen to the rest of the group and let the student drive the session from his or her vantage point. This technique was used frequently in the mathematics course analyzed.

7. Provide informative feedback

Feedback takes several forms in CDLI classes. First, as students complete activities, the correct answers are displayed at the bottom of the web page. Second, automated computer feedback is given on practice multiple-choice questions and end-of-section assessments (Figure 1.B.6).

Note that this feedback is of limited value because it only indicates the correctness of answers but does not help learners correct their errors. The feedback does not expand on why one choice is correct over the others. This type of limited feedback is also evident in the end-of-section assessments. According to Gagné's seventh event, informative feedback becomes yet another teaching method—showing students where their thinking processes were flawed and giving them varied ways to correct their errors.

Beyond computer-generated feedback, students at CDLI were able to get real-time feedback from instructors during synchronous sessions. Instructors provided feedback in a number of ways: posing questions and directing students to respond in the chat panel, asking students to mark their names visually if they did or did not understand a concept, and allowing a student to lead the session by sharing that student's screen and mouse actions. With all of these methods, the teacher provided verbal feedback to students' responses and performances.

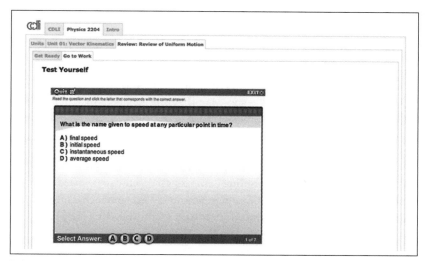

FIGURE 1.B.6 ▶ Example of informative feedback

8. Assess performance

At the end of each section, students take an assessment that ranges from four to 10 multiple-choice questions. While many of the questions require students to perform calculations, assessment questions are not open-ended. Additionally, as mentioned in the previous section, the feedback answers on the computer assessments are limited, as they only indicate which answers are correct and provide no additional explanations. Nor do they link students back to the portions of the material that they failed to grasp initially. Additionally, many courses offered end-of-unit assignments that were both computer graded and included teacher feedback. When teachers write feedback, they can remedy this weakness by providing additional explanations along with examples of material students need to review and understand before proceeding to the next level.

9. Enhance retention and transfer

Just as this lesson built on skills taught in previous lessons, the concepts around vector kinematics and uniform motion are reviewed in subsequent lessons, reinforcing the learning through a spiral curriculum that promotes long-term retention. Additionally, each course includes a set of multi-media learning objects; they are extensions of what is taught within the lesson to help students dig deeper into the material and understand core concepts in multiple contexts. Teachers' explanations overlay graphical animations to help students further master the concepts and transfer the learning.

Design and Delivery Considerations

There are several issues to consider when applying Gagné's nine events of instruction. In terms of design, the nine events are practical for teachers to use because they encapsulate the learning episode at a lesson plan or unit level. This enables teachers to easily adopt and adapt the different events in their lesson or unit-plan design. Second, the appeal of the nine events of instruction is how logically the principles translate into practice (Ertmer, Driscoll, & Wager, 2003). The nine events are practices that most teachers already apply in some form or another and are firmly grounded in research and theory.

In terms of delivery, Gagné's nine events used in an online context can capitalize on advancements provided by modern technologies. For example, computer-generated feedback can give students instantaneous feedback on simple assessments and practice activities. This facility, coupled with the practice of adaptive performance and assessment, has the power to tailor learning experiences to meet individual needs of students.

Despite its strengths, there are a few challenges with the model that may impact lesson design. First, the fact that these events appear ordered sequentially may give teachers the sense that they are to occur in linear order. In reality, teachers will continually find themselves attempting to gain attention, create opportunities for practice, provide feedback, maintain focus on the goal, and present new material. Also, these events are often cyclical and repetitive, as opposed to single-shot events. While Gagné's writing expresses the repeated nature of many of these steps, the sequential and prescriptive presentation of the model makes it easy to fall into the trap of designing these events as one-time occurrences in the lesson or unit plan design.

Another challenge related to online teaching is the absence of physical and verbal cues to guide teacher feedback. As mentioned by Hirumi in Chapter 2 of *Online and Hybrid Learning Design Fundamentals*, the first book in the series, the absence of physical cues makes it difficult to know whether particular students' inactivity is due to a busy schedule or confusion and frustration with the subject matter. Consequently, when designing online courses and lessons, teachers need to be more intentional as to how they plan on engaging students in practice and providing feedback on their performances. This is consistent with Hirumi's model in the series' first book for applying grounded strategies (and related interactions between the learner and instructor [Level III interactions]) to design and sequence interactions between the learner and human and nonhuman resources (Level II interactions), as well as analyzing planned interactions to ensure that they are repeated frequently enough with sufficient quality. As we know, interactions need to be frequent and ongoing rather than seldom and singular. In online environments, spontaneous conversations are rare. Consequently, interactions need to be intentional, premeditated, and planned.

Another challenge with feedback is the potential for delayed responses between students' questions and the teacher's responses. In asynchronous learning contexts, students may pose questions or state their understandings of material and then have to wait for delayed responses from the teacher to answer, correct, guide, or challenge their understandings—compared to the instantaneous responses possible in face-to-face learning environments. While these delay times vary from teacher to teacher, too many lengthy delays can be discouraging to students as they work to understand and progress through the online material.

It is important to note that Gagné's model may not be as applicable to learning situations for which the outcomes are less defined from the outset, as in discovery learning (Orey & Nelson, 1997). According to Orey and Nelson, the prescriptive and systematic nature of Gagné's approach "assumes that content can be sufficiently structured and that enough activities can be provided for the learners to acquire the desired knowledge and skills…" (pp. 283–284). However, discovery-based learning does not always follow a systematic instructional flow. Rather, the reality of this type of learning is that it is adaptive. That is, the activities, outcomes, and sequences evolve in unforeseen ways, depending on the learners' responses and creativity and on the various pathways they choose to take throughout the learning experience.

Conclusions

The practical, intuitive elements of Gagné's nine events of instruction make it an easy, practical instructional strategy to adopt for K–12 online and hybrid learning contexts. Whether done explicitly, as in the case of Connections Academy, or implicitly, as in the case of the Center for Distance Learning and Innovation, Gagné's method provides a systematic approach to structuring a learning experience for desired outcomes. Teachers who adopt this instructional design theory need to look at how they can overcome the limitations of linearity, teacher-centeredness, and feedback challenges in an online environment. Gagné's method is a simple tool that can guide teachers through designing and teaching courses and lead students through effective, lasting learning experiences.

References

Atkinson, R.C., & Shiffrin, R.M. (1968). Human memory: A proposed system and its control processes. In K. W. Spence, & J. T. Spence (Eds.), *The psychology of learning and motivation* (Volume 2, pp. 89-195). New York, NY: Academic Press.

Barbour, M. K. (2007). Principles of effective web-based content for secondary school students: Teacher and developer perceptions. *Journal of Distance Education, 21*(3), 93–114. Retrieved from www.jofde.ca/index.php/jde/article/view/30

Colvin, G. (2008). *Talent is overrated: What really separates world-class performers from everybody else.* New York, NY: Penguin.

Driscoll, M. P. (2000). *Psychology of learning for instruction* (2nd ed.). Boston, MA: Allyn and Bacon.

Ertmer, P. A., Driscoll, M. P., & Wager, W. W. (2003). The legacy of Robert Mills Gagné. In B. J. Zimmerman, & D. H. Schunk (Eds.), *Educational psychology: A century of contributions* (pp. 303–330). Washington, DC: American Psychological Association.

Gagné, R. M. (1974). *Principles of instructional design.* Toronto, Canada: Holt, Rinehart & Winston of Canada.

Gagné, R. M., Briggs, L. J., & Wager, W. W. (1992). *Principles of instructional design* (4th ed.). New York, NY: Harcourt Brace Jovanovich.

Hattie, J., & Timperley, H. (2007). The power of feedback. *Review of Educational Research, 77*(1), 81–112. Retrieved from http://rer.sagepub.com/content/77/1/81

McCown, R., Driscoll, M. P., & Roop, P. G. (1996). *Educational psychology: A learner-centered approach to classroom practice* (2nd ed.). Boston, MA: Allyn and Bacon.

Orey, M. A., & Nelson, W. A. (1997). The impact of situated cognition: Instructional design paradigms in transition. In C. R. Dills & A. J. Romiszowski (Eds.), *Instructional development paradigms* (pp. 283–296). Englewood Cliffs, NJ: Educational Technology Publications.

CHAPTER 2

Using WebQuests to Implement Inquiry-Based Learning

Kelley K. Rogers

IN THIS CHAPTER, I DISCUSS the benefits of using the student-centered, collaborative WebQuest instructional strategy to create inquiry-based lessons. Grounded in constructivist theory, WebQuests place the responsibility for learning in the hands of the students, as they explore predetermined websites to gain the knowledge necessary to solve a real-world task. In collaborative groups, students work sequentially though six key events, which are given to the students at the beginning of the project. Through the structured events, the instructor can scaffold the assignment as needed to accommodate individual learners. As shown by related research, students indicate an increase in motivation and collaboration skills as a result of using WebQuests in the classroom.

Following an overview of the WebQuest instructional strategy, I provide two complete lessons to illustrate how the strategy may be used to facilitate e-learning. The first is a high school lesson for a class offered entirely online, and the second is intended for middle school students in a hybrid (partially online, partially face-to-face) class. Both lessons model how to integrate the WebQuest strategy into required instruction, using the Common Core standards. The last section of the chapter addresses design and delivery issues, specifically, accommodating large classes, differentiating instruction online for exceptional education and English language learners, assessing the learner, and forming/norming teams. In each case, common problems with online learning in general and WebQuests in particular are addressed, and solutions, where possible, are suggested.

Created by Bernie Dodge and Tom March, WebQuests are inquiry-based activities designed for students to explore predetermined web resources to research a particular subject. Students analyze and synthesize the information and then present their findings in a designated format, usually one related to a real-life scenario. After their creation in 1995, WebQuests quickly became the go-to instructional strategy for instructors eager to integrate technology into lessons. All you have to do is enter the term "WebQuest" in your favorite search engine to find thousands of WebQuests created by teachers in every subject area on levels from elementary to post-secondary.

WebQuests provide an instructional framework to help teachers create meaningful online learning activities that promote higher-level thinking skills, such as analysis, synthesis, and evaluation (Zheng, Perez, Williamson, & Flygare, 2008). A WebQuest presents a high-interest scenario that requires students to work in small groups, using web-based research to complete a task. While the research is teacher-guided by way of preapproved web resources, this instructional strategy allows students to determine their own investigative process as they gather their information. Frequently, each member of the group is assigned a specific area of knowledge to study so that they can contribute their piece to the group when it comes time to complete the task.

Think about your own classroom. When do students show higher-level thinking? In my experience, it isn't when they are quoting my own information back at me. I see the highest level of thinking when students are required to take the available information and create their own answers from the evidence. My students are used to me saying, "There are many right answers … as long as you support your right answer with convincing evidence." When our students get into college and the real world, they will not be required to pick out the "one right answer"; they will be required to find available information and synthesize a solution or a response. Inquiry-based lessons train students to use the thinking and logical skills needed to complete these tasks.

The WebQuest instructional strategy is based on constructivist theory, where students "construct" knowledge through their own explorations of the material. Instead of orienting instruction around the teacher, students direct their own learning by investigating a teacher-given scenario or resource. They develop critical thinking skills through inquiry-based activities, in which the instructor acts more as a guide than a "sage on the stage." Rather than parrot back information given by the instructor, students must determine the research question, evaluate given resources, analyze and synthesize the found information, and then create a response.

Building on the constructivist theory, WebQuests further integrate two additional principles: social interaction through collaboration and instructional support through scaffolding. In the 21st century, collaboration is no longer an option; it is a necessity. Our students will be entering a world where they not only need to know how to interact appropriately face-to-face but also online. They need to have experience working with those who are different from themselves—those who aren't necessarily friends—to prepare them for the world they will enter after graduation. In creating authentic tasks for students, collaboration must be included. WebQuests incorporate these collaborative elements, as they are not intended to be completed in isolation. Instead, students should work in collaborative groups to divide the research before coming together to discuss the results and complete an end task.

WebQuests also integrate the principle of scaffolding instruction for struggling students. In any given class of 30 students, I may have 10 who are current or former English language learners (ELL) and another five who have some sort of learning disability. In terms of ability levels, I might have students who are barely literate in the same class as students who read at or above grade level. To get my students to the higher levels of learning, I need to scaffold my instruction, providing additional support until they are able to complete the task on their own.

Scaffolds are not intended to be permanent, of course. Instead, they are put in place only as long as the student needs them before they are gradually reduced. The idea is that students will be supported as they move to the next level in their achievement. WebQuests have built-in scaffolds that the instructor can increase or reduce as needed by class, by group, or by student. At the moment, I teach three levels of English classes: regular for students way below grade level, adequate yearly progress (AYP) for students at or just below grade level, and honors for students above grade level. Rarely do I have a lesson or project that works for all three. My students have come to expect and enjoy WebQuests. Because the six steps of a WebQuest are so clearly defined, my struggling students are given step-by-step instructions on how to complete the task successfully. While the task alone may seem overwhelming, once students walk through the WebQuest steps with their group, they gain confidence in their abilities and are able to complete the task.

In a WebQuest, students proceed through six steps or key events. All steps are made available to students at the beginning of the assignment, so the students have an overview of the entire process before they start. All six events are traditionally presented on a web page or wiki for the students to refer to throughout the assignment. The students then work sequentially through the steps as a collaborative group.

TABLE 2.1   ▶   Key Events of a WebQuest

EVENT	DESCRIPTION
1. Introduction	Creates interest in the WebQuest by describing the project's scenario, as well as giving an overview of the final product.
2. Task	Describes the specific, open-ended activity the students are to complete. It should be as realistic as possible and not have a simple solution, so no scavenger hunts or fill-in-the-blank worksheets are used. Students' roles should also be explained here.
3. Process	Sets the boundaries for exploration by giving thorough and complete steps for the students to complete. Also includes any background information and any assessment criteria.
4. Resources	Provides the specific web resources students should use for their research. All links should be screened by the teacher, annotated with brief descriptions, and checked regularly to make sure they still work.
5. Evaluation	Assesses the task and applicable elements of the process in a rubric that is as objective and measurable as possible.
6. Conclusion	Sets the stage for future learning by encouraging students to reflect about what they have learned and why the task was important.

(Schweizer & Kossow, 2007)

By using a six-step process, WebQuests scaffold learning with a structure that leads students through the inquiry process. I can also adjust the level of scaffolding within each step to create additional support for struggling students or increase the rigor by removing scaffolds within steps to challenge high-achieving students. In this way, I can use the same WebQuest for these three groups of students, adjusting the degrees of scaffolding within each level as needed.

But are WebQuests effective? WebQuests definitely tend to increase students' motivation compared with lectures and other teacher-centered instructional strategies. Strong evidence indicates that when WebQuests integrate groups, regular and special education students benefit from the collaboration component (Murray, 2006; Milson, 2002; Leahy & Twomey, 2005). At this time, though, no definitive evidence proves that WebQuests directly influence student achievement. In their survey of the available research, Abbitt and Ophus (2008) found no significant achievement difference between students who learned via WebQuest as opposed to traditional instruction. The one exception was a study by Tsai (2006), which found improvements in vocabulary performance for English language learners who used WebQuests versus those who did not.

Lesson Plan Examples

Two lesson plans are presented next. The first, a completely online lesson, is geared toward high school students, and the second is a hybrid lesson for middle school students. I deliberately chose to create a totally online experience for the high school students because more and more states are integrating online learning classes into their graduation requirements. Middle school students, in contrast, won't necessarily have the motivation or the maturity to complete an online course without significant teacher assistance. Working through a hybrid lesson introduces middle school students to an online learning environment while giving them in-class instructional support during several key events.

For the purposes of these example lessons, the key events of the WebQuest are written with students as the audience. I deliberately chose to do this so that teachers could immediately implement these lessons with very little modification. Any notes directed solely to teachers will be placed at the beginning of each lesson's individual stages and be prefaced by "Note to teacher."

Lesson Plan A

Equality in America: A Literary and Historical Review *(Online Lesson)*

OVERVIEW

This lesson is intended for eleventh grade students who are studying American Literature. In my state, eleventh grade students also take a course in United States History during their junior year, so this WebQuest could be a cross-curricular partnership with a teacher or teachers in the History Department. In terms of course sequence, I would use the WebQuest as an introductory activity before examining contemporary speeches, essays, short stories, and poems on race and equality. Although not included in this lesson plan, the historical perspectives of race and equality of others besides African Americans, such as Japanese Americans during the internment camps of World War II, could be included.

LESSON OBJECTIVE

Given a list of websites, students will integrate and evaluate multiple sources of information that address racial equality in the United States through a WebQuest. Students will present their research in the form of a self-playing PowerPoint presentation or video.

STANDARD ADDRESSED

The WebQuest is aligned to the eleventh/twelfth grade Common Core State standard in English Language Arts. RI.11-12.7: Integrate and evaluate multiple sources of information presented in different media or formats (e.g., visually, quantitatively) as well as in words in order to address a question or solve a problem. (See www.corestandards.org/ELA-Literacy/RI/11-12 for more information on this and other related standards.)

TIME TO COMPLETE

8–10 hours

Introduction

Racism. Hate crimes. Since the founding of the United States, racial equality has been an issue, whether it concerned slavery, segregation, or racism. You have been hired by the Martin Luther King, Jr. Center for Nonviolent Social Change to create an informative video for high school students. They are concerned that today's students don't understand the people and ideas that were foundational within our country's struggle for racial equality. Specifically, they want the video to include primary sources from political and literary figures throughout history, examining their perspectives on equality.

Task

You will create a 4- to 6-minute video or self-playing PowerPoint presentation that examines one political figure and one literary figure for each of the major historical periods in the struggle for civil rights. For each figure, you must articulate his or her specific message about equality and support your thoughts with related evidence from a primary source. Each person in your group will be assigned one of the following historical eras listed in Table 2.A.1.

TABLE 2.A.1 ▶ Sample research questions associated with historical eras

ERA	DATE RANGE	SAMPLE RESEARCH QUESTIONS
Pre-Civil War	1776–1859	How did the founding fathers of our country view slavery and racial equality?
		How did the writers of the Declaration of Independence rationalize slavery in a nation where "all men are created equal" and are guaranteed the rights of "life, liberty, and the pursuit of happiness"?
Civil War and Reconstruction	1860–1876	How did Harriet Beecher Stowe's *Uncle Tom's Cabin* influence the nation's thoughts on slavery?
		How did Abraham Lincoln's speeches, specifically his second Inaugural Address, express his thoughts on equality and slavery in relation to preserving the Union?
Segregation and Jim Crow Laws	1876–1955	How did the writers of the Harlem Renaissance influence public thought on racial equality?
		How did Booker T. Washington's Atlanta Exposition Address of 1895 affect how African Americans were treated in the South?
Civil Rights Movement	1955–1968	How did Dr. Martin Luther King, Jr.'s view of the Civil Rights Movement and racial equality differ from Malcolm X's?
		How do Maya Angelou's writings communicate the experience of African Americans during the Civil Rights Movement?

Your finished presentation must include the following:

- ▶ All four eras, equally represented
- ▶ A brief overview of each of the eras as it relates to the chosen political and literary figures
- ▶ Each political or literary figure's message on equality
- ▶ Primary sources from each political or literary figure that support the person's message
- ▶ Title and credits with sources

Process

1. Your teacher will assign you to a group and also to an era/event. You must include the following eras/events in your video:

   a. Pre-Civil War (1776–1859)

   b. Civil War and Reconstruction (1860–1876)

   c. Segregation and Jim Crow Laws (1876–1955)

   d. Civil Rights Movement (1955–1968)

2. Gather background information on your era. Questions to think through:

   a. What major events occurred in the country?

   b. What are the attitudes of people of the two major racial groups in terms of race and equality?

3. Investigate major political and literary figures of the time who wrote about or spoke about equality and race relations or whose writings/speeches were influenced by race or equality.

4. Choose one political figure and one literary figure to research more in depth.

5. Research each figure's biography and read samples of the person's work.

6. Determine his or her views of race relations and equality using primary sources (i.e., the individual's speeches or writings).

7. Come together with your group to create your presentation. You may use Google+, Google Docs, Dropbox, or other collaboration software to meet online as a group.

Resources

Note to teacher: In Tables 2.A.2–2.A.5 web page titles would be hyperlinked when posted online, using the long link listed in the third column. The final WebQuest would include only the web page title and description columns. Also, the resources listed in these tables can supplement any subscription-based resources that your school already pays for, such as online encyclopedias, databases, or search engines. Keep in mind that while these resources were active links at the time of publication, web pages and addresses are constantly changing. Please ensure that all links are still active before providing them to your students.

TABLE 2.A.2   ▶   Resources for All Roles

WEB PAGE TITLE	DESCRIPTION	LINK
African American Odyssey	Online exhibits of the African American experience from slavery to the Civil Rights Movement (Library of Congress).	http://memory.loc.gov/ammem/aaohtml/exhibit/aointro.html
African American World	Timeline with linked stories covering the African American experience from the 1400s to present (PBS).	www.pbs.org/wnet/aaworld/timeline.html
Africans in America	History of Africans in America from 1450–1865. This resource bank is especially helpful as it outlines the contents of each section (PBS Online).	www.pbs.org/wgbh/aia/home.html
American Rhetoric	Transcripts of American speeches. Some speeches include audio when available.	www.americanrhetoric.com
Poets.org	Poems and poets' biographies are listed by poet and by topic. Includes some audio recordings of the poems as well (The Academy of American Poets).	www.poets.org (General Site) www.poets.org/viewmedia.php/prmMID/20281 (Poems of the American Revolution) www.poets.org/viewmedia.php/prmMID/20047 (Poems about Politics and Patriotism)
Bio	Includes biographies on historical and contemporary figures (A&E Television Networks).	www.biography.com

TABLE 2.A.3   ▶   Pre-Civil War and Civil War Resources

WEB PAGE TITLE	DESCRIPTION	LINK
Slavery and the Making of America	Primary and secondary sources related to both the political side and the daily routine of slavery are cited (PBS).	www.pbs.org/wnet/slavery
Stories from the Revolution: African Americans in the Revolutionary Period	Text-heavy overview of African Americans in the Revolutionary War (National Park Service & U.S. Department of the Interior).	www.nps.gov/revwar/about_the_revolution/african_americans.html
Slavery in America	Large collection of resources including key people, themes, and events of this era (The History Channel, A&E Television Networks).	www.history.com/topics/slavery
"To Light Us to Freedom and Glory Again": The Role of Civil War Poetry	List of major Civil War poets and poems (Library of Congress Poetry Resources).	www.loc.gov/rr/program/bib/lcpoetry/cwvc.html
Literature of the Civil War	List of Civil War-era authors with brief biographies and links to their writings (National Endowment for the Humanities).	http://edsitement.neh.gov/feature/literature-civil-war
American Civil War	Large collection of resources (text and videos) that includes the people, themes, and events of the Civil War (The History Channel, A&E Television Networks).	www.history.com/topics/american-civil-war

TABLE 2.A.4 ▶ Resources for Segregation/Jim Crow Era and the Civil Rights Movement

WEB PAGE TITLE	DESCRIPTION	LINK
African American Odyssey	A digital exhibit including information on the African American experience from slavery through the Civil Rights Movement (Library of Congress).	http://memory.loc.gov/ammem/aaohtml/exhibit/aointro.html
The Rise and Fall of Jim Crow	An online companion to the PBS documentary. Includes a timeline, historical context, and biographies and key people (PBS).	www.pbs.org/wnet/jimcrow
The Civil Rights Movement	A Timeline of the Civil Rights Movement (CNN Interactive).	www.cnn.com/EVENTS/1997/mlk/links.html

Evaluation

You will be evaluated on the final PowerPoint presentation or video using the rubric in Table 2.A.5.

TABLE 2.A.5 ▶ Assessment rubric used to evaluate final project

	EFFECTIVE	SATISFACTORY	INEFFECTIVE
Message	Video clearly and explicitly connects the historical context to the political and literary figures' writings in all four eras.	Video connects the historical context to the political and literary figures' writings in at least two of the eras.	Video does not connect the historical context to the writings.
Point of View	All four eras are included and equally represented.	Three of the four eras are included. Eras are generally given equal time, though one era might be concentrated on more than others, or one is left out.	Fewer than three eras are included, or one era is given substantially more time than the others.
Completeness	Includes a brief historical overview and writings from one related political figure and one related historical figure for all four eras.	Includes two of the following for three eras: a brief historical overview, writings from one related political figure or from one related historical figure.	Includes information for fewer than three eras, or information includes only one of the three required elements.
Production Values	Includes appropriate background music and/or audible narration throughout the video. Has clear and smooth transitions between eras.	Includes background music and/or narration in the video. Has transitions between eras, though they may sometimes be rough or unclear.	Lacks background music and narration in the video. Transitions between eras are rough or nonexistent.
Sources/Credits	Includes titles and credits for all of the information used.	Includes titles and credits for some of the information used.	Titles and credits not included.

Conclusion

In this task you should have learned a little more about the history of race relations in America. As we examine contemporary speeches and writings, keep this historical context in mind. See how today's political and literary figures mention those in our country's past as having affected their lives and viewpoints.

Lesson Plan B
Great Britain Welcome Wiki *(Hybrid Lesson)*

OVERVIEW

This lesson is intended for use with seventh grade students, though it could easily be adapted for older or younger students. Often before beginning a novel with my students, I want to give them some background information about the setting, particularly if it is somewhere unfamiliar or takes place in an earlier era. In this case, we were about to begin reading Agatha Christie's classic mystery *And Then There Were None*. The action takes place on an island off the coast of Devon in England and includes many references to 1930s British society and culture, so I found it helpful to explain some of that decade's cultural and historical background to help my students understand the text better.

LESSON OBJECTIVE

Given a list of websites, students will research the geography, society, political system, and technology of 1930s Great Britain through a WebQuest. Students will present their research in the form of a wiki.

STANDARD ADDRESSED

WebQuest will be aligned to the seventh grade Common Core standard in English Language Arts, RL.7.9: Compare and contrast a fictional portrayal of a time, place, or character and a historical account of the same period as a means of understanding how authors of fiction use or alter history.

TIME TO COMPLETE

9–10 hours (3 in class, 6–7 online)

Introduction *(In Class)*

Have you ever traveled to a foreign country (or even a new, unfamiliar part of town) and felt completely out of place? Did you notice the people spoke a different language or used unfamiliar slang, ate different kinds of food, and followed different rules? For this project, you work for the U.S. Embassy in London in the 1930s. Employees in the Consular Service have noticed that many Americans who move to England face culture shock. Your task is to help make the transition easier for these newcomers. Working with a team, you will create an online resource for Americans living in Great Britain that will explain some basic information to help smooth the transition into life in a new country.

Task *(In Class)*

Each person in your group will be assigned one of the following roles listed in Table 2.B.1. The group will create a wiki of five or more pages that introduces Americans to life in Great Britain in the 1930s. You must have at least one page for each role plus a reference page for your sources, though you are free to create additional pages if needed. Be sure to cite sources appropriately for any information you post in your wiki.

TABLE 2.B.1 ▶ List of WebQuest roles and related research questions and ideas

ROLE	RESEARCH QUESTION(S)	IDEAS FOR RESEARCH
Historian	How does the geography and climate of Great Britain compare to that of the United States?	What is the British Empire? What geographical areas did it include in 1939? What is the typical climate?
Political Scientist	How does the British political system compare to the one in the United States?	What type of government do they have? (democracy, dictatorship, monarchy, republic, etc.) What is Scotland Yard? How did it come into existence? What does it do?
Sociologist	How is living in Great Britain different from living in the United States?	What type of money denominations were used in the 1930s? What is the class system? What are the general levels?
Scientist	How do the technology, transportation, and scientific achievements of Great Britain in 1939 compare with those of today?	What kind of communications technology was available? What major scientific achievements occurred in the 1920s and 1930s?

Your finished presentation must include the following:

▶ Accurate information from all four roles equally represented

▶ Answers to both questions given plus development of two additional ideas chosen by you

▶ Comparisons between the British system and its American equivalent when possible

▶ Information that will be useful to an American audience

▶ Proper in-text citations and a reference page

Process *(Online unless otherwise noted)*

1. Your teacher will assign you to a group and also to a role. (In class)

2. As a group, add to the existing list of questions to answer while researching. Additional questions can be added during the research process. (In class)

3. On your own, use the provided resources to research your assigned topic. (Online)

    a. Use Cornell Notes (http://coe.jmu.edu/LearningToolbox/cornellnotes.html), with your questions on the left-hand side and your notes on the right-hand side.

    b. In your notes, indicate the sources of your information.

4. Meet with your group to share your information and identify any areas you may have missed. This is also a time when you can ask your teacher any questions. (In class)

    a. As you are working, your teacher will be checking your group's progress to make sure everyone is contributing.

5. Work with your team to create your wiki. You may use Wikispaces or another wiki host to post your project. Each teammate is responsible for the page in your wiki that corresponds to that person's role.

6. Once a draft is complete, read through all the pages. In the comment box, give any suggestions for revisions or editing. You should include at least one good comment and one revision for each page, including your own.

7. Before turning in the project, all members of the group should check over the final product to make sure it satisfies all the requirements.

8. When finished, post a link to your wiki in the Discussion Board thread labeled "Great Britain Welcome Wiki."

Resources *(Online)*

Note to teacher: Students should have access to at least one encyclopedia. If your school does not subscribe to an online encyclopedia, consider allowing the students to use Wikipedia. Personally, I do not allow my students to use Wikipedia if they have access to an encyclopedia that is fact checked. Table 2.B.2 lists resources to be provided to students during their WebQuest. Please ensure that all links are still active before providing them to your students.

TABLE 2.B.2 ▶ List of resources for students going on Great Britain WebQuest

WEB PAGE TITLE	DESCRIPTION	LINK
British Life and Culture	A comprehensive site that includes many aspects of British life. Information can be difficult to find because the site is so big, so make use of the search box (Woodlands Junior School in Kent, United Kingdom).	www.projectbritain.com
Encyclopedia Britannica	Comprehensive articles about Great Britain's history and political structure (Requires school subscription).	http://school.eb.com
Judiciary of England and Wales: Links for Students	The official government site for the British court system. This page lists links to information written especially for students (UK Judicial Office).	www.judiciary.gov.uk/interactive-learning/quick-links-for-students
Technology Timeline	A technology timeline from 2400 B.C. to A.D. 2001 gives an overview of the available technology (History Timelines).	www.history-timelines.org.uk/events-timelines/12-technology-timeline.htm
The History Channel: Inventions	Includes links to important inventors, eras, events, and other related topics. Tends to be focused on America, but many inventions were shared between the United States and Great Britain, so it is still useful (The History Channel; A&E Television Networks).	www.history.com/topics/inventions
The World Factbook: United Kingdom	Includes primarily statistical information on topics such as the government, economy, and population. Updated often and extremely current (Central Intelligence Agency).	www.cia.gov/library/publications/the-world-factbook/geos/uk.html

Evaluation *(Online)*

You will be evaluated on the final wiki using the following rubric (Table 2.B.3):

TABLE 2.B.3 ▶ Assessment rubric used to evaluate final project

	EFFECTIVE	SATISFACTORY	INEFFECTIVE
Accuracy	All information is accurate and addresses the topic.	Some information is accurate. Most addresses the topic.	Most information is inaccurate. Little addresses the topic.
Completeness	Information is included for all four categories. Information answers the questions given by the instructor plus at least two more created by the student. All four team members commented on all wiki pages.	Information is included for at least three categories. Information answers the questions given by the instructor. At least two team members commented on each wiki page.	Information is included for fewer than three categories. Only one team member commented on each wiki page.
Organization	Information is easy for the reader to find and understand. Information is in logical, short paragraphs and bulleted when necessary. Subtitles are used to categorize information.	The reader sometimes gets lost or can't find related information. Information is chunked in large paragraphs. Bullet points and subtitles are used but are either inconsistent or illogical.	The reader frequently gets lost. Information is presented in one large block with no paragraphs, bullet points, or subtitles.
Grammar and Spelling	All words, with only one or two exceptions, are spelled correctly. Sentences and paragraphs show proper use of grammar and punctuation.	Commonly used words are spelled correctly. There are some problems with grammar and punctuation, but the reader can still understand the text without frequent stops.	Commonly used words are spelled incorrectly. There are massive problems with grammar and punctuation so that the reader cannot understand what the writer is trying to say.
Sources/Credits	Includes sources and credits for all information used. Sources cited correctly.	Includes sources and credits for some of the information used. Sources cited incorrectly.	Sources and credits not included.

Conclusion *(In Class)*

Note to teacher: Give the students an opportunity to share their wikis with their classmates. Depending on your class and technology resources, this could be a gallery walk, with the wikis pulled up on classroom computers, or a short presentation to the class.

Through the research and the wiki, you should have learned a bit more about British society and culture. As we start reading Agatha Christie's classic mystery, *And Then There Were None,* you will now understand many of the references to British language and culture, allowing you to enjoy her suspenseful story all the more.

Design and Delivery Issues

If you choose to apply the WebQuest instructional strategy to design and deliver totally online or hybrid lessons, you should consider a number of issues, including (a) addressing large classes, (b) differentiating instruction for exceptional education students and English language learners, (c) assessing the learners, and (d) forming/norming teams.

Addressing Large Classes

As with any class, determining how to balance quality assessment with the time required to grade it is an issue. With the collaborative nature of WebQuests, the teacher only needs to grade one project for every four students, dramatically decreasing the paper load. As the teacher grades the projects, he or she is also freed up to give more in-depth feedback because the number of assignments to grade has decreased when compared with a traditional assignment that every student completes individually. In addition, the teacher will need to monitor student progress on the assignment prior to the final product, but this monitoring could take place during a short team conference (hybrid) or through wiki comments or discussion board or blog posts (online). In the end, using the WebQuest instructional method is one strategy for effectively instructing a large class of students.

Differentiation: Exceptional Education Students and English Language Learners

With the passage of the IDEA act, requiring the least restrictive environment for Exceptional Education (Ex Ed) students, regular education teachers are facing an influx of students with disabilities who are mainstreamed into our classes. In addition, with the increasing number of English language learners (ELLs) in our school systems, we also must address students with widely varying levels of English proficiency. Therefore, we must provide ways to accommodate these students, even in an online or hybrid environment.

In addition to these challenges, a huge emphasis has been placed on differentiated instruction in our classrooms for students who are low-performing. I'm not going to speak to adaptive technology needs, as these would be required no matter the instructional strategy. But, how might you provide accommodations for the WebQuest instructional strategy in an online environment?

When assigning roles, the teacher may differentiate instruction by giving low-performing students the roles with more available resources. In these WebQuest examples, I would assign the Civil War or Civil Rights Movement Role (online lesson) or the Sociologist Role (hybrid lesson) to those struggling students as the requirements are more straightforward. As many students with disabilities struggle with note-taking, the teacher could also provide a graphic organizer or note-taking form to assist the students during research (Skylar, Higgins, & Boone, 2007). The instructor could also further limit the number of websites, directing the Ex Ed students to the specific sites needed for their roles or parts of the assignment.

For gifted students, the teacher might reduce the scaffolding by having them create their own guiding questions as well as their own research questions. If needed, the instructor could increase the expected depth of research or require students to embed related multimedia in their projects. For any group requiring differentiation, the teacher can use strategic grouping to accommodate both struggling and advanced learners (see Forming/Norming Teams).

Learner Assessment

As with most group projects, there is always the concern about making sure all students in the group do their fair share. I purposely did not include this element in the rubric for each WebQuest because this goal can be achieved in several ways, depending on the teacher's preference. The teacher could have students complete teamwork evaluations on themselves and their teammates that are submitted at the end of the assignment. The downside of this is that, in my experience, students often will not be honest because they are concerned about the opinions of their classmates. Making this evaluation as private as possible helps and can provide some needed information, but it should be accompanied by other teacher-observed measures as well.

Teachers can also choose to grade the individual research the students do before completing the group task. This could take the form of checking notes that the students are required to take as they research. If the teacher wanted to assess the research process, the students could create a blog to document their research process, challenges, and successes. The teacher could then trace each student's thinking process as he or she completes the project. This also adds an element of student reflection into the WebQuest. The downside, of course, is the additional grading, but assignments such as these could be an option in classes where student accountability is an issue.

Forming/Norming Teams

Creating teams, particularly with middle and high school students, can be challenging. In general, I have found that when asked to partner with students they don't know or don't like, some will complain or refuse. At this point in their social development, students are still learning how to collaborate with people who aren't necessarily their friends. If given the choice, the students will almost always choose to work with their friends, whether it is best for them academically or not.

Despite student complaints, though, I rarely allow students to choose their own groups. I do this for two reasons. First, if we, as educators, are truly preparing our students for the 21st century, then we need to break up their cliques, if only temporarily, and provide students the opportunity to work with others outside their friend groups. Second, I usually group my students heterogeneously, so that there are students of varying ability levels in each group. When I allow students to choose their own groups, inevitably all the high-performing students form a group, while all the low-performing students group together and form another. If this happens, the high-performing students are generally on top of the project and learning, but the low-performing students are generally lost because they do not have someone in their group to model the project and hold them accountable. As the teacher, I can model the assignment, but instruction tends to be much more powerful when it is student to student.

Therefore, grouping students should be teacher-directed to create heterogeneous groups that contain students of differing abilities and social groups. If a teacher is concerned about the ability of the low-performing student to complete the task due to being ELL or exceptional education, the teacher can choose to differentiate the WebQuest within the group, as mentioned earlier in this chapter.

Concluding Thoughts

In this chapter, I have shown how WebQuests can successfully be used in middle and high school language arts and history classes as an alternative to teacher-lead instruction. Although I focused on these two subjects, I hope you can see how WebQuests can be modified for any content area or subject. This instructional strategy is one of the most flexible I have found in terms of subject-area application.

As WebQuests, by their very nature, are student-driven, they can be somewhat intimidating to try in the classroom. But when teachers hand over some of the responsibility for learning to the students, they will learn how to conduct research in a collaborative environment that mirrors, to some extent, that which they are likely to find in the workplace. In addressing some of the common concerns and difficulties with integrating WebQuests into the classroom, I hope I have assuaged some of the fears in implementation so you can confidently integrate technology, collaboration, and student-centered learning in your instruction. If this chapter sparked your interest, but you feel like you need to see more examples or would like to know more about the instructional strategy, you are encouraged to visit http://webquest.org for the most complete and current source of information about the WebQuest Model.

References

Abbit, J., & Ophus, J. (2008). What we know about the impacts of WebQuests: A review of research. *AACE Journal, 16*(4), 441–456.

Leahy, M., & Twomey, D. (2005). Using web design with preservice teachers as a means of creating a collaborative learning environment. *Educational Media International, 42*(2), 143–151.

Milson, A. J. (2002). The Internet and inquiry learning: Integrating medium and method in a sixth grade social studies classroom. *Theory and Research in Social Education, 30*(3), 330–353.

Murray, R. (2006). WebQuests celebrate 10 years: Have they delivered? *Action Research Exchange, 5*(1).

Schweizer, H., & Kossow, B. (2007). WebQuests: Tools for differentiation. *Gifted Child Today, 30*(1), 29–35. Retrieved from the EBSCOhost Research Database.

Skylar, A. A., Higgins, K., & Boone, R. (2007). Strategies for adapting WebQuests for students with learning disabilities. *Intervention in School and Clinic, 43*(1), 22–28.

Tsai, S. (2006, March). Integrating WebQuest learning into EFL instruction. Paper presented at the Society for Information Technology and Teacher Education International Conference 2006, Orlando, FL.

Zheng, R., Perez, J., Williamson, J., & Flygare, J. (2008). WebQuests as perceived by teachers: Implications for online teaching and distant learning. *Journal of Computer Assisted Learning, 24*(4) 295–304.

CHAPTER 3

The 5E Instructional Model
Developing 21st-Century Skills through Online and Hybrid Course Work

Shelly Wyatt, Natalie Dopson,
Yana Keyzerman, and Janet Daugherty

INFLUENCED BY HIGH LEVELS of Internet use and digital literacy, educators have increased interest in and commitment to learner-centered approaches to lesson design. The cultural and technological shift to learner-centered instruction has also generated increased demand for online and hybrid course work that taps into digital skills and literacy. The 5E Model of instructional design offers educators a scaffold for developing learner-centered instruction that supports student inquiry and knowledge construction. For this chapter, we review the five components of the 5E Model: engagement, exploration, explanation, elaboration, and evaluation. We summarize research on the 5E Model, illustrating its applications across subjects and the use of tools, such as wikis, online learning management systems, texting, open source website hosting, and online document sharing sites to support collaboration and the sharing of information. We then provide two examples of lesson plans that focus on social science objectives—one example for mixed-mode delivery and one for totally online delivery. Finally, we explore the design and delivery issues inherent in the model.

earners at all levels of K–12 education report consistent use of the Internet, with preteens and teens logging in more hours than their younger schoolmates (Cloney, 2010). Indeed, teens (ages 12–17), along with young adults (ages 18–29), spend more time online than any other group (Lenhart, 2009). In an average day, approximately 33% of eight- to 18-year-olds use a computer for schoolwork with an average time of 16 minutes spent on academics (Rideout, Foehr, & Roberts, 2010). According to the Pew Internet & American Life (2010), 93% of teens use the Internet; these same teens will continue to utilize the Internet in college and beyond. Not surprisingly, the skills associated with high levels of Internet use—utilization of search engines, creation of web-based content, and online collaboration—create a demand for online and mixed-mode instruction that taps into and reinforces these skills.

One response of educators to the shift in student skills and expectations is the 5E Instructional Model. An instructional approach grounded in research, the 5E Model is learner centered, emphasizing student inquiry and knowledge construction through interaction with the instructor, peers, and selected course content. The 5E Model is also flexible and may be effectively applied across disciplines.

We begin this chapter by reviewing the components of the 5E Model and explaining its theoretical foundation. We then summarize research related to the 5E Model and provide samples of online and hybrid K–12 lesson plans. Sample lesson plans illustrate applications of the 5E Model to National Geography Standards (http://education.nationalgeographic.com/education/standards/national-geography-standards/?ar_a=1), specifically Standard 16, which focuses on resource use and its meaning around the world. We conclude the chapter with a discussion on key design and delivery issues. In addition, the International Standards for Quality Online Courses are considered as guiding standards for course development (International Association for K–12 Online Learning [iNACOL], 2011).

Phases and Benefits of the 5E Model

Funded by a grant from IBM, the Biological Sciences Curriculum Study (BSCS) model, commonly known as the BSCS 5E Instructional Model or the 5E Model, was first developed over twenty-five years ago to enhance science curriculum development and the creation of instructional materials for professional training (Bybee, Taylor, Gardner, Van Scotter, Powell, & Westbrook, 2006). This model consists of five distinct phases: engagement, exploration, explanation, elaboration, and evaluation. According to Bybee et al. (2006, p. 1):

> Each phase has a specific function and contributes to the teacher's coherent instruction and to the learners' formulation of a better understanding of scientific and technological knowledge, attitudes, and skills. The model frames a sequence and organization of programs, units, and lessons. Once internalized, it also can inform the many instantaneous decisions that science teachers must make in classroom situations.

Although initially developed for science education, the 5E Model works equally well for other disciplines, including social sciences, mathematics, and technology-related fields of study. The reason for its broad applicability is that the model supports students' grasp of new concepts and enhances the connections among various instructional activities, thus leading to learners making more connections (Bybee et al., 2006). The utility of the 5E Model resides in the relationships between and among its core phases. Taken alone, these phases clearly support the teaching and learning process. Used together, these phases provide a powerful instructional approach. Table 3.1 briefly paraphrases each phase.

TABLE 3.1 ▶ Phases of the BSCS 5E Instructional Model (Bybee et al., 2006, p. 2)

PHASE	DESCRIPTION
Engagement	Learners engage the new concept by participating in short activities that elicit prior knowledge and pique their interest.
	Activities make connections between previous and new learning experiences, reveal present conceptions related to a new learning objective, and focus the learners' minds on the "learning outcomes of current activities."
Exploration	Learners participate in "exploration experiences" that identify and challenge current knowledge (including "misconceptions"), skills, and processes to facilitate "conceptual change."
	Activities within this phase may consist of lab activities or other hands-on activities that encourage use of current understandings to generate new ideas, "explore questions and possibilities," and "design and conduct a preliminary investigation."
Explanation	Learners focus more deeply on a particular aspect of their exploration experiences.
	In this phase, demonstrations of skills, knowledge, and understandings of concepts are emphasized.
	Activities ask learners to work individually or in groups to explain what they have learned from their exploration experiences.
Elaboration	Instructors provide opportunities for learners to elaborate on, correct mistakes or misconceptions, and otherwise extend their understandings of concepts.
	Activities include applying concepts to real-world problems.
Evaluation	Learners assess their mastery of skills and understandings associated with learning objectives.
	Instructors evaluate students' progress.

The benefits of the 5E Model correspond with its focus on higher-order thinking skills that constitute a strong component of the 21st-century skills. According to Bybee (2009), the following skills are included in the model:

- ▶ Adaptability
- ▶ Complex communication/social skills
- ▶ Nonroutine problem solving
- ▶ Self-management/self-development
- ▶ Systems thinking

The 5E Model supports a learner-centered approach that emphasizes the role of the students in creating their own learning. While many instructional models have the goal of supporting learner-centered instruction, the 5E Model provides clear steps to making the identified goal a reality. Another important strength of the 5E Model is that it can be applied within different instructional formats, including on-site, on-site with an online component (called hybrid, blended, or mixed mode), and completely online. The tools that are available for online learning, including learning management systems, Web 2.0 tools such as wikis, virtual study halls, Google docs, email, texting, and Skype, make the implementation of learner-centered approaches a more successful reality than ever before.

Theoretical Foundations of the 5E Model

The theoretical basis for the 5E Model resides squarely in the constructivist camp; within this camp, three main areas of emphasis are inquiry based, learner centered, and cooperative learning. In general, constructivist learning theory promotes the idea that learners must actively participate in—or construct—their own understandings of the content matter, rather than having the teacher tell them what they are supposed to know. The redirection of instructional emphasis from teacher to learner represents a radical shift from traditional, instructor-centered models to one in which instructors and learners cooperate and collaborate (Boddy, Watson & Aubusson, 2003). However, the idea that learners must participate in their own learning is not new. For example, in the 1930s, John Dewey recognized that passive learning develops passive minds and stunts creativity. The industrial age model of education, patterned more closely after behaviorist and information-processing models, embraced the goal of developing workers who were able to work in factories and to follow rules and guidelines in the manufacturing of goods for mass consumption. Constructivism responds to the needs of a new century and a new economy that demands creative thinking, problem solving, and well-developed interpersonal skills (Bybee et al., 2006).

As the guiding theory of the 5E Model, constructivism acknowledges that learning is "individually constructed and socially co-constructed by learners based on their interpretations of experiences in the world" (Jonassen, 1999, p. 217). Constructivism, as an explanation of how learning takes place, provides a broad view of the learning process that has generated numerous approaches to teaching and learning, including learner-centered, experiential, and inquiry-based instructional strategies. Constructivism is the product of multiple theorists. Early supporters of constructivism reasoned that learners utilize past experiences to make sense of new experiences, fitting these new ideas and experiences into already existing frameworks. Learners then accommodate these new concepts by developing new frameworks to accommodate their new ideas and experiences (Harcombe, 2001). Influential constructivist Lev Vygotsky (English translation, 1962) focused his analysis of learning on the social element, emphasizing the importance of learning through socially constructed activities; this collaborative space, with boundaries determined by the personal understanding of peers and teachers, provides rich opportunities to explore and develop new ideas and understandings.

Application of the 5E Model across Subjects

Various studies support the use of the 5E Model to enhance science curriculums (Bybee et al., 2006) as well as across subjects. For example, in Turkey, researchers compared a group of high school students who were taught science using the 5E Model and a control group of students taught with the traditional methods. The researchers found that the 5E group scored an average of two percentage points higher on a test for Reasonable Thinking Ability and "developed more positive attitudes towards the subject" (Ergin, Kanli, & Unsal, 2008, p. 47). The study by Ergin et al. (2008), along with other research studies (e.g., Kukula & Harbor, 2009; Saka & Akdeniz, 2006), support use of the 5E Model within classrooms to improve student outcomes.

Kukula and Harbor (2009) provide an example of how the 5E Model was implemented with students in a middle school lesson on biometric technology about fingerprinting technology. The 5E Model divided the information into categories: "The lesson was developed in this fashion to create interest and curiosity about biometrics (*engage*), encourage students to work together without direct instruction from the fellow or teacher (*explore*), enable students to explain difficult concepts and definitions in their own words (*explain*), enable transferability of knowledge by having students apply what they have learned in biometrics to a new situation (*elaborate*), and measure the effectiveness (*evaluation*)" (Kukula & Harbor, 2009, p. 202).

Similarly, Saka and Akdeniz (2006) found positive outcomes with high school students on learning about genetics when teachers used the 5E Model and integrated computer-assisted materials, using Flash Player to help them better understand chromosomes. This study provides another example of how the 5E Model is grounded in constructivist theory—allowing children to explore via experimentation and linking new information to their prior knowledge. Although originally used for science lessons, the 5E Model has expanded to other subject areas, including the social sciences.

Sample Lessons Using the 5E Model

In this section, we illustrate how you can apply the 5E Model to facilitate learning. We present an example of a hybrid lesson, integrating online and on-site (in class), face-to-face learning activities, as well as an example of a totally online lesson.

Lesson Plan A
Fish as a Natural Resource *(Hybrid Learning)*

Fish as a Natural Resource is a hybrid instructional unit, based on the 5E Model, that leads learners in an exploration of fish as a vital natural resource around the world. It incorporates both on-site and online instructional elements and materials. This unit is designed to support learners' use of critical thinking skills in exploring and evaluating one of the most important issues facing our growing world population: the depletion of fish stocks at the same time the global demand for fish is increasing. The five components of this lesson engage learners in activities that challenge their current assumptions and challenge them to confront a real-world issue in terms that are accessible and engaging.

Fish constitutes one of the most important sources of nutrition for human beings; demand for this resource is increasing along with world populations. The ways people view natural resources vary around the world, including how fish are regarded. After reflecting on their current experiences with natural resources in their homes and at school, learners will view, discuss, and interact with media related to the pressures on fish populations. Learners will then explore the current conditions of specific species of fish and will generate a business plan or presentation that addresses fish as a natural resource under pressure from human demand.

Fish as a Natural Resource addresses National Geography Standard 16: By the end of the eighth grade, the student should know and understand the changes in the meaning, use, and importance of natural resources. Although geared toward middle-school learners, both sample lessons can be revised to accommodate and challenge more mature learners. This lesson also conforms to iNACOL (2011) standards in its use of digital content and resources, a combination of on-site and online assessment, and the development of digital content. This hybrid lesson is designed to be completed in five or six 50-minute classes, plus time outside class to complete the online activities and report or blog.

We used several online tools, including websites sponsored by National Geographic and PBS, as well as a free website-building tool called Webs. This free website was used to create online discussions (using the "forum" feature) and to host student blogs. Please note that there are other free online tools available, including Wikispaces and Wix, many of which are interactive.

Engagement

To engage learners, we begin the lesson with an activity that asks learners to identify several natural resources that are familiar to them and post their findings to an online discussion forum. Figure 3.A.1 depicts the web page posted to facilitate the event, followed by a copy of the instructions that were given to the learners.

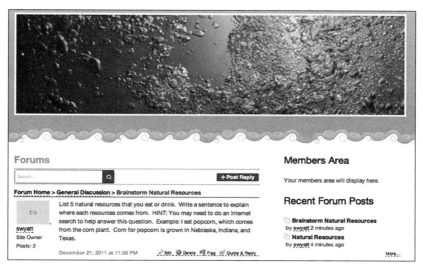

FIGURE 3.A.1   ▶   Screenshot of online discussion of natural resources

ACTIVITY 1 *(Online Discussion)*

A *natural resource* is any material found in nature that people use and value. Look around your home. What natural resources do you and your family use every day? List five natural resources that you eat or drink. Write a sentence to explain where each resource comes from. After you have posted your lists, respond to at least one classmate's postings; you may wish to ask a question, or you may simply make a comment. *Hint:* You may need to do an Internet search to help answer this question.

Example: I eat popcorn, which comes from a special type of corn plant. Most popping corn is grown in Nebraska, Indiana, and Texas.

Exploration

After engaging learners, the lesson exposes them to key concepts related to natural resources. Exploration consists of two activities, one that takes place in the online environment and the other that takes place in the classroom. The online discussion asks learners to make the distinction between renewable and nonrenewable resources. In this online discussion, we advise the instructor to participate actively, encouraging learners to use examples to explain their answers and to redirect the discussion as necessary. We also recommend assigning the discussion at the beginning of the week so that it takes place before the on-site activity.

ACTIVITY 2 *(Online Discussion)*

There are two types of natural resources. Renewable resources are resources that the Earth replaces naturally. Nonrenewable resources are resources that cannot be replaced. One natural resource that people all over the world use for food is fish.

Question: Do you think fish are a renewable or nonrenewable resource? Explain your answer. Be sure to respond to at least one classmate's posting.

The in-class activity consists of showing a video segment from National Geographic titled *Oceans: Declining Fish,* followed by a class discussion. The purpose of the activity is to encourage learners to explore the concept of natural resources in depth by distinguishing between types of resources and discussing real-world issues related to fish as a natural resource. In short, the instructor shows the video from National Geographic (depicted in Figure 3.A.2) and asks students to take notes and determine why fish populations around the world are declining.

FIGURE 3.A.2 ▶ Screenshot of *Oceans: Declining Fish* video clip

ACTIVITY 3 *(In-Class Discussion)*

Fish are a renewable resource because more fish can hatch to replace ones that have been caught. However, fish populations around the world are declining due to overfishing. Overfishing occurs when people catch so many fish that the fish cannot reproduce fast enough to replace those that are caught. Watch the *Oceans: Declining Fish* video from the National Geographic website (http://video.nationalgeographic.com/video/player/environment/habitats-environment/habitats-oceans-env/declining-fish.html) to find out some of the reasons why fish populations are falling. Use the questions below to take notes (in a notebook or on a computer) about the video. The instructor will then lead a discussion related to the video. You are to share your notes with the class during the discussion.

1. What problem does the video describe?

2. What solution does Dr. Jackson propose?

3. Why does he think this solution will be difficult to accomplish?

4. Dr. Jackson states that protecting parts of the ocean from fishing will hurt some people. What does he mean by that statement?

Explanation

The third instructional event of this lesson constitutes a mix of online and on-site activities, including an assignment that begins in the classroom and concludes with an online assignment. The purpose of this event is for learners, with the support of the instructor, to explain in detail the issues and challenges related to overfishing and the growing demand for fish products around the world. The first activity, facilitated in class, asks learners to interact with a virtual sushi bar sponsored by National Geographic Education. The instructor begins with a whole-class discussion with students about sushi, explaining that sushi is a traditional Japanese dish of rice topped with raw fish or other sea products. Although Japan accounts for only 3% of the world's population, it consumes 16% of the world's seafood. In recent years, sushi has become popular in many other countries, adding strain to an already declining fish supply. After the class discussion, learners explore and interact with the website and are asked to answer the questions provided below. At the end of this activity, learners may share their answers with the class.

ACTIVITY 4 *(In-Class Group Discussion)*

Although Japan accounts for only 3% of the world's population, it consumes 16% of the world's seafood. In recent years, sushi has become popular in many countries, adding strain to an already declining fish supply. Work in groups of four or five in class to interact with the Sushi Bar activity from National Geographic Education (http://education.nationalgeographic.com/archive/xpeditions/lessons/16/g68/sushi.html?ar_a=1). Discuss the following questions with your group:

1. Where do some of the seafood products for sushi come from?

2. Which fishing practices contribute to the decline of the world's fish populations?

3. How is fishing in foreign waters similar to piracy? What are countries doing to protect their fish resources?

4. How are the high prices paid for fish contributing to the problem?

5. What are the implications of sushi's growing popularity around the world?

The second activity begins in the classroom and concludes online. In accordance with the purpose of this event—to explain in detail issues related to overfishing and increased demand for fish products—learners work in teams to research the status of different types of fish that are in high demand. In teams, learners select a species of fish from the list provided and will research their selected species using suggested websites (included below). They then report their findings using the Webs.com site created for this lesson (illustrated in Figure 3.A.3). The instructor may respond directly to the blog or may ask learners to present their blogs to the class in the classroom.

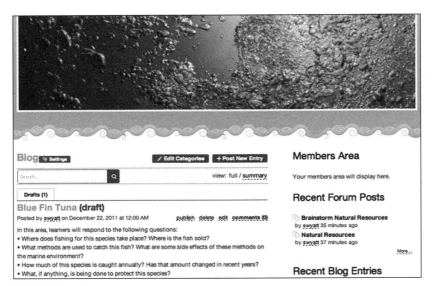

FIGURE 3.A.3 ▶ Screenshot of sample blog

ACTIVITY 5A (In Class)

Working with your group, choose an overfished species in the United States from this list:

bluefin tuna

Atlantic cod

salmon

halibut

red snapper

ACTIVITY 5B (Online)

Create a short report or blog about your chosen species. Use Internet resources to research information for your report. Use charts and graphs to help present information. Reports should include the following information:

1. Where does fishing for this species take place? Where is the fish sold?

2. What methods are used to catch this fish? What are some side effects of these methods on the rest of the marine environment?

3. How much of this species is caught annually? Has that amount changed in recent years?

4. What, if anything, is being done to protect this species?

Please use the following list of resources to research your report or blog post:

KidSafe Seafood: www.kidsafeseafood.org

Monterey Bay Aquarium Seafood Watch—Ocean Issues:
www.montereybayaquarium.org/cr/cr_seafoodwatch/issues

National Geographic—Seafood Decision Guide: http://ocean.nationalgeographic.com/ocean/take-action/seafood-decision-guide/#/seafood-decision-guide

National Oceanic and Atmospheric Administration (NOAA): www.nmfs.noaa.gov/sfa/domes_fish/StatusoFisheries/SOS8%20-05.htm

NOAA National Marine Sanctuaries: http://sanctuaries.noaa.gov

Shifting Baselines videos on ocean decline: www.shiftingbaselines.org/videos/

Sustainable Fishery, Wikipedia entry: http://en.wikipedia.org/wiki/Sustainable_fishery

World Resources Institute—Decline in Fish Stocks: www.wri.org/publication/content/8385

Elaboration

The fourth instructional event of this hybrid lesson provides an opportunity for students to use and *elaborate* on what they have learned. More specifically, learners apply what they have learned in previous sections to complete an extension activity. In this single activity, learners will select one of the following two assignments (selections below). Working in teams, this activity consists of learners developing an informed response to a specific problem or question. This activity may begin in the classroom and then may be completed as homework to be presented later to the class or posted in the course's website. The role of instructors is vital to the success of this step as their feedback will support learners' deepening understanding of the topic and synthesis of ideas already addressed in the previous instructional events.

ACTIVITY 6 *(In Class)*

Working with your group, complete one of the activities below. Present your results to the class. The instructor will assign one of the two prompts below. In your group, record your possible responses to the assigned prompt and then develop a plan or presentation that satisfies the prompt requirements. This activity may be completed over two class periods or may be assigned as homework.

1. Imagine that your team is opening a restaurant that features sustainable seafood. Write a business plan that includes a background section and a proposed menu. Make sure to explain how the various fish on your menu come from sustainable sources.

2. Imagine that you are a team of scientists working for a conservation organization. Create a presentation that you might give to government leaders explaining why they should pass a law banning a harmful fishing method.

Evaluation

This event consists of two activities to evaluate learners' mastery of the lesson's objectives. The first activity presents learners with an online opportunity to review materials associated with fish as a natural resource (Figure 3.A.4). The second activity consists of a test that may be administered online or in the classroom. The questions below correlate with Standard 16 of the National Geography Standards (http://education.nationalgeographic.com/education/standards/national-geography-standards/16/?ar_a=1).

FIGURE 3.A.4   ▶   Screenshot of net results activity, *Empty Oceans, Empty Nets*, from Habitat Media (2002–2013), PBS Marine Fisheries & Aquaculture Series (www.pbs.org/emptyoceans)

Background for Teachers: See the following link (www.pbs.org/emptyoceans/educators/activities/net-results.html) to review materials found on the home page of PBS's Marine Fisheries & Aquaculture Series. The link About the Films has a trailer for *Empty Oceans, Empty Nets* and information on how to purchase the film.

TEST *(Individual Online Activity)*

Directions: Go to *Empty Oceans, Empty Nets* (www.pbs.org/emptyoceans/eoen), and click on the links to the five types of fish listed. Follow the links to Overview, Case Study, and Viewpoints for more detailed information. Then write a short paragraph to answer each of the following questions.

1. **Define.** Explain how fish and other marine life are natural resources. Are they renewable or nonrenewable resources?

2. **Cause and Effect.** What are the effects of overfishing on people around the world?

3. **Compare and Contrast.** Compare the effects of overfishing on people in developing nations with those in developed nations.

4. **Recall.** Why are more fish being caught than ever before?

5. **Analyze.** How are the methods used to catch fish today harmful to the marine environment?

6. **Draw Conclusions.** What can governments do to address the problem of overfishing? What can citizens do to be responsible fish consumers?

Lesson Plan B

Oil as a Natural Resource *(Online Learning)*

Oil as a Natural Resource is an online instructional unit that leads learners in an exploration of oil as a vital natural resource around the world. This lesson is designed to support learners' use of critical thinking skills in exploring and evaluating one of the most important issues facing our world today: the increasing demand for oil as developing economies continue to grow. The five components of this lesson engage learners in activities that challenge their current assumptions and challenge them to confront a real-world issue in terms that are accessible and engaging.

Oil is one of the most important natural resources in the world, providing the energy to fuel the industrialization of nations in the developing world, as well as the continued economic growth of developed nations. Although there may be agreement as to the importance of this resource, considerable disagreement surrounds the impacts of oil's extraction and sale on the environment, politics, and human rights. After reflecting on their current understanding of renewable and nonrenewable resources, learners view, discuss, and interact with media related to the pressures on oil. Learners then explore the history and impacts of the oil industry and conduct research concerning an aspect of the oil industry. To develop a deeper understanding of oil as a resource, learners engage in a debate and then, as an evaluation, complete an online assessment.

Oil as a Natural Resource addresses National Geography Standard 16: By the end of the eighth grade, the student should know and understand the changes in the meaning, use, and importance of natural resources. This lesson conforms to iNACOL (2011) standards in its use of digital content and resources; ease of use of online resources, including learning management systems (LMSs) for e-learning; and the development of digital content. Although geared toward middle school learners, this lesson, as well as the previous lesson, can be revised to accommodate and challenge more mature learners. This online lesson is to be completed in approximately five hours online, plus three hours outside class to conduct research and collaborate with classmates.

We used several online tools, including websites sponsored by the History Channel (www.history.com); the Paleontological Research Institution (www.priweb.org/ed/pgws/); and the Public Broadcasting Service (PBS, www.pbslearningmedia.org). We also used a free website-building tool called Webs (www.webs.com). This free website was used to create online discussions (using the forum feature) and to host student blogs. Other free online tools are available, including Wikispaces (www.wikispaces.com) and Wix (www.wix.com), many of which are interactive.

The following five instructional events associated with the 5E Model appear below as a hybrid lesson that focuses on the utilization of natural resources.

Engagement

In this first instructional event, learners explore their current understanding of renewable and nonrenewable resources. The goal of this event is to engage students' interest in the lesson's learning objectives and to activate previous knowledge. The first of two activities associated with this event is an online discussion that requires participation by the instructor in order to keep the discussion on track and to provide clarification as necessary (Figure 3.B.1). Activity 2 engages learners by clarifying the uses of oil and natural gas in people's lives.

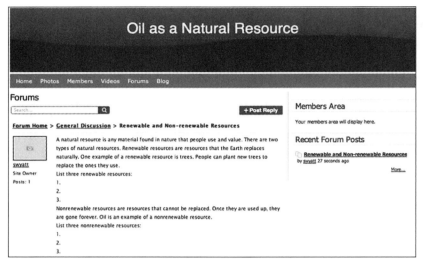

FIGURE 3.B.1 ▶ Screenshot of Activity 1 discussion used to engage learners

ACTIVITY 1

A natural resource is any material found in nature that people use and value. There are two types of natural resources. Renewable resources are resources that the Earth replaces naturally or resources that humans can help to replace. One example of a renewable resource is trees. Some seeds that fall from trees grow into new trees, and people can plant new trees to replace the ones they use. List three other renewable resources:

1.

2.

3.

Nonrenewable resources are resources that cannot be replaced. Once they are used up, they are gone forever. Oil is an example of a nonrenewable resource. List three other nonrenewable resources:

1.

2.

3.

ACTIVITY 2

Oil is used to make a lot of things we use every day. Check out the link below to learn about everyday objects made from oil and natural gas:

www.adventuresinenergy.org/Oil-and-Natural-Gas-in-Your-Life/

Exploration

The second instructional event of this lesson contains two activities to facilitate learners' exploration of key concepts and principles. Each activity requires learners to view and interact with online resources from the History Channel and PBS. The first activity (Activity 3 in this lesson) consists of learners viewing a streaming video titled *Black Gold*; this video explores the challenges of drilling for oil and demonstrates the technology involved in extracting oil from the land and seabed. Learners complete the first activity by participating in an online discussion (see questions below). The instructor may participate in the discussion, encouraging learners to provide details and examples in their posts and redirecting the discussion as necessary.

ACTIVITY 3

Watch this video to find out how the discovery of oil affected America.

History.com—Black Gold video (2:41):
www.history.com/topics/oil-industry/videos#black-gold

Write a paragraph answering the following questions:

1. Why do you think oil became known as "black gold"?

2. In what way were the discoveries of gold and oil similar?

3. How did "black gold" change America?

The second activity (Activity 4 in this lesson) asks learners to explore a timeline titled *Extreme Oil* and post answers to questions related to the assigned media (Figure 3.B.2). As instructors provide feedback on student blogs, learners are encouraged to use examples to explain their answers and to provide more details as necessary. This is also a good opportunity to draw a contrast between oil as a nonrenewable resource and renewable resources, such as fish or timber. The purpose of this event, to encourage learners to explore the concept of nonrenewable resources beyond a surface level, is achieved through distinguishing among types of resources and discussing real-world issues related to oil. People use oil in many different ways. In addition to being used to make products, oil is processed to make fuel for heating homes or for moving people and goods from place to place. However, people didn't always use oil in the same ways we do today.

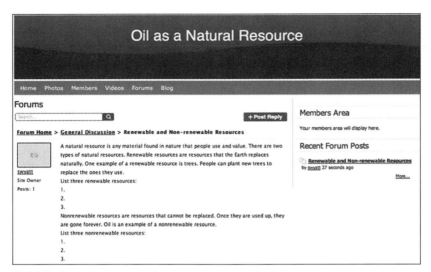

FIGURE 3.B.2 ▶ Screen shot from online course blog for Extreme Oil

ACTIVITY 4

Learn about the history of oil by looking at this timeline:

www.pbs.org/wnet/extremeoil/history/

Post answers to the following questions in the online course blog.

1. Who is known as the "Father of the Petroleum Industry"? Why?

2. Where was the first oil well in the United States located?

3. What happened in 1968?

4. Give examples of two events that affected oil prices.

Explanation

The third instructional event of this lesson constitutes two activities, each one requiring learners to investigate, interpret, and explain concepts related to the drilling of oil. The purpose of this event is for learners, with the support of the instructor, to explain in detail the issues and challenges related to the drilling of oil and the growing demand for products around the world. The first activity in this event asks learners to work in teams to investigate the mechanics involved in the extraction of oil. The instructor may begin with a whole class discussion about the extraction of natural resources in general, explaining that extraction affects many countries around the world, including the United States. Good examples are the BP oil spill and the Exxon Valdez spill. Ask students what effects they think these spills have had on the environment and on the political discourse surrounding oil. As learners explore websites related to oil extraction, learners respond as a team to the questions. The instructor as well as other teams may wish to respond to each team's posts, creating a robust dialogue. Next, as a continuation of this activity, learners in teams create a simple diagram of either a land-based or offshore oil rig. Teams may use PowerPoint or any other kind of simple drawing software, labeling the major parts of the rig and posting the diagram in the discussion area.

The second activity asks learners to explain the data contained in the assigned interactive map. In accordance with the purpose of this event—to explain in detail issues related to oil extraction and use—learners identify and explain the distribution of oil reserves around the world. After exploring the map, learners respond to the questions and post their answers in the discussion area.

ACTIVITY 5

In this activity, you will work with a partner to investigate how oil is drilled on land and offshore. Use the resources below to research your assigned topic.

Resources

Adventures in Energy: Exploration and Production—Drilling Rigs:
www.adventuresinenergy.org/Exploration-and-Production/Drilling-Rigs.html

History.com—Hoover Dam videos: www.history.com/topics/hoover-dam

History.com—Oil Drilling Ships video (2:53):
www.history.com/topics/oil-industry/videos#oil-drilling-ships

PBS—Extreme Oil: www.pbs.org/wnet/extremeoil/science/interactive.html

Captain tour—a virtual tour to a North Sea oil platform:
http://resources.schoolscience.co.uk/SPE/

Part A

In the discussion area, both partners will write separate posts on what each of you has found out. Your explanations should answer the following questions on the assigned topic:

1. What kind of equipment is used in this method of drilling?

2. What are the advantages of using this method?

3. What are the disadvantages?

Part B

Respond to your partner's posting. Discuss how your methods compare.

Part C

Work with your partner to create a simple diagram of either a land-based or an offshore rig. Use PowerPoint or any kind of simple drawing software. Label the major parts of the rig. Post your diagram to the discussion area.

ACTIVITY 6

Using the interactive maps on the U.S. Energy Information Administration's website (www.eia.gov/countries/), answer the following questions:

1. What are the world's top five oil-producing countries?

2. What countries are the top five oil consumers?

3. Which country has more proven oil reserves, Saudi Arabia or Canada?

4. Which country in South America produces the most oil?

5. In the future, where will most of the United States' oil come from?

Elaboration

The fourth instructional event of this hybrid lesson, the elaboration event, provides an opportunity for students to use what they have learned. More specifically, learners will be applying what they have learned in previous sections to complete an extension activity. In this single activity, learners, in teams of three or four, engage in a debate regarding drilling for oil in protected wilderness areas in Alaska. Working in teams, this activity asks learners to assume roles (see below) within teams to delve more deeply into a specific problem or question. Team members may use resources already identified and utilized within this lesson or may engage in additional online research. Teams engage in a debate within the context of an online discussion. The role of instructors is vital to the success of this step, as their feedback will support learners' deepening understandings of the topic and syntheses of ideas addressed in the previous instructional events.

ACTIVITY 7

Work with your team to decide who will play which role. Using the scenario below, engage in a debate on your group's discussion board. Back up your statements with facts from this unit or online research. Based on the arguments presented, your team should make a decision either to open the areas to drilling or to keep them protected. Explain your decision.

Scenario

Oil Company X wants to open protected wilderness areas in Alaska to drilling.

Roles

▶ An Oil Company X executive

▶ An oil industry lobbyist

▶ An Alaskan government representative

▶ A U.S. Environmental Protection Agency (EPA) representative

Evaluation

During the final event, learners evaluate their mastery of the lesson's objectives, and the instructor evaluates learners' progress and mastery as well. This event consists of one activity in two parts; the first part provides learners with an online opportunity to review what they have learned, and the second part provides learners with an opportunity to demonstrate their knowledge. The review consists of crossword puzzles that students may complete (links below). Learners then complete an online exam (below).

REVIEW

To review what you have learned in this lesson, complete these crossword puzzles. You can use the Hints in the puzzles or search the Internet to find any terms you cannot remember.

www.eia.gov/kids/energy.cfm?page=cwp_nonrenewables

www.eia.gov/kids/energy.cfm?page=cwp_petroleum

TEST

Directions: Write a short paragraph to answer each of the following questions.

1. **Define.** Explain why oil is a natural resource. Is it a renewable or nonrenewable resource?

2. **Cause and Effect.** What was the effect of the discovery of oil at Spindletop?

3. **Compare and Contrast.** What are the advantages and disadvantages of drilling on land versus offshore drilling?

4. **Recall.** Which country is the world's top oil producer?

5. **Analyze.** How is oil important in our everyday lives? Name three products you use that are made from oil.

6. **Draw Conclusions.** What can we do to lessen our dependence on oil?

Design and Delivery Issues

For many of you currently in the field, the demand for online instruction is growing, but training and experience have not kept pace. Often you may not have the time, resources, training, or support to incorporate technology effectively into your curriculum or instruction (Lear, 2007). The urgency associated with delivering high-quality online and hybrid (blended) instruction permeates school districts across the nation. This urgency arises from the promises associated with these delivery methods, including increased course offerings and a more individualized approach to learning (International Association for K–12 Online Learning [iNACOL], 2011). Teaching online or within a blended learning environment may present certain challenges for you. It is important to become aware of these challenges.

Pock (2011) found that a difference between teaching online and face-to-face is that teachers who teach online may not get immediate feedback from their students compared with face-to-face classrooms. Particularly, you may not see your students' facial expressions or nonverbal reactions, making it more difficult to determine whether students are grasping concepts or whether you need to make adjustments to your instruction. To prevent possible confusion within the online environment, it is critical for you to provide a typed copy or voice/video recording of instructions, activities, and other materials or topics at all times. Teachers can also create or use existing online tutorials. For example, if teachers want to embed an online wiki into a lesson to support a collaborative group project, they should include a tutorial to ensure that students have access to step-by-step instructions on how to create the wiki. As a result, teachers will reduce the number of questions such as, "What is a wiki, and how do I create one?" By making these simple adjustments, teachers can spend more time on ensuring that students are actively engaged in the learning process and assisting students with questions related to the content or interactive group work.

Students also face challenges with online or partially online learning environments. Pock (2011) found that students often have difficulty with self-discipline and time management. You must be cognizant of this and help students by creating timelines showing when assignments are due, communicating clear expectations, and offering suggestions on how to improve time management.

According to iNACOL (2011), in its publication titled "National Standards for Quality Online Courses," design and delivery issues associated with blended and online courses include resource diversity and quality, responsiveness to multicultural environments, and freedom from bias and advertising. Access to online and blended course content for all learners remains a core issue, ensuring that "course materials and activities are designed to provide access to all students" (p. 16). Another important issue relates to the need for clear communication between students and instructors, as well as between instructors and parents. Positive, open, respectful communication among all participants greatly enhances the effectiveness of online or blended learning.

Palloff and Pratt (2001) share the following lessons learned after teaching in the cyber classroom:

- ▶ Course development should focus first on facilitation and interactivity to ensure delivery of content rather than the instructor simply lecturing;

- ▶ Teachers' and students' roles need to continue to evolve, especially in terms of embracing the potential of Web 2.0 technologies (for example, blogs, social media, wikis) to decentralize the learning process. While acting more as a facilitator of learning rather than a dispenser of information, teachers can encourage students to build on pre-existing knowledge and skills to generate new knowledge and skill sets through generating and sharing online content;

- ▶ Adequate administrative support for faculty and students must be provided in a timely manner; and

- ▶ Good institutional planning is critical to the success of online courses and programs.

Each of these lessons learned by effective online instructors should be addressed during each of the five events associated with the 5E Model.

Engagement

In the 5E Model, engagement entails finding out students' background knowledge to help them understand the course's new concepts and objectives. Usually in a face-to-face class, you can ask questions to determine students' prior knowledge and see facial expressions and gestures that indicate whether they are familiar with a topic. This presents a challenge for the online environment, where you may not readily see whether students are learning. You can develop a pre-assessment survey/questionnaire or quiz to measure students' prior knowledge of a topic. Based on students' responses, you can adjust the level of instruction to meet their different learning needs. Some of the pre-assessment tools found online are free and open source, and others can be purchased.

Another obstacle that you may encounter is that students engage in different ways; therefore, it is critical to provide options and different ways for students to engage in the learning environment. Teachers must design learning environments that are accessible and engaging for all students, including those with disabilities and those who are English language learners. One way teachers can do this is by using principles of the Universal Design for Learning covered by Straub and McKinney in Chapter 6 of the first book in this series, *Online and Hybrid Learning Design Fundamentals*, and accessible online at www.cast.org/udl/.

Exploration

During the exploration stage, teachers are to provide opportunities for students to experience the learning process and to interact with course content firsthand. How can students experience hands-on learning within an online environment? Certain tools are necessary. For example, teachers can use interactive e-books so that students can interact with the text by manipulating three-dimensional objects, interactive images, and galleries. Instructors can also assign videos related to the topic. In an online biology class, for example, students can dissect a frog by interacting with the images instead of using a real frog. Students who would find pithing and dissecting an actual frog to be cruel or disgusting can now participate in simulated dissections and learn about the anatomy of a frog. Online instruction offers a wealth of interactive information and allows students to apply skills in a hands-on manner. (Check out http://images.apple.com/education/ibooks-textbooks for resources that may be used to facilitate student exploration online). An obstacle for online learning may be that some schools do not have adequate funding to purchase interactive e-books, the necessary hardware (electronic tablets, iPads, and laptops), or technology support. However, most students can participate in hands-on learning activities with the support of technology tools.

Explanation

During this stage, students are to explain what they have learned from their explorations. You can give students a number of options to demonstrate or explain what they have learned. Some valuable tools for facilitating student explanations within online or hybrid environments include Skype, iMovie, YouTube, and other live and recorded video streaming applications. You may also ask students to fill out Venn diagrams or other visual organizers to explain what they have learned. Furthermore, you can ask questions to scaffold students' explanations and help ensure that all are learning and deepening their knowledge.

Elaboration

Probably the most challenging of the events in the 5E Model to facilitate totally online is elaboration, which may be particularly difficult with a large number of students. After students explain what they have learned from their explorations, you are to assess their explanations, correct misconceptions, and fill in any potential gaps by asking students to elaborate on their newly acquired skills and knowledge. Assessing, providing corrective feedback, and asking 10 to 20 students to elaborate on their work may not be too taxing in a traditional, in-class environment because all or most communications may be facilitated in person in real time. But once you have more than 20 students in a course, elaboration may be challenging to facilitate, particularly online, because the communications are predominately asynchronous and in writing.

To elaborate, students may also be asked to apply their new knowledge and skills to real-world problems. To do this, the Internet can be a valuable resource for students. However, even though the Internet is a great place to find current world news and information on many topics, students need to be able to determine whether some websites are legitimate or not. A caution is for teachers to inform students that certain websites cannot be trusted. Sometimes schools have filters that allow students to see only approved websites. Students should be taught how to detect legitimate information from reputable sources versus opinions from blogs. A good resource for learning how to evaluate websites may be found at http://lib.nmsu.edu/instruction/evalcrit.html. Assessing and providing written feedback to the level of detail necessary to correct misconceptions, fill in the gaps, and otherwise elaborate on the content is the key issue that must be considered if you are going to apply the 5E Model to design and deliver a totally online course or lesson.

Evaluation

In the evaluation part of the 5E Model, you are to assess students' achievement of specified learning objectives and their mastery and application of related skills and knowledge. Some of the different assessment tools you can use include rubrics for individual and group projects, surveys, questionnaires, quizzes, and tests. The assessments should match the learning goals and objectives of the lesson as discussed by Hirumi in Chapter 1, "Aligning Learning Objectives and Learner Assessments: An Essential Precursor for Grounded Design," of the first book in this series, *Online and Hybrid Learning Design Fundamentals*. In essence, teachers should ask, "What do I want my students to learn from this lesson? Why are these objectives relevant and applicable to their lives?" Teachers need to create or find assessment tools that will measure student learning. The Internet has several resources that are open source or free, as well as some that can be purchased. Some useful assessment tools can be found on the website of Northern Arizona University's Office of Curriculum, Learning Design, and Academic Assessment (http://nau.edu/OCLDAA/Assessment-Process) and at RubiStar (http://rubistar.4teachers.org), a free tool for teachers to create rubrics from specific subject matter templates.

Conclusion

The technology revolution has significantly changed the way students learn. Many children have access to information and technology tools at an early age. Concurrently, education has become more learner centered. Effective styles of teaching and learning have shifted from the teacher being the epistemological center of authority to students having access to abundant sources of information. Students are becoming active participants who contribute to courses' knowledge and fellow students' learning experiences. As schools increasingly offer hybrid learning and fully online learning options for students, it is important for teachers and students to prepare for this transition and to clarify their new roles within new learning environments (Ash, 2011; Palloff & Pratt, 2001). The 5E Model offers teachers a dynamic, learner-centered instructional model that is responsive to the changing interests of today's students and society. The benefits of the 5E Model include robust student engagement and an inquiry-based focus that support critical thinking and collaborative learning (Boddy, Watson, & Aubusson, 2003; Bybee et al., 2006), making this model appropriate and beneficial for many subjects, including science, literature, and social science.

References

Ash, K. (2011, November 9). Blended learning on the rise, report says [Blog post]. Retrieved from http://blogs.edweek.org/edweek/DigitalEducation/2011/11/blended_learning_on_the_rise_r.html

Boddy, N., Watson, K., & Aubusson, P. (2003). A trial of the five Es: A reference model for constructivist teaching and learning. *Research in Science Education, 33,* 27–42.

Bybee, R. W., Taylor, J. A., Gardner, A., Van Scotter, P., Powell, J. C., Westbrook, A., & Landes, N. (2006). *The BSCS 5E instructional model: Origins and effectiveness.* Colorado Springs, CO: Biological Sciences Curriculum Study (BSCS). Retrieved from www.bscs.org/sites/default/files/_legacy/BSCS_5E_Instructional_Model-Full_Report.pdf

Bybee, R. W. (2009). *The BSCS 5E instructional model and 21st century skills.* Paper prepared for the Workshop on Exploring the Intersection of Science Education and the Development of 21st Century Skills, National Research Council. Retrieved from http://itsisu.concord.org/share/Bybee_21st_Century_Paper.pdf

Choney, S. (2010, February 3). Most younger net users get there wirelessly. Retrieved from www.nbcnews.com/id/35206710/ns/technology_and_science-tech_and_gadgets/t/most-younger-net-users-get-there-wirelessly/#.UapMbJW1lUM

Ergin, I., Kanli, U., & Unsal, Y. (2008). An example for the effect of 5E Model on the academic success and attitude levels of students: Inclined projectile motion. *Journal of Turkish Science Education 5*(3), 45–59.

Harcombe, E. S. (2001). *Science teaching/science learning: Constructivist learning in classrooms.* New York, NY: Teachers College Press.

Heffron, S., & Downs, R. (Eds.). (2012). *Geography for life: National geography standards* (2nd ed.). Washington, DC: National Council for Geographic Education. Examples from the standards and ordering information are available at www.ncge.org/geography-for-life

International Association for K–12 Online Learning (iNACOL). (2011). *National standards for quality online courses* (2nd ed.). Vienna, VA: author. Retrieved from www.inacol.org/cms/wp-content/uploads/2013/02/iNACOL_CourseStandards_2011.pdf

Jonassen, D. H. (1999). Designing constructivist learning environments. In C. M. Reigeluth, (Ed.), *Instructional-design theories and models: A new paradigm of instructional theory* (Vol. II, pp. 215–239). Mahwah, NJ: Lawrence Erlbaum.

Kukula, E. P., & Harbor, J. M. (2009, March). Biometric technology program to promote STEM education for the K–12 environment. Paper presented at the meeting of VI International Conference on Engineering and Computer Education, Buenos Aires, Argentina. Retrieved from www.gk12.org/files/2010/04/158_kukula_gk12_ICECE.pdf

Lear, S. (December, 2007). *No teacher left behind: Overcoming teacher barriers to technology use within the secondary school classroom* (Unpublished master's thesis). Sierra Nevada College, Incline Village, Nevada.

Lenhart, A. (2009). Teens and social media: An overview presentation. Pew Internet & American Life Project. Retrieved from www.pewInternet.org/~/media//Files/Presentations/2009/Teens%20Social%20Media%20and%20Health%20-%20NYPH%20Dept%20041009nnAMREVISE.ppt

National Geography Standards Index. Retrieved from http://education.nationalgeographic.com/education/standards/national-geography-standards/?ar_a=1

Palloff, R. M., & Pratt, K. (2001, August). Lessons from the cyberspace classroom. Paper presented at the 17th Annual Conference on Distance Teaching and Learning. Madison, WI: The Board of Regents of the University of Wisconsin System. Retrieved from www.uwex.edu/disted/conference/resource_library/proceedings/01_20.pdf

Pew Internet & American Life Project. (2010). *Generations 2010.* Retrieved from www.pewInternet.org/~/media/Files/Reports/2010/PIP_Generations_and_Tech10.pdf

Pock, R. (2011, March 21). Cyber-school: The challenges of teaching and learning online from one English instructor's perspective. *The Journal of Education, Community, and Values, 11*(2). Retrieved from http://bcis.pacificu.edu/journal/article.php?id=773

Rideout, V. J., Foehr, U. G., & Roberts, D. F. (2010, January 1). Generation M2: Media in the lives of 8- to 18-year-olds. A Kaiser Family Foundation Study. Retrieved from http://kaiserfamilyfoundation.files.wordpress.com/2013/01/8010.pdf

Saka, A., & Akdeniz, A. R. (2006, January). The development of computer based material about genetic[s] and application according to [the] 5E model. *The Turkish Online Journal of Educational Technology (TOJET), 5*(1), 129–141.

Vygotsky, L. S. (1962, 1986). *Thought and language* (Rev. ed. by A. Kosulin). Cambridge, MA: MIT Press.

Watson, J. (2008). Blended learning: The convergence of online and face-to-face education. *Promising practices in online learning.* Vienna, VA: North American Council for Online Learning (NACOL).

CHAPTER 4

Using Scaffolded Vee Diagrams to Enact Inquiry-Based Learning

Kent J. Crippen,
Leanna Archambault, and Cindy Kern

IN THIS CHAPTER, WE DISCUSS how educators can use the principles of scientific inquiry to support student learning by creating lessons with scaffolded Vee diagrams. Our method involves the blending of two powerful frameworks: the Vee diagram and the principles of scaffolded knowledge integration. The scaffolded Vee diagram is a tool for the science-learning environment that includes strategies that support autonomous student work and collaborative argumentation. Working through a series of conceptual and methodological steps, students address a research question by constructing a scientific argument in the form of a claim that is supported by reasoning and evidence. The lesson plan examples provided in this chapter offer a tangible guide to implementing scaffolded Vee diagrams as a grounded approach for inquiry-based science courses in hybrid (i.e., blended) and online learning environments.

One grounded approach to inquiry-based learning uses Vee diagrams, named for their structure in the form of the letter "V," as a method to create a learning environment that parallels the conceptual and methodological practice of science. According to Gowin and Alvarez (2005), "The Vee diagram was developed as a way to aid in the understanding of meaningful relationships among events, processes, or objects. It is a tool that helps one observe the interplay between what is known and what needs to be known or understood" (p. 35). As a representation, the Vee diagram identifies the epistemic elements of scientific knowledge as they are used in a scientific investigation (e.g., asking research questions, conducting an analysis). The general shape of the diagram uses the open portion of the Vee to illustrate the role of research questions in framing an investigation, while the tip of the Vee points directly to the object, events, or material under investigation. A completed Vee diagram is a rich source of information about the process and products of a scientific investigation. As a learning scaffold, students use the Vee diagram as a guide, following a series of steps for identifying and documenting the elements of an investigation. In a parallel fashion, these steps serve to reinforce the process and products of learning from an investigation and make these steps explicit. The form and process of completing a Vee diagram illustrate its utility as a grounded approach for inquiry-based learning in science.

In this chapter, we use the term "scaffold" to describe a support that is provided to afford autonomous student work and collaborative argumentation. Scaffolds are the underlying parts of the Vee diagram written beneath each main label of the diagram provided to students. Scaffolds are created by teachers to guide students on how to start and continue working through the parts of the diagram. Our teacher-supplied scaffolds take many different forms: multimedia for students to view and comment on; resources for students to read, such as a link to a file folder containing a Word document or URLs for students to access on the Internet and comment on; and sentence-starter prompts for students to complete. Our scaffolded Vee diagrams support and guide students individually, as they learn to think logically, assess and compile datasets, construct and defend arguments, and reflect upon what they have learned—all of which help them to internalize the practices of science.

The Vee diagram has a rich history of use in education and has been modified into various forms and evaluated through research in numerous ways (Novak, 1990). Of primary importance to this chapter, the Vee diagram has been used successfully as a scaffold for learning in undergraduate science laboratories (Passmore, 1998), as well as in more traditional applications, including K–12 science classrooms (Alvarez & Risko, 2007).

Vee diagrams were first proposed by Gowin (1981) to describe the structure of knowledge involved in any educational event. Gowin viewed knowledge about knowledge as enduring, deeply meaningful, and a basic component of the process of educating. The Vee diagram was created as a "sense-making structure" that afforded "…relating events, facts and concepts to other elements of knowledge…" (p. 34).

Recently, Knaggs and Schneider (2011) demonstrated a positive relationship between improved procedural and conceptual understandings in science as a function of multiple, repeated learning experiences with Vee diagrams. In the context of online learning, Nussbaum and colleagues have been using a form of the Vee diagram that they call an argumentation Vee diagram to support collaborative argumentation in online discussions (Nussbaum, 2008; Nussbaum & Edwards, 2011; Nussbaum, Winsor, Aqui, & Poliquin, 2007). Regardless of the particular format of the Vee diagram, prior empirical research has established its effectiveness as a support for inquiry-based learning in face-to-face, hybrid, and online learning environments that span the educational continuum from elementary to graduate school.

In this chapter, we discuss how K–12 educators can use the principles of scientific inquiry to support student learning by creating online lessons using a method we call the scaffolded Vee diagram.

Our method involves a blending of two powerful frameworks, the Vee diagram, used by Gowin and Alvarez (2005) as a framework for science teaching and learning, and the principles of scaffolded knowledge integration, developed by Linn and colleagues (Linn, 2000; Linn, Bell, & Davis, 2005).

As a representation, the Vee diagram delineates the process of inquiry as a flow of conceptual and methodological steps that are used to address a research question with a scientific argument. This scientific argument contains a claim that is supported by reasoning and evidence. As a powerful learning environment tool, the Vee diagram is enhanced to include learning scaffolds that support autonomous student work and collaborative argumentation. We call this enhanced Vee diagram the scaffolded Vee diagram. As K–12 professional development leaders and classroom science teachers in hybrid and online-learning environments, our experiences have demonstrated the success of scaffolded Vee diagrams with students and teachers.

The Scaffolded Vee Diagram

A scaffolded Vee diagram serves as a guide for autonomous learning. The diagram supports students as they generate a scientific argument while focusing on the elements of scientific knowledge (Figure 4.1). Our diagram builds upon the work of Roehrig, Luft, and Edwards (2001), who also proposed the use of a Vee diagram as an alternative to the traditional science laboratory report, as well as the Vee diagram used by Gowin and Alvarez (2005). Our diagram departs from a general framework for a laboratory activity by including directed scaffolding for knowledge integration. Specific to each investigation, students are directed to fill in partially completed charts, tables, and diagrams to aid their production of valid scientific argument. In addition, whenever student input is required, sentence-starter prompts are used to help students elucidate their thinking, to guide them as they work through the lesson on their own, and to connect with other students by presenting and defending their arguments.

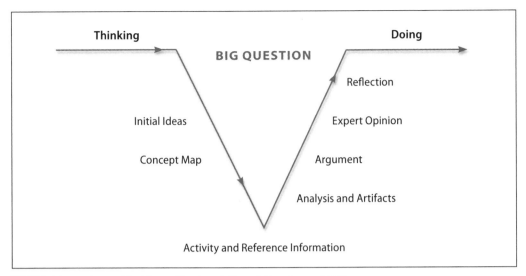

FIGURE 4.1 ▶ Our modified form of Gowin and Alvarez's Vee diagram (2005)

Note that the Vee diagram is to be read from the upper left Thinking side down and through the point of the Vee, and then up along the narrow right side, up to the Doing top right side of the Vee.

Table 4.1 describes additional theoretical frameworks and strategies that support our scaffolded Vee diagrams.

TABLE 4.1 ▶ The components and supporting theoretical frameworks involved in the scaffolded Vee diagram

COMPONENT	THEORETICAL FRAMEWORK	STRATEGIES
Lesson Structure	Inquiry-Based Learning, as defined by the five essential features of inquiry (Olson & Loucks-Horsley, 2000)	Vee diagram
Technology	Computer Supported Collaborative Learning (CSCL) (Stahl, Koschmann, & Suthers, 2006)	Data analysis Production of inscriptions (e.g., charting, graphing, mashup)
Learning Mechanism	Collaborative Argumentation (Andriessen, Baker, & Suthers, 2003) Scaffolded Knowledge Integration (Linn, 2006)	Knowledge integration environment (e.g., claim scaffolds, sentence-starter prompts)
Learning Outcomes	Self-Regulated Learning (cognition, metacognition, belief) (Schunk, 2001)	Evaluation and reflection (e.g., learning strategy use, efficacy for science learning)

In this chapter, we describe the components of the scaffolded Vee diagram and illustrate their functions with two practical examples, one for hybrid learning and one for online learning. First, we outline the general flow of a lesson and detail each of the components, including the function, task, and types of scaffolds that are used. Next, we outline the current technologies used to transform the scaffolded Vee diagram into an autonomous science-learning environment. As the scaffolding of students' responses plays such a critical role in achieving the primary goals of student autonomy and high-quality learning, we offer additional details on how teachers can construct effective sentence-starter prompts.

The Flow of a Lesson

Within a scaffolded Vee diagram, each lesson is focused on addressing a *Big Question*. These questions are based on real-world problems and are written by the teacher so that students understand that the scientific problems apply to their daily lives. Following the big question, the lesson progresses down from the left, *Thinking* side of the Vee diagram with *Initial Ideas* and *Concept Map*, through the point of the Vee. The resources at the point of the Vee diagram that serve as the focus of the inquiry (i.e., the data to be analyzed) are included under the *Activity and Reference Information* as hyperlinked objects. The Vee diagram then proceeds upward along the narrow part of the right, *Doing* side with the activities in the scaffolds under *Analysis and Artifacts, Argument, Expert Opinion,* and *Reflection*.

As students work through the Vee diagram, they will begin at the top of the *Thinking* (left) side of the process with a scaffold titled *Initial Ideas;* it contains a link to a form of multimedia relevant to the big question, such as a video provided by the teacher. After viewing the video (or other type of multimedia), students write their initial ideas by completing the sentence-starter prompts in the initial ideas scaffold.

At the next scaffold down, constructing a *Concept Map*, students are given no more than 12 concepts to work with. The teacher provides these concepts as nodes in a concept mapping software program; students are limited to working with only the given list. (A concept mapping software program we like is IHMC Cmap Tools [http://cmap.ihmc.us]; more details about this program will be given later.) Students first arrange the nodes of the concept map in a meaningful way with similar and related concepts closer together and then link related concepts with an arrow indicating the direction of the relationship. Students add a verb or phrase to each linking arrow to show the nature of the relationship. They are encouraged to revisit and update their concept maps at any time during the inquiry in a recursive fashion (Kern & Crippen, 2008). This mapping exercise focuses students' attention and leads into gathering the resources to be studied, located at the point of the Vee as *Activity and Reference Information*. Table 4.2 summarizes the elements of the *Thinking* side of the scaffolded Vee diagram that precede the activity and reference information.

TABLE 4.2 ▶ The components, their functions, general task descriptions, and explanations of learning scaffolds used in the *Thinking* side of the scaffolded Vee diagram

COMPONENT	FUNCTION	TASK	SCAFFOLD
Big Question	Contextualizes the inquiry and triggers motivation.	Throughout the activity, students are encouraged to develop an evidence-claim-reason (ECR) statement that addresses the big question.	The big question, written by the teacher from the students' perspective, is based on their interests and experiences.
Initial Ideas	Capture students' ideas related to the concepts associated with the big question.	Students are provided with two to three elements of engaging, rich media and are asked to consider what the big question means to them.	Self-monitoring sentence-starter prompts.
Concept Map	Offers a semantic representation in graphic form of each student's understanding.	Students construct a linked, two-dimensional representation of their understanding; they continually update the map as they research the big question.	Provided list of up to 12 concepts.

The activities and reference information at the point of the scaffolded Vee diagram serve a single purpose: to generate a set of data (i.e., evidence) that each student will use to construct an argument. The argument includes reasons for how the evidence supports a claim. Appropriate activities for gathering reference information might include viewing a web-based simulation or other multimedia resource(s), such as a movie or visualization; using a data mashup tool; or participating in a virtual laboratory experiment. Two to three high-quality websites that offer different perspectives on the big question topic may be listed on the scaffold to guide students to valid reference information.

Using data mashup tools (commonly known as "mashups") can be an imaginative way of gathering information and will aid students and educators as they develop 21st-century research skills—needed to fulfill the vision of cyberlearning (NSF, 2008). Mashups provide an array of graphic and text information on a selected subject, combining more than one dataset. Mashups use an analysis and visualization process to create a completely new dataset (Archambault, Tsai, & Crippen, 2011). If you have not yet accessed mashups, these resources serve as visual representations that provide a wealth of engaging, information-rich data sources. Be sure to try the MyEnvironment tool from the U.S. Environmental Protection Agency (www.epa.gov/myenvironment). Other common mashup sources include maps (such as Google Map), videos (such as YouTube), photos (such as Flickr), searches (such as Google), and widgets (such as Widgetbox). Various mashups can be created using services such as Yahoo! Pipes, Google Public Data Explorer, and IBM's Many Eyes (Table 4.3). These applications and data form numerous combinations that can be used by students to create evidence for their scientific arguments.

TABLE 4.3 ▶ Examples of web-based mashup tools and resources

NAME	SOURCE	GUIDE
Yahoo! Pipes	http://pipes.yahoo.com/pipes	http://pipes.yahoo.com/pipes/docs
Google Public Data Explorer	www.google.com/publicdata/	https://support.google.com/publicdata/answer/1100640?hl=en&ref_topic=1100622
IBM Many Eyes	www-958.ibm.com/software/analytics/manyeyes/	www-958.ibm.com/software/analytics/manyeyes/page/Tour.html

After students have participated in research-gathering activities and compiled a dataset, the *Doing* side of the scaffolded Vee diagram begins at the lower right side of the Vee with an *Analysis* of activities and reference information they have accumulated. This analysis, in turn, will generate an *Artifact*. Students' work within the structured activities is not open-ended; instead, it is teacher-directed with steps that guide them to explore and collect scientific evidence related to the big question. This evidence is compiled into something separate and visible—a chart, diagram, or other data representation that serves as the artifact (i.e., product) of their analysis. Later in the process, this artifact functions as a focal point for each student's critical discussion and collaboration. In most schools now, students will produce their artifacts on their computers. Artifacts need to be created so they can be maximized into a larger form for others to view in groups and as an entire class. If the technology is available, students may project their artifacts onto a whiteboard.

The next component of the *Doing* side of the Vee diagram involves making an *Argument* in the form of an evidence-claim-reason (ECR) statement. In an ECR statement, evidence is connected to support a claim by a reason. The reason is an explanation of why the connection exists and is often the most difficult part of the ECR statement. ECR statements may be scaffolded with a three-column table and a series of sentence-starter prompts.

Collaborative argumentation guides how students communicate and justify their individual arguments (Andriessen, Baker, & Suthers, 2003). This process involves comparing and justifying individual arguments (evidence-claim-reason statements) against the accepted scientific understanding, as presented by valid, authoritative multimedia sources and experts whose opinions are published in reference books, textbooks, and online resources. Each student's arguments are also measured against competing claims offered by other students who are working as peer investigators. Each student's arguments (ECR statements) will also be measured against competing arguments offered by other peers, who are simultaneously gathering data and formulating their own arguments.

Once ECR statements are written, students compare them against what scientists (experts) accept as a valid argument (opinion). This *Expert Opinion* is generally provided as a short piece of narrative text. The narrative text may come from a few elements of multimedia, material selected from the course's textbook, two to three reference websites, and/or special reports found online. The key is to offer a valid, declarative statement of an aspect of the accepted scientific knowledge related to the big question. At this point, students are also encouraged to re-evaluate their concept maps and update them to reflect any new ideas or changes they need to make, based on new information they have gathered. The *Doing* side of the Vee diagram continues with students presenting their arguments—including artifacts, claims, and analyses of expert opinions to their peers. Students' presentations include a justification for the decisions they made; fellow students offer critical peer-reviews. Following each student's presentation, peer critiques, and the presenter's arguments in defense of his/her claim, students complete the scaffolded Vee diagram with *Reflection,* as they reflect (in writing and/or a class discussion) upon how their ideas compare and contrast with those of their peers. Table 4.4 includes a summary of the components of the *Doing* side of the scaffolded Vee diagram.

TABLE 4.4 ▶ The components, their functions, general task descriptions, and example learning scaffolds used in the *Doing* side of the scaffolded Vee diagram

COMPONENT	FUNCTION	TASK	SCAFFOLD
Analysis and Artifacts	Analyzes a dataset based on research to produce an artifact that will be used in constructing a scientific argument.	Students are guided to perform the analysis and construct the artifact.	Partially completed diagram, table, or other data graphic
Argument	Describes an evidence-claim-reason related to addressing the big question.	Students explain their reasoning by using their evidence to construct an argument with a specific claim.	Evidence-Claim-Reason table or argument prompt
Expert Opinion	Describes the accepted scientific knowledge related to the big question.	Students use teacher-provided multimedia or web resources to compare their arguments against what scientists say about the question.	Self-evaluation prompts Self-monitoring prompts
Reflection	Analyzes and critiques how each student's ideas are similar and different from those of other students.	Students present, compare, and critique their arguments; then they respond by writing about or discussing how their ideas compare with those of other students.	Activity prompts

Next we describe our experiences and current applications of freely available technology to deliver the scaffolded Vee diagram as an autonomous science-learning environment.

The Scaffolded Vee Diagram as an Autonomous Science-Learning Environment

With the use of appropriate learning technologies, the scaffolded Vee diagram can fulfill the vision of an autonomous science-learning environment. This environment must offer a high degree of engagement, support students' autonomy, and focus their efforts on proven strategies that build deep, integrated knowledge structures in a transparent manner consistent with the nature of science. Practically, this requires a set of technologies that afford a seamless integration of concept mapping, the utility of hyperlinking to external resources, and a medium for providing student scaffolding in a read/write format.

Over time and with varying degrees of success, we have experimented with a range of technologies, including the use of a Microsoft Word version of the Vee diagram as described by Coffman and Riggs (2006). However, the need for seamless concept mapping and the restricted space of a single page in a word processing document were serious limitations. Currently, we are using the software IHMC Cmap Tools (http://cmap.ihmc.us) for the following reasons:

▶ Students are able to save their work on a server that is accessible from home and school across various platforms.

▶ Teachers can electronically distribute a single activity file for all students.

▶ The software offers seamless integration of concept mapping, an essentially unlimited two-dimensional workspace, the utility of hyperlinking to resources, and a mechanism for providing student scaffolding in a read/write form.

▶ Most encouraging, IHMC Cmap Tools is currently distributed free for education. Based on our experience, this is the best medium to use with the scaffolded Vee diagram to create an autonomous science-learning environment.

With Cmap Tools, we have created a template of the scaffolded Vee diagram that teachers can tailor for individual lessons. Tailoring this template is as simple as editing a word processing document. Use the "Shared Cmaps in Places" feature from within Cmap Tools to find the server named "UNLV COE (NV-USA)" and the folder titled "Chapter—Vee Diagrams Enact Learning." Within this folder is supplementary material, including a general template for the scaffolded Vee diagram, as well as the full activity files for the two example lessons presented in the next section.

Lesson Plan A

What is the Current Risk for Indoor Radon in Our Community? *(Hybrid Lesson)*

In this inquiry, students use web-accessible data from the U.S. Environmental Protection Agency (EPA) and testing results from their state and local agencies to develop an evidence-claim-reason statement in response to the big question, "What is our current risk for indoor radon in our community?" The following sections present the narrative elements that are provided to students in a scaffolded Vee diagram (Figure 4.A.1).

This inquiry addresses all eight content standards from the National Science Education Standards (NRC, 1996). The inquiry involves assessing personal risk for exposure to radon, a chemically inert gas that is produced through the radioactive decay of naturally occurring uranium found in soil. The amount of uranium in the soil is highly dependent upon local geology, but all soils have some level of uranium. The half-life of radon is quite short (3.8 days), and if it decays while in the lungs, it is deposited as a solid that further decays, emitting alpha particles. Alpha particles are highly damaging to the soft tissue of the lungs. After smoking, radon is the second leading cause of lung cancer in the United States (EPA, 2011). Content standard one, *Unifying Concepts and Processes,* is addressed through the multidisciplinary science needed for assessing the risk for indoor radon. As illustrated by the description of the issue, students must be able to understand the connections among the traditional scientific disciplines of life, earth, and physical science. Content standard two, *Science as Inquiry,* as well as content standard eight, *History and Nature of Science* are also addressed with the elements of the scaffolded Vee diagram.

The explicit use of an evidence-claim-reason statement for describing the risk for indoor radon means that students communicate their understanding of the nature of science as well as their understanding of the science concepts. The science content of this activity includes the states of matter, radioactive decay, the Earth's surface geology, and the interaction of energy and matter in the form of human tissue and cancer cells. These topics address content standards three, *Physical Science;* four, *Life Science;* and five, *Earth and Space Science.*

Once radon levels are assessed, mitigating one's risk for indoor radon involves decision making about changes to the home in the form of technologies used in home construction. This establishes a connection between the natural and designed. This form of decision making addresses content standards six, *Science and Technology,* and seven, *Science in Personal and Social Perspectives.* The standards addressed by the inquiry, "What is the current risk for indoor radon in our community?" illustrate the utility of the scaffolded Vee diagram for creating a powerful science-learning environment.

ASSESSING THE LOCAL RISK FOR INDOOR RADON

Thinking

Doing

Focus Question

What is the current risk for indoor radon in our community?

Initial Ideas

View the video linked to this box, then complete the two statements.

The video is a news story from the *Dr. Oz Show*. Dr. Oz is a medical doctor who offers advice related to health issues. The video explains about radon and why it is important to have your home tested.

1. Based upon this news story and what I already know, I think the current risk for indoor radon in our community is...

2. I think this is accurate because...

3. Watching this video news story has also made me wonder about...

Concept Map

Create a concept map of the terms below.

Reflection

After watching or reading the presentations provided by other groups, update your concept map to reflect your current understanding and complete this inquiry by finishing the following statements:

1. My ideas are similar to other people's ideas in the following ways...

2. Ways that my ideas differ from the ideas of others include...

3. As I worked on this project, I wish I would have spent more time on...

Expert Opinion

Consider the expert opinion on indoor radon by viewing the references attached to this node and then reconsider your argument. Restate your argument by finishing the following sentence-starter prompts (even if it doesn't change).

1. As evidenced by...

2. I claim that the risk for indoor radon in my community is...

3. Because...

4. After considering the expert opinion, the reason I chose to change (or not to change) my claim is because...

Argument

Use your analysis results to generate an argument by finishing the following sentence-starter prompts.

1. As evidenced by...

2. I claim that the risk for indoor radon in my community is...

3. Because...

Analysis and Artifacts

Once you complete your analysis, attach the artifacts as files that you have created or include them as URLs, then finish the following statements.

1. I analyzed the reference information in the following ways...

2. The attached artifacts illustrate my analysis by...

Collect Evidence

View the reference information linked to this node and devise a scientific way to analyze the information.

Your analysis should require you to create a couple of artifacts that illustrate your process of analysis and results. Acceptable artifacts include: charts, graphs, and diagrams.

FIGURE 4.A.1 ▶ An image of the scaffolded Vee diagram for the Risk for Indoor Radon inquiry

The scaffolded Vee diagram is designed for autonomous learning where all of the components occur online. For a hybrid learning environment, as is described with this example, use of the diagram could occur on a continuum from the teacher serving solely as lesson facilitator to more directed, face-to-face, teacher-led activities. The role of lesson facilitator implies that the teacher moves among student groups, answers questions, checks for understanding, and modifies the lesson where appropriate. For the components of the *Thinking* side, the teacher encourages collaboration and the deliberate completion of the starter prompts and concept map. For the *Doing* side, the teacher acts as a sounding board for ideas about the relationships among evidence and claims. If desired or needed, the expert opinion and reflection components could be face-to-face activities.

Next, we detail each of the narrative elements from the scaffolded Vee diagram and include a *Teacher Note,* offering suggestions for how to deliver this lesson in a hybrid learning environment.

Risk for Radon—Initial Ideas

View the video below, and then complete the statements that follow.

The video is a news story from the *Dr. Oz Show.* Dr. Oz is a medical doctor who offers advice related to health issues. The video explains about radon and why it is important to have your home tested.

FIGURE 4.A.2   ▶   News story from the *Dr. Oz Show* on radon and home testing
(www.doctoroz.com/videos/ask-dr-oz-anti-cancer-edition-pt-2)

1.   Based upon this news story and what I already know, I think our current risk for indoor radon in our community is...

2.   I think this new report is accurate because...

3.   Watching this video news story has also made me wonder about....

Risk for Radon—Concept Map

Create a concept map of these terms.

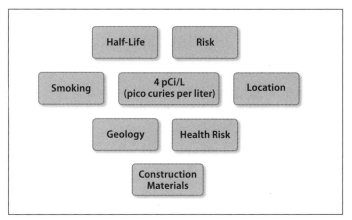

FIGURE 4.A.3 ▶ Concept map terms

Arrange the concepts in a meaningful way where similar and related concepts are closest together. If you do not know what a concept is, then move it to the left side of your map.

Link related concepts with an arrow indicating the direction of the relationship. Arrows may point from one concept to the other (unidirectional) or they may have two heads, one pointing at each concept (bidirectional).

Create a linking phrase between concepts by adding a verb or phrase to each linking arrow that describes the relationship between the concepts.

Risk for Radon—Collect Evidence

View the reference information at the following websites and devise a scientific way to analyze the information. Your analysis should require you to create a couple of artifacts that illustrate your process of analysis and results. Acceptable artifacts include charts, graphs, and/or diagrams.

EPA Map of U.S. Radon Zone: www.epa.gov/radon/zonemap.html

EPA Map of State Radon Zones: www.epa.gov/radon/whereyoulive.html

Google Map of State Radon Levels by State: www.radon.com/maps

Teacher Note: Use whole class or small group instruction to help students interpret the EPA map of the radon zones. This discussion is an opportune time to discuss how EPA scientists use multiple, varying representations to communicate their data meaningfully to the public.

Risk for Radon—Analysis and Artifacts

Once you complete your analysis, attach the artifacts as files that you have created or include them as URLs. Finish the following statements:

1. I analyzed the reference information in the following ways...

2. The attached artifacts illustrate my analysis by...

To enhance this lesson, students can test their own homes using relatively inexpensive commercial test kits. With the test results, use Google Earth to create a spatial representation of the entire set of student data by entering each point as a place mark.

Risk for Radon—Argument

Use your analysis results to generate an argument by finishing the following sentence-starter prompts:

1. As evidenced by...

2. I claim that the risk for indoor radon in my community is...

3. Because...

Teacher Note: Once students have determined their personal risk for indoor radon, they can be assigned to determine the risk for a family member or friend who lives elsewhere in the United States. These arguments can be presented along with their personal risk for radon.

Risk for Radon—Expert Opinion

Consider the expert opinion on indoor radon by viewing this reference:

EPA—A Citizen's Guide to Radon: www.epa.gov/radon/pubs/citguide.html

Reconsider your argument. Restate your argument by finishing the following sentence-starter prompts (even if it doesn't change).

1. **Evidence:** As evidenced by...

2. **Claim:** I claim that the risk for indoor radon in my community is...

3. **Reasoning:** Because...

4. After considering the expert opinion, the reason I chose to change (or not to change) my argument is because...

Teacher Note: Use a whole group discussion to elaborate on the big ideas of the expert opinion. Use a poster walk by having student groups present their arguments on a single PowerPoint slide. Rotate the class through each group's poster, allowing them to read and make notes about similarities and differences in each argument. Consider presenting an argument for a high-risk radon region in your state and having a discussion about potential actions individuals in the region might take to mitigate the risk.

Risk for Radon—Reflection

After watching or reading the presentations provided by others, update your concept map to reflect your current understanding and complete this inquiry by finishing the following statements:

1. My ideas are similar to other people's ideas in the following ways…

2. Ways that my ideas differ from the ideas of others include…

3. As I worked on this project, I wish I would have spent more time on…

The sentence-starter prompts used in the scaffolded Vee diagram are a critical attribute for developing deep and integrated knowledge. Depending upon the focus of each component in the scaffolded Vee diagram, one of three types of prompts may be used. The next section describes each category of prompts and provides examples.

Achieving Knowledge Integration with Sentence-Starter Prompts

The use of sentence-starter prompts as a learning scaffold facilitates knowledge integration and self-regulated learning (Schraw, Crippen, & Hartley, 2006). The sentence-starter prompts fall into three categories: activity prompts, self-monitoring prompts, and self-explanation prompts. A solid empirical basis exists for the strategy of sentence-starter prompts as well as these particular categories of prompts for promoting high-quality learning (Berthold, Eysink, & Renkl, 2009; Berthold, Nuckles, & Renkl, 2007; Davis & Linn, 2000).

Activity prompts encourage reflection on individual progress by guiding students to consider their own activities within the context of a large project (Davis & Linn, 2000). These prompts are used in nearly all components of the scaffolded Vee diagram as embedded elements. Activity prompts are constructed to have meaning for each student, to require a student to consider specific elements of an individual component of the Vee diagram (e.g., evidence, claims, reasoning), and to connect these elements to the larger goal of the inquiry (i.e., addressing the big question).

Following are examples of activity prompts:

▶ The reasons I chose to (support/not support) the Yucca Mountain project are…

▶ The scientific understanding contributing to my decision about the Yucca Mountain project includes…

> ▶ The claim made by the presenter is...

> ▶ Evidence the presenter used to support his/her claim included...

Self-monitoring prompts are used for planning and formative evaluation. They involve evaluation of planning for learning, strategy implementation during learning, and reflection and elaboration after learning.

Examples of self-monitoring prompts used for planning:

> ▶ In order for me to do a good job on this project, I must...

> ▶ As I worked on this project, I wish I would have spent more time on...

> ▶ One part of the project that I am most proud of is...

Examples of self-monitoring prompts used for evaluation:

> ▶ One concept I still do not understand involves...

> ▶ When thinking about the claims made by the expert, I am confused about...

> ▶ One piece of evidence I still do not understand is...

> ▶ The part of collecting evidence that I find difficult is...

Self-explanation is a strategy that involves a personal dialogue or self-talk during problem solving (Ainsworth & Loizou, 2003). These prompts encourage students to talk to themselves about a specific aspect or process of a problem or situation. Self-explanation prompts are designed to guide students as they work to develop a deeper understanding of a concept, procedure, or representation (Berthold, Eysink, & Renkl, 2009).

Examples of self-explanation prompts:

> ▶ When I look at the two representations of photosynthesis, I see the following similarities...

> ▶ The similarities in the two representations are important because...

> ▶ The reason I calculated _____ first is...

To achieve the highest possible learning gains, it is critical that the teacher constructs and applies the three types of sentence-starter prompts as scaffolding. In the next section, we describe a second example of a lesson written as a scaffolded Vee diagram intended for online learning. As you read and view this learning activity, it may be helpful to explain to yourself the classification and purpose of each type of sentence-starter prompt that is used. Imagine yourself as a student working through this activity, and think about how the starter prompts help effectively use the resources that are provided in order to build understanding while developing a strong argument.

Lesson Plan B

How Are Humans Affecting the Groundwater in Pocatello, Idaho? *(Online Lesson)*

In this inquiry, students use three different sources of data that are mashed up in Google Earth: (1) the boundary of the Lower Portneuf River Valley Aquifer near Pocatello, Idaho, (2) the location and nitrate level readings for selected groundwater collected in 2006, and (3) the relative number of septic permits issued in a given area (septic permit density). These data are used to develop an evidence-claim-reason statement in response to the big question, "How are humans affecting the groundwater in Pocatello, Idaho?" Our collaborators at the Boise Center Aerospace Laboratory and Idaho State University generously provided the evidence that students analyze in this activity. The following sections of the lesson plan present the narrative elements that are provided to students in a scaffolded Vee diagram (Figure 4.B.1).

By focusing on the socio-scientific issue of humans as components of the freshwater system, this inquiry addresses all eight content standards from the National Science Education Standards (NRC, 1996). The inquiry involves understanding how human activity affects groundwater in the small, rural community of Pocatello, Idaho. Pocatello serves as a model for the larger issue of understanding the origin of our local water, our involvement as a component of the freshwater system, and the role of human actions in maintaining a supply of quality drinking water, regardless of location.

Groundwater makes up 30% of the available freshwater on Earth, and for many people, groundwater is the primary source of drinking water (USGS, 2011). The lack of available, safe drinking water continues to be a major global issue (Maddocks, 2011). Content standard one, *Unifying Concepts and Processes,* is addressed through the multidisciplinary science needed for assessing the impact of humans on the freshwater system in Pocatello. As illustrated by the description of this issue at the beginning of the lesson plan, students must understand the connections among the traditional scientific disciplines of life, earth, and physical science. Within the scaffolded Vee diagram, the evidence-claim-reason argument statements for how humans are affecting the local groundwater addresses content standards two, *Science as Inquiry,* and eight, *History and Nature of Science.* The science content of this activity includes Earth surface geology, hydrology, solution chemistry, and ecology. These topics address content standards: three, *Physical Science;* four, *Life Science;* and five, *Earth and Space Science.* Minimizing human impact on the freshwater system is a socio-scientific issue at the interface of the natural and designed worlds and involves decision making about potential changes to our lifestyles, developing new technologies for purifying wastewater, as well as policy making about how humans dispose of their waste. Engagement in this issue addresses content standards six, *Science and Technology,* and seven, *Science in Personal and Social Perspectives.*

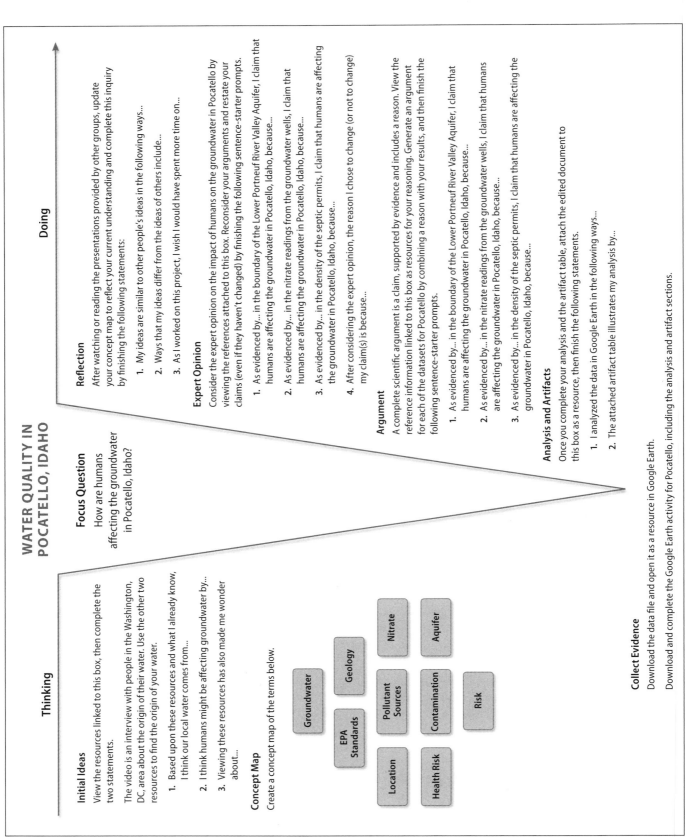

FIGURE 4.B.1 ▲ An image of the scaffolded Vee diagram for the Water Quality in Pocatello, Idaho, inquiry

Next, we detail each of the narrative elements from the scaffolded Vee diagram and include a *Teacher Note,* offering suggestions for how to deliver this lesson in a fully online-learning environment.

Water Quality in Pocatello—Initial Ideas

View these resources then complete the three statements below:

Where Does Your Water Come From?
www.youtube.com/watch?v=YtdCbHR1zoQ
> This is a video of interviews with people in the Washington, D.C., area, asking what they know about the origin of their water.

Groundwater: The Hidden Source of Life: www.thewaterchannel.tv/index.
php?option=com_hwdvideoshare&task=viewvideo&Itemid=53&video_id=208
> This video illustrates the importance of groundwater to humans on Earth.

Groundwater Contamination: www.youtube.com/watch?v=5xs1jLlbztE
> In this video Barb Mahler of the U.S. Geological Survey and the University of Texas describes the process of groundwater contamination.

Where Does Your Water Come From?:
www.nature.org/all-hands-on-earth /where-does-your-water-come-from-3.xml
> This is an interactive map that shows the sources of water from 493 cities in the world; for explanations of the map, see http://blog.nature.org/ conservancy/2012/10/18/the-science-behind-mapping-our-water

EPA—Water: Local Drinking Water Information: http://water.epa.gov/drink/local
> This page provides data about your local drinking water system.

Complete the following statements:

1. Based upon these resources and what I already know, I think our local water comes from...

2. I think humans might be affecting groundwater by...

3. Viewing these resources has also made me wonder about...

Water Quality in Pocatello—Concept Map

Create a concept map of the terms in Figure 4.B.2.

Arrange the concepts in a meaningful way, so that similar and related concepts are closest together. If you do not know what a concept is, then move it to the left side of your map.

Link related concepts with an arrow indicating the direction of the relationship. Arrows may point from one concept to the other (unidirectional), or they may have two heads, one pointing at each concept (bidirectional).

Create a linking phrase between concepts by adding a verb or phrase to each linking arrow.

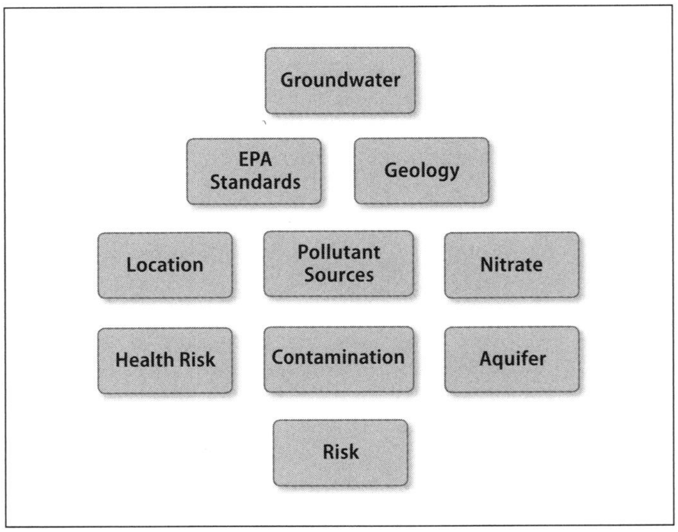

FIGURE 4.B.2 ▶ Concept map terms

Water Quality in Pocatello—Collect Evidence

Download the data file and open it as a resource in Google Earth.

Download and complete the Google Earth activity for Pocatello, including the analysis and artifact sections.

Three different datasets are displayed in Google Earth for your 3-D interactive exploration of water quality in the Pocatello area. Edit the Google Earth Activity file, and complete the Analysis and Artifact sections below; then attach this file to your Vee map as a resource. Please note the following:

▶ The boundary of the Lower Portneuf River Valley Aquifer is displayed as a thick blue line.

▶ Selected IDEQ and USGS groundwater wells are displayed as points with nitrate values collected in 2006. Wells are colored green for low nitrate values, yellow for medium, and red for high.

▶ Septic permit density is shown using an image that is dark blue in areas of higher density (more permits) and light blue in areas of lower density (fewer permits).

Analysis

This activity will involve using the three sets of data from Pocatello to support the claim that humans are affecting the local groundwater. Use Google Earth to explore the data and to answer the following questions:

1. What is the name of the well with the highest nitrate value?

2. What do you see under the areas with a high density of septic permits? To answer this, zoom into one or more of the dark blue areas and toggle the density image on and off.

3. What do you see under the areas with a low density of septic permits? To answer this, zoom into one or more of the light blue areas and toggle the density image on and off.

4. In what area of the aquifer are there generally higher nitrate values?

5. What features do you see at the edges of the aquifer boundary?

6. What can you see in Google Earth in and around Pocatello?

Artifact

Organize your experiences with the data in Google Earth and your responses to the questions above in the artifact table below as evidence to support the scientific argument that humans are affecting the local groundwater.

DATASET	Evidence for the influence of human activity	RELATIONSHIPS AMONG THE DATASETS		
		Relationship to human activity found on the boundary of the aquifer	Relationship to the nitrate readings from the groundwater wells	Relationship to the density of septic permits
Boundary of the Lower Portneuf River Valley Aquifer				
Nitrate readings from the ground-water wells				
Density of septic permits				

Water Quality in Pocatello—Analysis and Artifacts

Once you complete your analysis and the artifact table, attach the edited document as a resource, and then finish the following statements.

1. I analyzed the data in Google Earth in the following ways...

2. The attached artifact table illustrates my analysis by...

Teacher Note: This lesson could be further enhanced by having students test groundwater or surface water in their own area, using relatively inexpensive commercial test kits and then using Google Earth to create a spatial representation by entering each data point as a place mark (http://bit.ly/fbTR1U [https://support.google.com/earth/answer/148142]).

Water Quality in Pocatello—Argument

A complete scientific argument is a claim, supported by evidence and includes a reason. View the reference information linked to this box as resources for your reasoning. Generate an argument for each of the datasets for Pocatello by combining a reason with your results, and then finish the following sentence-starter prompts.

1. As evidenced by... in the boundary of the Lower Portneuf River Valley Aquifer, I claim that humans are affecting the groundwater in Pocatello, Idaho, because...

2. As evidenced by... in the nitrate readings from the groundwater wells, I claim that humans are affecting the groundwater in Pocatello, Idaho, because...

3. As evidenced by... in the density of the septic permits, I claim that humans are affecting the groundwater in Pocatello, Idaho, because...

Water Quality in Pocatello—Expert Opinion

Consider the expert opinion on the influence of humans on the groundwater in Pocatello by viewing the following references.

Portneuf River Basin Pulse: www.portneufriver.org
> This site is the home of the live monitoring program for the Portneuf River Basin and provides a gateway to access data and information about the Portneuf River Basin, its monitoring program, and related activities.

Water Quality Protection—Pocatello: www.idahogeology.org/services/Hydrogeology/ PortneufGroundWaterGuardian/my_drinking_water/water_quality_reports/reports_ text/poky_protect.html
> This site, from the Pocatello Water Department, describes processes the city uses to purify the local water.

Reconsider your arguments, and restate them (even if they haven't changed) by finishing the following sentence-starter prompts.

1. As evidenced by... in the boundary of the Lower Portneuf River Valley Aquifer, I claim that humans are affecting the groundwater in Pocatello, Idaho, because...

2. As evidenced by... in the nitrate readings from the groundwater wells, I claim that humans are affecting the groundwater in Pocatello, Idaho, because...

3. As evidenced by... in the density of the septic permits, I claim that humans are affecting the groundwater in Pocatello, Idaho, because...

4. After considering the expert opinion, the reason I chose to change (or not to change) my claim(s) is because....

Water Quality in Pocatello—Reflection

After watching or reading the presentations provided by other groups, update your concept map to reflect your current understanding, and complete this inquiry by finishing the following statements:

1. My ideas are similar to other people's ideas in the following ways...

2. Ways that my ideas differ from the ideas of others include...

3. As I worked on this project, I wish I would have spent more time on...

Conclusion

In this chapter, we described how K–12 educators can use the scaffolded Vee diagram as an instructional tool to design interactive, inquiry-based learning activities to support student learning in hybrid or online courses. Depending on the instructional needs, the process can be differentiated with the amount of teacher scaffolding, including the complete conversion of components to face-to-face, teacher-led activities. The scaffolded Vee diagram is an amalgam of the Vee diagram (Gowin & Alvarez, 2005) and the principles and techniques of scaffolded knowledge integration (Linn, 2000). The scaffolded Vee diagram serves as a guide for autonomous learning, supporting students as they generate and defend a scientific argument. Carefully designed charts, tables, and diagrams are coupled with sentence-starter prompts to encourage engagement and focus student thinking. As such, it addresses all five of the essential features of inquiry identified by the National Science Education Standards (Olson & Loucks-Horsley, 2000, Tables 2–5, p. 25):

1. Learners are engaged by scientifically oriented questions.

2. Learners give priority to evidence, which allows them to develop and evaluate explanations that address scientifically oriented questions.

3. Learners formulate explanations from evidence to address scientifically oriented questions.

4. Learners evaluate their explanations in light of alternative explanations, particularly those reflecting scientific understanding.

5. Learners communicate and justify their proposed explanations.

The scaffolded Vee diagram is a valuable tool for enacting inquiry-based learning. Contemporary models for inquiry-based learning emphasize the use of learning cycles that are supported by our understanding of how students learn science concepts and skills (Donovan & Bransford, 2005). This includes the development of reasoning and understanding of the nature of science (NRC, 2006). In the modern era, leveraging the availability of data-using resources from the web is an important component for students to be able to gather information, develop claims, and measure their evidence-based arguments against each other and experts. The scaffolded elements of the

Thinking and *Doing* sides of the Vee diagram are designed to address each of these stages explicitly, as well as the essential features of inquiry-based learning. The examples provided in this chapter offer a tangible guide to implementing a scaffolded Vee diagram as a grounded approach to designing interactive activities to support 21st-century learning.

Funding for this work was provided by the National Science Foundation (EPS-0919123, EPS-1006797) and the State of Nevada Department of Education under Title II, part B, of the United States Department of Education's Math and Science Partnership (MSP) program. Thanks to Sara Ehinger, Carol Moore, and Nancy Glenn at Idaho State University and to Kasey Guthrie at the Idaho Department of Environmental Quality for the rights to use the water quality data in the second example, Water Quality in Pocatello.

References

Ainsworth, S., & Loizou, A. T. (2003). The effects of self-explaining when learning with texts or diagrams. *Cognitive Science, 27,* 669–681.

Alvarez, M. C., & Risko, V. J. (2007). The use of Vee diagrams with third graders as a metacognitive tool for learning science concepts. *Teaching and Learning Presentations, Paper 5.* Department of Teaching and Learning, Tennessee State University. Retrieved from http://e-research.tnstate.edu/pres/5

Andriessen, J., Baker, M., & Suthers, D. D. (Eds.). (2003). *Arguing to Learn: Confronting cognitions in computer-supported collaborative learning environments.* Dordrecht, The Netherlands: Kluwer Academic Publishers.

Archambault, L., Tsai, W. T., & Crippen, K. (2011). Exploring cyberlearning: Inquiry-based mashups combining computer science with STEM. In M. Koehler & P. Mishra (Eds.), *Proceedings of society for information technology & teacher education international conference 2011* (pp. 3867–3874). Chesapeake, VA: Association for the Advancement of Computing in Education.

Berthold, K., Eysink, T., & Renkl, A. (2009). Assisting self-explanation prompts are more effective than open prompts when learning with multiple representations. *Instructional Science, 37*(4), 345–363.

Berthold, K., Nuckles, M., & Renkl, A. (2007). Do learning protocols support learning strategies and outcomes? The role of cognitive and metacognitive prompts. *Learning and Instruction, 17*(5), 564–577.

Coffman, C., & Riggs, L. (2006). The virtual Vee map: A template for Internet inquiry. *Journal of College Science Teaching, 36*(1), 32–39.

Davis, E. A., & Linn, M. C. (2000). Scaffolding students' knowledge integration: Prompts for reflection in KIE. *International Journal of Science Education, 22*(8), 819–837.

Donovan, S. M., & Bransford, J. D. (2005). *How students learn: Science in the classroom.* Washington, DC: National Academies Press.

EPA (United States Environmental Protection Agency). (2011). Radon (Rn): Health risks. Retrieved from www.epa.gov/radon/healthrisks.html

Gowin, D. B. (1981). *Educating.* Ithaca, NY: Cornell University Press.

Gowin, D. B., & Alvarez, M. C. (2005). *The art of educating with V diagrams*. New York, NY: Cambridge University Press.

Kern, C., & Crippen, K. J. (2008). Mapping for conceptual change. *The Science Teacher, 75*(September), 32–38.

Knaggs, C. M., & Schneider, R. M. (2012). Thinking like a scientist: Using Vee-maps to understand process and concepts in science. *Research in Science Education, 42*(4), 609–632.

Linn, M. C. (2000). Designing the knowledge integration environment. *International Journal of Science Education, 22,* 781–796.

Linn, M. C. (2006). The knowledge integration perspective on learning and instruction. In R. K. Sawyer (Ed.), *The Cambridge handbook of the learning sciences* (pp. 243–264). New York, NY: Cambridge University Press.

Linn, M. C., Bell, P., & Davis, E. A. (2005). *Internet environments for science education*. Mahwah, NJ: Lawrence Erlbaum.

Maddocks, A. (2010, March 15). Taking the pulse of global freshwater issues. *Circle of Blue*. Retrieved from www.circleofblue.org/waternews/2010/world/taking-the-pulse-of-global-freshwater-issues

National Research Council (NRC). (1996). *National Science Education Standards*. Washington, DC: National Academies Press.

National Research Council (NRC). (2006). *America's lab report: Investigations in high school science*. Washington, DC: National Academies Press.

National Science Foundation (NSF). (2008). *Fostering learning in the networked world: The cyberlearning opportunity and challenge*. Arlington, VA: NSF Task Force on Cyberlearning. At www.nsf.gov/pubs/2008/nsf08204/nsf08204.pdf

Novak, J. D. (1990). Concept maps and vee diagrams: Two metacognitive tools to facilitate meaningful learning. *Instructional Science, 19*(1), 29–52.

Nussbaum, E. M. (2008). Collaborative discourse, argumentation, and learning: Preface and literature review. *Contemporary Educational Psychology, 33*(3), 345–359.

Nussbaum, E. M., & Edwards, O. V. (2011). Critical questions and argument stratagems: A framework for enhancing and analyzing students' reasoning practices. *Journal of the Learning Sciences, 20*(3), 443–488.

Nussbaum, E. M., Winsor, D. L., Aqui, Y. M., & Poliquin, A. M. (2007). Putting the pieces together: Online argumentation vee diagrams enhance thinking during discussions. *International Journal of Computer-Supported Collaborative Learning, 2*(4), 479–500.

Olson, S., & Loucks-Horsley, S. (Eds.). (2000). *Inquiry and the national science education standards: A guide for teaching and learning*. Washington, DC: National Research Council & National Academy Press. Retrieved from www.nap.edu/catalog.php?record_id=9596

Passmore, G. G. (1998). Using Vee diagrams to facilitate meaningful learning and misconception remediation in radiologic technologies laboratory education. *Radiologic Science & Education, 4*(1), 11–28.

Roehrig, G., Luft, J. A., & Edwards, M. (2001). Versatile vee maps: An alternative to the traditional lab report. *The Science Teacher, 33*(1), 28–31.

Schraw, G., Crippen, K. J., & Hartley, K. D. (2006). Promoting self-regulation in science education: Metacognition as part of a broader perspective on learning. *Research in Science Education, 36*(1–2), 111–139.

Schunk, D. H. (2001). Social cognitive theory and self-regulated learning. In B. J. Zimmerman & D. H. Schunk (Eds.), *Self-regulated learning and academic achievement: Theoretical perspectives* (Vol. 2, pp. 125–152). Mahwah, NJ: Lawrence Erlbaum.

Stahl, G., Koschmann, T., & Suthers, D. D. (2006). Computer-supported collaborative learning. In R. K. Sawyer (Ed.), *The cambridge handbook of the learning sciences* (pp. 409–425). New York, NY: Cambridge University Press.

U.S. Geological Survey (USGS). (2011). The water cycle: Groundwater discharge. The USGS Water Science School. Retrieved from http://ga.water.usgs.gov/edu/watercyclegwdischarge.html

CHAPTER 5

Conducting Authentic Historical Investigations in the Digital Age

Scott M. Waring

TRADITIONALLY, SOCIAL STUDIES EDUCATION has focused on the memorization of historical dates and figures taken from secondary sources of past events. Students often fail to see the relevance of such knowledge and perceive history as a boring subject. Emerging technology and digital repositories now allow teachers and students to access primary sources of history. However, new instructional strategies are necessary to engage students with such sources and facilitate critical thinking about issues that are important to them as well as to the community and society. Authentic Historical Investigations consist of seven basic events that mirror what historians do in the field. This strategy makes history more meaningful and relevant to students than traditional methods of history instruction and allows them to inquire about and discover the past in an authentic and engaging manner. A lesson example illustrates how a repository, such as the Virginia Center for Digital History's Valley of the Shadow project, can engage students in Authentic Historical Investigations that facilitate both asynchronous online interactions and synchronous classroom interactions.

Far too frequently, students view social studies and, more specifically, history as a boring subject that does not relate to their lives and does not provide them with any skills that they see as necessary for being productive in modern life (Allen, 1994; Black & Blake, 2001; Jensen, 2001; Steffey & Hood, 1994; Zhao & Hoge, 2005). It is essential to expose students to history in ways that are authentic and true to the methods used by those conducting historical investigations and to make explicit connections that illustrate how the learned skills are directly related to those needed for daily life, including being a participatory citizen. Effective history instruction involves students in engaging educational experiences that allow them to make comparisons, analyze a variety of sources, and construct plausible narratives. As they learn in this way, students are compelled to think critically about issues of importance to them.

Think for a moment about how students learn content in other disciplines. In science class, students use microscopes, measure liquids, build models of human bodies, and complete other activities that are performed by professionals in the fields of science. In language arts class, students read and write poetry, may pretend to be authors for the *New York Times,* and learn how to communicate with others. During mathematics time, students are asked to see how fractions and decimals are present around them during an average day, determine distances and travel times from one location to the next, and learn other computational and logical skills helpful to being successful in life. Unfortunately, when it comes to many traditional history classes, students are just defining vocabulary words, reading textbook chapters, and completing multiple-choice examinations. I have yet to meet a professional historian who conducts research in this manner. History must be more than names and dates. To fully engage students in the content and to have them retain the information and concepts, history instruction must shift from memorization of facts toward instruction that includes investigation of primary sources and construction of authentic historical narratives. These narratives, or stories of the past, present the most plausible explanations for historical events based on available evidence rather than depicting history as a series of unequivocal facts. It is vital that educators find ways to allow students to conduct authentic historical investigations to help them see the importance of learning history and to gain the skills necessary for conducting historical inquiry.

History students need to be given in-depth, authentic opportunities to engage in work that mirrors the intellectual work conducted by professionals in the field (King, Newmann, & Carmichael, 2009). If done properly, this authentic intellectual work allows for the application of knowledge and skills specific to the discipline, rather than a routine regurgitation of names, dates, and facts and the use of mundane procedures devoid of authentic practices used by historians.

However, an inquiry-based instructional approach to history and the process of thinking histori-cally do not come naturally to most people (Wineburg, 2001). Educators must recognize that authentic historical thinking is not an inherent human capability, nor is it a process that typical students would initiate. Many of the processes needed for authentic historical thinking are in competition with many of the approaches typically utilized in the average history class and those used in the acquisition of content in other subject areas. King, Newmann, and Carmichael (2009) suggest how this authentic intellectual work approach may look in the social studies classroom. The following discussion provides an adaptation of this authentic approach to a more specific context, the history classroom.

Teachers can introduce the historical inquiry approach to students by using three vital elements in their lessons. First, the approach should include the use of prior knowledge, specific to the discipline of history: particular facts, vocabularies, concepts, theories, and other conventions necessary to conduct rigorous historical inquiry. Second, teachers must lead students past superficial awareness of the subject matter (such as answering questions at the back of the book) and strive for in-depth knowledge of the content. In this case, depth versus breadth is a preferred outcome. This is contrary to the type of middle school and secondary education that simply dashes through the textbook's contents in the least amount of time necessary so that students can pass standardized, fact-based tests. For teachers to shift their instructional approach from traditional to one that is inquiry-based, they need to require learners to create authentic questions, not necessarily those found in the textbook, seek verifiable information, and perform research that tests relationships among facts, events, concepts, and claims to resolve inconsistencies and to corroborate probable accounts of the past. This is a recursive process that should ultimately lead the learners to the individual construction of a narrative that is most probable, based on the available evidence. As a final product of each major unit of study, students should have opportunities to develop and express their findings through various forms of elaborated communication, including verbal, symbolic, graphic, and visual presentations that are most closely aligned with their learning styles (Gardner, 1983, 1993; Gardner & Hatch, 1989).

A Continuum, from Novice to Expert Level

It is imperative for history educators to view each of their students as being somewhere along a continuum—from novice to expert—in regard to level of historical thinking and understanding. It is not productive for classroom teachers to view each student's capabilities as being exclusively related to the student's age or grade level or to force all instruction to meet a certain narrow daily criterion. Curriculum designed for the historical inquiry-based classroom presupposes an understanding of how novices and experts differ. Experts have a clear understanding of key concepts in the field of history and have a more developed understanding of how, when, and where to apply these concepts (Chi, 1976; Sternberg & Horvath, 1995). In many history classrooms, students are forced to memorize names, dates, and given "facts" without understanding their underpinning concepts and principles or even having an idea of how the events' meanings were constructed. Thus, they never have the opportunity to progress along the continuum, to start as novices and to become experts or near-experts as they conduct a series of historical investigations.

To better understand the novice to expert level continuum present in history students, it is helpful for history teachers to be aware of the Bradley Commission on History in Schools' (1995) History's Habits of Mind and understand how the development of each habit is facilitated throughout students' instruction. The Bradley Commission posits that, as history students move toward the expert side of the continuum, they should have learning experiences that allow them to:

1. Understand the significance of the past to their own lives, both private and public, and to their society;

2. Distinguish between the important and the inconsequential, to develop the "discriminating memory" needed for a discerning judgment in public and personal life;

3. Perceive past events and issues as they were experienced by people at the time, to develop historical empathy as opposed to present-mindedness;

4. Acquire at one and the same time a comprehension of diverse cultures and of shared humanity;

5. Understand how things happen and how things change, how human intentions matter, but also how their consequences are shaped by the means of carrying them out, in a tangle of purpose and process;

6. Comprehend the interplay of change and continuity, and avoid assuming that either is somehow more natural, or more to be expected, than the other;

7. Prepare to live with uncertainties and exasperating, even perilous, unfinished business, realizing that not all problems have solutions;

8. Grasp the complexity of historical causation, respect particularity, and avoid excessively abstract generalizations;

9. Appreciate the often tentative nature of judgments about the past, and thereby avoid the temptation to seize upon particular "lessons" or history as cures for present ills;

10. Recognize the importance of individuals who have made a difference in history, and the significance of personal character for both good and ill;

11. Appreciate the force of the non-rational, the irrational, the accidental, in history and human affairs;

12. Understand the relationship between geography and history as a matrix of time and place, and as context for events; and

13. Read widely and critically in order to recognize the difference between fact and conjecture, between evidence and assertion, and thereby to frame useful questions.

Fundamental Elements of Historical Inquiry

Proper history instruction is not just a process of transmitting knowledge; the teacher must work collaboratively with the students to "uncover" history (Wiggins & McTighe, 2001) and together ask, "what is the evidence or reason for believing" what was read in the historical narratives and other sources encountered during the historical inquiry process (Calder, 2006)? As students have opportunities to deconstruct and construct their own historical narratives, they begin to understand that history is not a predetermined, definitive story, with a series of "facts" threaded together.

Many useful strategies have been developed for historical inquiry. Like the History's Habits of Mind posited by the Bradley Commission, Calder (2006) asserts that students should be independently skilled in six historical cognitive habits before engaging in historical inquiry-based learning experiences. These habits are questioning, connecting, sourcing, making inferences, considering alternate perspectives, and recognizing limits to one's knowledge. When students engage with various sources related to a historical topic, Wineburg (2010) suggests that students should use the following specific, history-related strategies for reading and understanding the sources: sourcing, contextualizing, close reading, using background knowledge, reading the silences, and corroborating. Hicks, Doolittle, and Ewing (2004) propose that students use their SCIM-C strategy, which focuses on five broad phases: summarizing, contextualizing, inferring, monitoring, and corroborating.

Based on all of these approaches and in order to move them forward along the novice–expert continuum, I would suggest that history students should have learning opportunities that allow them to:

1. **Create authentic questions.** Students must have opportunities to ask questions of personal interest related to history.

2. **Utilize a variety of sources.** A variety of sources (i.e., published documents, unpublished documents, oral histories, visual documents, artifacts, etc.) should be sought to answer the question posed.

3. **Scrutinize the sources.** Each source must be examined to determine who constructed it and why.

4. **Determine the context of each source.** Context for the document is vital. A document taken out of context can lead to invalid conclusions.

5. **Read the sources.** Sources should be read closely, and efforts should be made to "read between the lines."

6. **Consider alternative perspectives.** Multiple alternative perspectives must be considered. Finding just the polar extremes is not sufficient.

7. **Corroborate the sources.** Corroborating sources need to be found.

8. **Construct narratives.** Opportunities should be presented for students to have a chance to construct historical narratives, utilizing the spectrum of sources, while noting where gaps in the sources' or the author's (that is, the student's) knowledge exist.
   (Waring, 2011, p. 14)

To offer these opportunities and cover these eight elements in a cogent manner, history teachers need to have an instructional strategy for what is to be accomplished during instructional time. More importantly, the strategy should be made explicit to the students to facilitate their progress from novice to expert levels of historical thinking and understanding.

Authentic Historical Investigations: An Instructional Strategy for Facilitating Historical Inquiry

Once an understanding of the elements necessary for instruction have been established, history teachers should think critically about how instructional time will be used to allow students opportunities to engage in authentic historical inquiry. Approaches should vary, depending upon the content and level of understanding. For students at a lower level of expertise, it may be helpful to discuss the structure of stories and narratives prior to engaging in historical inquiry-based activities. For these students, teachers should begin instruction by encouraging them to think about a typical story structure; most stories have a beginning, middle, end, setting, characters, problem, and resolution (Levstik & Barton, 2011). Through an in-depth examination of available evidence, an author of history will construct the most probable historical narrative. When students have opportunities to examine a variety of historical sources and to construct narratives, they will begin to see that history and historical narratives often have more than one beginning, middle, end, setting, characters, problem, and resolution, unlike like a typical storybook.

To begin a discussion of narrative in history and the need to examine the narrative from multiple perspectives, I suggest sharing a piece of children's literature that follows a typical story structure but also shows an alternative perspective. An excellent book to share with students is Scieszka's *The True Story of the 3 Little Pigs* (1995). This story presents the well-known story of the three little pigs and the big bad wolf from the perspective of the wolf. The story provides a good entry point for discussing the elements vital to constructing a plausible narrative and to a successful and authentic historical inquiry-based investigation.

The Authentic Historical Investigation instructional strategy consists of seven basic events that can and should be modified according to the content to be covered and the needs of the students. When it comes to history instruction, there is no cookbook-style, foolproof method. But part of the beauty of authentic historical inquiry-based approaches is that mistakes and tangential paths often inform as much or more than the initial planned approach and original list of sources.

Following are the instructional events associated with each Authentic Historical Investigation:

1. Begin with a hook

2. Identify fundamental question(s)

    a. non-dichotomous questioning

    b. questions that encourage inquiry

3. Engage with primary and secondary sources

4. Consider multiple perspectives and historic causation

    a. battling mono-causal history

    b. battling historical presentism

5. Construct a plausible narrative

6. Complete authentic assessments

7. Reflect on the experience

To engage students, history instruction should move through several events, as outlined in the Authentic Historical Investigation instructional strategy. In the following sections, I provide a short description of each event followed by a detailed example of a complete lesson applying the strategy to further illustrate the design of Authentic Historical Investigations.

Begin with a Hook

Instruction should begin with a hook to interest students in the content to be covered. You can hook students with a thought-provoking image, document, or other source related to the content or an activity that involves a process or concept similar to what is needed in the inquiry. For example, you could begin a lesson on immigration by playing a game of hide and seek with an image of Mulberry Street in New York City from around 1900 (Figure 5.1). You would ask students to find the best hiding place within the image, allowing them to be anything in size from a gnat to their current height. You would then find the students. Once a student is found, you should ask questions focusing on the senses (What do you hear? What do you smell?) or journalistic questions (i.e., who, what, where, when, why, and how?). As students are found, they could help the teacher try to find the rest of the hidden students, asking similar questions.

FIGURE 5.1 ▶ Image of Mulberry Street, New York City (ca. 1900)

Identify Fundamental Question(s)

The next step is to determine the question(s) that will focus the inquiry. For instance, you may ask, "What was life like in the United States of America during the Second World War?" or "How did American independence impact various segments of the population?" It is important that the question is not dichotomous. Far too often, history-based activities require students to answer a question that can be answered with a simple "yes or no." To truly engage a student, the question should be open-ended, be non-dichotomous, encourage deep and ongoing inquiry, and be of personal interest to the learner.

Engage with Primary and Secondary Sources

Essential to any authentic historical inquiry-based activities are the primary and secondary sources of information. Unfortunately, there is much confusion about what constitutes a primary source and how it differs from a secondary source. To make it as simple as possible, history teachers should use the topic of study or the fundamental question to be answered by the investigation as the basis for determining whether a source is primary or secondary. If the source is directly from the time under study or related to the topic, then it is considered a primary source. Conversely, if analysis, commentary, or modifications have been done to the source or the author is removed from the time under study, then it is considered a secondary source. For example, a history textbook is generally considered a secondary source because if one is reading and learning about the Battle of Gettysburg, it would be quite clear that the author of a textbook published in 2012 would not have been present at the battle and would have utilized a variety of sources in the construction of the narrative. However, if I were interested in investigating how textbooks from the twenty-first century were depicting the Battle of Gettysburg, then the textbook would be considered a primary source because it is from the time under study and the author is part of the group of authors constructing history textbooks in the twenty-first century.

It is important to remember that some sources may be considered both primary and secondary, and some will change over time or depending upon the question of study. Students often find it difficult to determine whether a source is primary or secondary if they don't remind themselves of the essential question of their study. The following list includes some items typically considered primary sources (though many could be considered secondary depending on the question of study): letters, books, pamphlets, government documents, cookbooks, diaries, furniture, buildings, clothing, photographs, maps, music, audio recordings, websites, emails, texts, and blogs. Don't immediately discount any source because, depending upon the question posed, any source can be worthy of inquiry. Ways to increase understanding of primary and secondary sources include activities and descriptions found on the Library of Congress' website (www.loc.gov); the Using Primary Sources website (www.loc.gov/teachers/usingprimarysources); and the National History Education Clearinghouse website (http://teachinghistory.org), which is depicted in Figure 5.2.

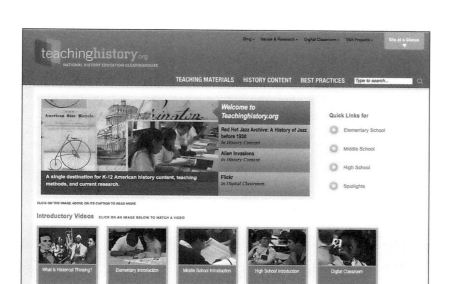

FIGURE 5.2 ▶ National History Education Clearinghouse website

Once students understand the differences between primary and secondary sources, it is vital that they have multiple and sustained opportunities to engage with various types of sources. However, reading and analyzing sources requires somewhat different skills from reading most other types of text and it may be difficult for learners, wherever they may be on the novice–expert continuum, to analyze, classify, and interpret sources of information properly without adequate scaffolding.

For example, a teacher-designed scaffold may be necessary to demonstrate to students how to read a letter analytically instead of in the typical, highly structured, left to right and top to bottom manner. A historian analyzing the letter would want to determine when it was written, who was the author, and any other details that would make the content of the letter understood in its particular historical context. The reader may start at the bottom of the letter to look at who wrote it, flip it over to look for distinguishing marks, analyze the envelope, and perform many other steps prior to reading the body of the letter. It is important for the reader to know that, if put into context correctly, a letter that was written in 1861 would be read differently from one written on September 12, 2001. Furthermore, a letter written by Sojourner Truth would be read differently from a letter written by Elvis Presley or Adolf Hitler. Thus, it is important for teachers to instruct students on how to read and analyze sources and how to recognize and take into consideration various related elements. Different sources may require different scaffolds.

One way a teacher can scaffold the learning process is by providing source analysis worksheets; these help structure the source analysis process and give students a place to record their observations and thoughts. Source analysis worksheets can be found on numerous websites, including the National Archives and Records Administration (NARA) (www.archives.gov/education/lessons/worksheets) (Figure 5.3); the Library of Congress (www.loc.gov/teachers/usingprimarysources); and the Maryland Historical Society (www.mdhs.org/education/teachers/primary-source-worksheets).

Reset Form	Written Document Analysis Worksheet	Print Form
1.	TYPE OF DOCUMENT (Check one):	

1. TYPE OF DOCUMENT (Check one):

- ○ Newspaper   ○ Map   ○ Advertisement
- ○ Letter   ○ Telegram   ○ Congressional Record
- ○ Patent   ○ Press Release   ○ Census Report
- ○ Memorandum   ○ Report   ○ Other

2. UNIQUE PHYSICAL CHARACTERISTICS OF THE DOCUMENT (Check one or more):

- ☐ Interesting Letterhead   ☐ Notations
- ☐ Handwritten   ☐ "RECEIVED" stamp
- ☐ Typed   ☐ Other
- ☐ Seals

3. DATE(S) OF DOCUMENT:

4. AUTHOR (OR CREATOR) OF THE DOCUMENT:

   POSITION (TITLE):

5. FOR WHAT AUDIENCE WAS THE DOCUMENT WRITTEN?

6. DOCUMENT INFORMATION (There are many possible ways to answer A-E.) |Limit response for each question to 3 lines of text|

   A. List three things the author said that you think are important:

   B. Why do you think this document was written?

   C. What evidence in the document helps you know why it was written? Quote from the document.

   D. List two things the document tells you about life in the United States at the time it was written.

   E. Write a question to the author that is left unanswered by the document:

**Designed and developed by the
Education Staff, National Archives and Records Administration,
Washington, DC 20408**

Reset Form		Print Form

FIGURE 5.3 ► Worksheet developed by the NARA

Consider Multiple Perspectives and Historic Causation

Many problems can be encountered throughout the historical inquiry process, but three of the most prevalent and troubling issues are the lack of multiple perspectives, mono-causal history, and historical presentism.

First, history is often presented from one perspective when it should be viewed and examined from multiple perspectives. Most would agree that if students only read letters from a pro-slavery plantation owner when trying to understand social issues of the first half of the nineteenth century, they would miss much of the story. It is vital that students are given an opportunity to view a variety of sources from differing perspectives when learning about the past.

The second problem that arises in the history classroom is mono-causal history, which suggests that there is only one cause for historical events. Unfortunately, standardized tests and poorly written standards can encourage teaching mono-causal history, as if there were only one "correct" answer or "fact" to be conveyed to the students. One of the more common events from American history typically presented in a mono-causal format is the involvement of the United States in the Second World War (World War II). It is far too easy to point to one cause, the bombing of Pearl Harbor. While that event was a key factor, many more events and conditions need to be discussed, so that students understand that World War II had multiple causes.

Third, the students should become aware of, and move away from, the idea of historical presentism, the act of viewing the past through a lens of the present, that is, from the viewpoint of the generally accepted morals, values, and understandings present in today's world. Students should be encouraged to move toward a more empathic view of the past, one that respects primary and secondary sources from the social and cultural contexts during the time they were constructed. It is difficult to understand or fully appreciate an image taken during the Great Depression if the viewer has no background knowledge of the time period or insists on viewing it through a present-day lens. Properly constructed Authentic Historical Investigations attend to these weaknesses as well as a plethora of others.

Create a Plausible Narrative

As the students engage with and analyze primary and secondary sources of history, they should work toward creating a plausible narrative, using the available evidence that most accurately answers the initial fundamental question(s) posed by the students. As students gradually construct their narratives, they should seek sources that contradict as well as corroborate their thesis. Typically, at the K–12 level, a student's analysis of sources is not exhaustive, but a sufficient number of sources should be consulted so that each student can confidently present a plausible narrative for the question. The appropriate number and types of sources will vary from one investigation to the next.

Plausible narratives can be constructed in a number of ways. Students should be given opportunities to present the information in a verbal, symbolic, graphic, and/or visual manner. For example, students may choose to present findings through a traditional written report, a website, museum-like exhibit, dramatic performance, or multimedia documentary. The important aspects of a plausible narrative are that they include various sources and perspectives and are not mono-causal or mired in historical presentism. Students must remember that when they are constructing a narrative, they need to find a sufficient amount of evidence, which means that corroborating as well as refuting sources must be sought, examined, and considered throughout the process of creating the narrative. Thus, the goal should be to construct the most plausible narrative for the historical topic of study based on the available evidence.

Complete Authentic Assessments

If students are given the freedom to choose the method of presentation, they may enjoy the process more and retain the information longer and more accurately. So, no matter how students choose to present their plausible narrative, you must be able to assess their work fairly. Based on the basic instructional design principle espoused by Hirumi throughout this Grounded Designs for Online and Hybrid Learning Series (namely, the way instructors design and deliver instruction should be based on the desired learning outcomes), the type/s of instruments used to assess student learning should depend on the instructor's goals and objectives. As such, based on the fundamental goals and objectives of historical inquiry (e.g., critical historical thinking and creative problem solving) and the assessment guidelines provided by Hirumi in Chapter 1, "Aligning Learning Objectives and Learner Assessments: An Essential Precursor for Grounded Design," of the first book in the series, *Online and Hybrid Learning Design Fundamentals,* instructors should consider using either an analytic or holistic performance assessment rubric to measure what students learned from their Authentic Historical Investigations.

Analytic rubrics are product specific and may be used if students are asked to complete certain assignments (e.g., make a presentation or write a report). Holistic rubrics, in contrast, are useful for assessing development of fundamental skills that are reflected in and transcend products and work samples. Table 5.1 presents a sample holistic rubric that may be used to assess plausible narratives generated by students from their Authentic Historical Investigations.

TABLE 5.1　▶　Sample assessment rubric for plausible narrative

Exemplary (90–100 pts)	Narrative presents plausible explanations/answer(s) to fundamental question that attends to alternatives.
	Narrative manipulates and integrates the use of various sources to support explanations/answer(s).
	Explanations for events/answer(s) to question are presented from multiple perspectives.
	Explanations for events/answer(s) to question demonstrate historical empathy.
	Explanations for events/answer(s) to question are based on multiple causes.
Proficient (80–89 pts)	Narrative presents plausible explanations/answer(s) to fundamental question.
	Narrative uses various sources to support explanations/answer(s).
	Explanations for events/answer(s) to question are presented from two perspectives.
	Explanations for events/answer(s) to question demonstrate historical understanding.
	Explanations for events/answer(s) to question are based on two causes.
Developing (<80 pts)	Narrative fails to provide plausible explanation/answer(s) to fundamental question.
	Narrative uses one or few sources to support explanation/answer.
	Explanation for events/answer to question is presented from one perspective.
	Explanation for events/answer to question is mired in presentism.
	Explanation for event/answer to question is based on one cause.

As you facilitate Authentic Historical Investigations, you may also choose to present students with analytic assessment rubrics, performance checklists, and conventional criterion-referenced tests to help them monitor their own progress toward targeted skills and knowledge. For example, you may allow students to complete a quiz to help them assess their acquisition of basic historical facts and concepts covered in the investigation. You may also generate and ask students to complete a checklist for locating and analyzing primary sources, as shown in Table 5.2.

TABLE 5.2 ▶ Sample student performance checklist for locating and analyzing primary sources

Characteristics of primary sources in the KWL chart and checklist	Does your KWL chart and checklist exhibit each characteristic?		Comment
	Yes	No	
I have contemplated fundamental question(s) to consider what types of sources may be used to formulate and support my answer.			
I have defined the criteria for determining the validity of source(s).			
I have identified relevant repositories for finding valid sources.			
I have located valid source(s) for supporting my narrative.			
I have observed source(s) and described their physical characteristics.			
I have reflected on source(s) to interpret the meanings of their physical characteristics.			
I have reexamined source(s) to identify any remaining questions.			
I have found additional source(s) to corroborate or refute my original explanation and have answered remaining questions.			

Then, at the end of an investigation (or series of investigations) students may be asked to select work samples and assessments completed during their historical inquiries and put together a portfolio to demonstrate what they learned. The teacher may then assess student portfolios using a holistic assessment rubric, like the sample provided in Table 5.1. Whether you decide to ask your students to prepare a portfolio or to focus solely on creating a plausible narrative to demonstrate their historical thinking and understanding, you should ask them to reflect on their experiences. Ask them, as they reflect, to interpret the meanings of their sources' physical characteristics, to reexamine their sources to identify any remaining questions, and to find additional sources—if they have not already done so—to corroborate or refute their original explanations and answer any remaining questions.

Reflect on the Experience

The last thing that students should do is reflect on their individual experiences. They should ask themselves, "What actions and decisions were particularly useful for creating my plausible narrative?" "What actions and decisions were less useful?" and "What would I do differently the next time I perform a historical investigation?" Possibly the most important questions students should answer at the end of their inquiry are these: "What did I learn from the experience?" and "What else do I want to know?" These last questions are necessary for students to understand that good historical investigations are never truly finished, and new questions worthy of inquiry often arise from an investigation. The beauty of teaching history in this manner is that student interest in and retention of historical content is increased. Authentic historical inquiry also facilitates the development of necessary daily life skills, including critical thinking, the ability to analyze various types of corroborating and contradicting sources, knowledge of how narratives are constructed, and the need to seek and understand multiple perspectives.

Lesson Plan Example

One of the earliest and most respected repositories of primary digital sources is The Valley of the Shadow project, constructed by a team at the Virginia Center for Digital History (VCDH; http://vshadow.vcdh.virginia.edu) at the University of Virginia (Figure 5.4). This project documents the lives of people who were living in Augusta County, Virginia, and Franklin County, Pennsylvania, during the American Civil War era.

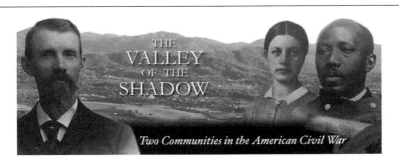

The Valley Project details life in two American communities, one Northern and one Southern, from the time of John Brown's Raid through the era of Reconstruction. In this digital archive you may explore thousands of original letters and diaries, newspapers and speeches, census and church records, left by men and women in Augusta County, Virginia, and Franklin County, Pennsylvania. Giving voice to hundreds of individual people, the Valley Project tells forgotten stories of life during the era of the Civil War.

FIGURE 5.4 ▶ The Valley of the Shadow website

Through The Valley of the Shadow website, users may access thousands of original documents, such as letters and diaries, census and government records, newspapers, and speeches, all of which record different aspects of daily life in those two counties before, during, and after the American Civil War. The creators of the site see this as "… more like a library than a single book. There is no 'one' story in the Valley Project." Many stories are told, and countless lives are documented through the primary sources available on this site. For example, users "can flip through a Valley resident's Civil War diary, read what the county newspapers reported about the Battle of Gettysburg, or even search the census records to see how much the average citizen owned in 1860 or 1870." The following example illustrates how a repository, such as the Valley of the Shadow, can be used to engage students in an authentic digital-based inquiry. This is a hybrid instructional unit containing asynchronous online interactions and synchronous classroom interactions, but elements that are used to facilitate the face-to-face portions of the lesson may be facilitated through the use of the Internet to create a totally online version.

Lesson Plan A

Who Was Thomas Garber, and How Was He Involved in the American Civil War?
(Hybrid Lesson)

This lesson is based on the work of Mason and Carter (1999), who worked closely with the Virginia Center for Digital History during their time at the University of Virginia. This lesson uses the Authentic Historical Investigation approach to learn about the life of Thomas Garber, a private in the 12th Virginia Cavalry during the American Civil War. Students use various sources, such as letters, newspapers, census data records, Google books, and the website Find a Grave (www.findagrave.com) to conduct an historical inquiry to learn more about this individual, to construct a narrative about who he was, and to engage in a discussion about his involvement in the American Civil War.

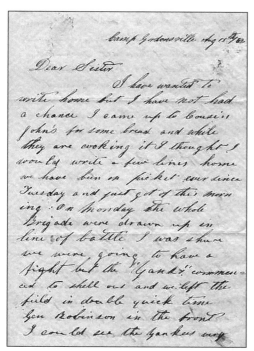

FIGURE 5.A.1 ▶ Copy of Thomas Garber's letter to his sister Addie

Event 1. Begin with a Hook

The lesson starts with a hook: having students read and carefully examine a letter (http://etext.lib.virginia.edu/etcbin/civwarlett-browse?id=A0806) online. This letter is found within the Garber family letters section (http://valley.lib.virginia.edu/VoS/personalpapers/documents/augusta/p2garberletters.html) of the Valley of the Shadow website. The Valley site provides images of the letter, transcriptions, a modern-day version that uses present-day vernacular, and a bibliographic record. This particular letter is from an individual named Thomas Garber, who is writing a letter dated August 15, 1862, to his sister (Addie Garber) to inform her about the military company he has joined. The letter, pictured in Figure 5.A.1, includes fascinating elements, such as details of battles, his role, and mentions of military officers (e.g., General Thomas "Stonewall" Jackson), but it is written in the plain, everyday prose that appeals to students, as they see that

Thomas is just like them or like some of their classmates or family members. It is the personal connection that should be sought when engaging students in historical inquiry-based activities.

Event 2. Identify Fundamental Question(s)

I begin an online discussion by posting the thoughts that occurred to me as I read the letter. For example, I want to know who Thomas Garber was and how was he involved in the American Civil War. I then ask students to help construct a know/want to know/have learned (KWL) chart (Ogle, 1986). This can be done on online forums, such as a class website, blog, or wiki. This approach requires students to think about what they know (K), what they want to know (W), and later, at the end of the unit, what they have learned (L). While seemingly rudimentary, this process of asking the students what they know and what they want to know engages them in the learning process. Typically, students pull out all of the major details from the letter for the K column, and for the W column, most want to know more about Thomas and his family, if he survived the war, battles in which he was involved, and many other questions related to Thomas. If students are reluctant to respond or express their thoughts, the teacher could pose questions, such as:

What did you learn about Thomas Garber from reading this letter?

What does this tell you about the life of a Civil War soldier?

What else would you like to know about Thomas Garber?

How could you find the answers to these questions?

Do you think Thomas was afraid?

Do you think Thomas missed his family?

What do you think was Thomas's job in the army?

How old do you think Thomas was when he wrote this letter?

Was Thomas killed in the war?

Did Thomas have other brothers and sisters?

Who were Thomas's parents?

What was life like during the Civil War for the average family?

What was it like to be a teenager during the Civil War?

Once the instructor is comfortable with the number of responses and with the K and W columns students have constructed in their KWL charts, the students should be asked to think about the letter, the class discussion, and what they will list in their W columns. Then they'll be ready to construct their own questions that could guide an inquiry lesson to help them learn about who Thomas Garber was and how was he involved in the American Civil War. These questions can be recorded in a number of ways, but a simple foldable worksheet or some other sort of scaffolding worksheet to be used throughout the lesson is needed.

Events 3 and 4. Engage with Primary and Secondary Sources and Consider Multiple Perspectives and Historic Causation

The next event of the Authentic Historical Investigation is for students to engage with a series of primary sources. This can be done online or in a face-to-face manner. Because of the authentic discussions and questions that can arise from examining the sources together as a class, this examination process is perfect for a whole class or small group investigation. The first step in this stage is to use the 1860 U.S. Population Census (http://valley.lib.virginia.edu/population_census) to learn more about Thomas and his family. Figure 5.A.2 depicts the basic search options of the U.S. Census database made available by The Valley of the Shadow project.

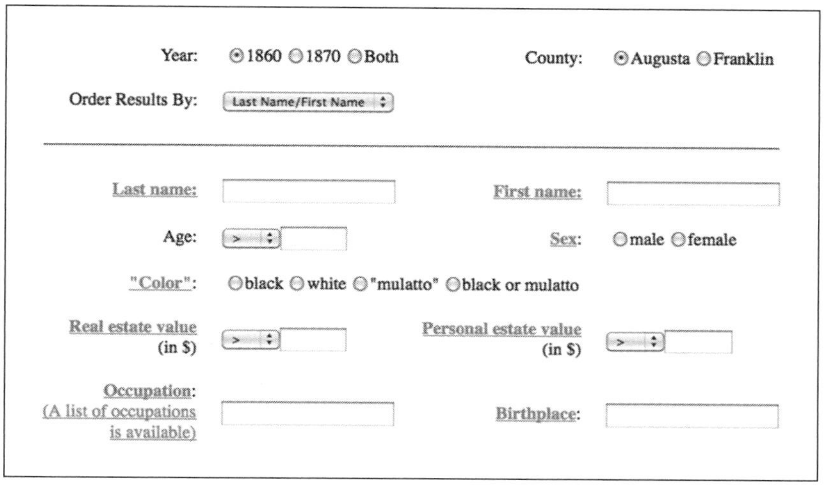

FIGURE 5.A.2 ▶ The Valley of the Shadow U.S. Census database search screen

Students will find out that Thomas was fourteen in 1860 and that he attended school in the past year, but according to the census (Figure 5.A.3), Thomas could not read or write.

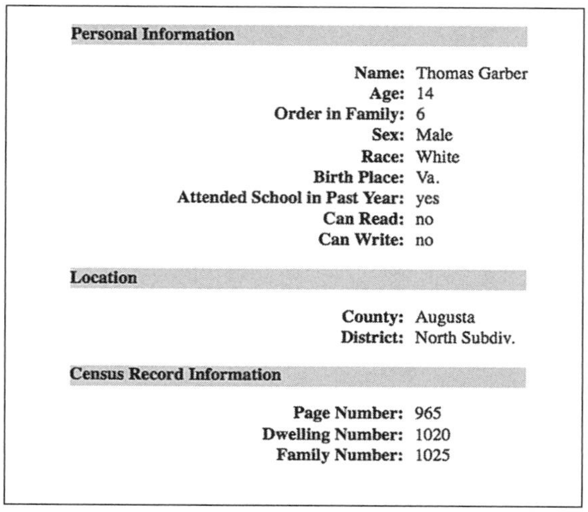

Personal Information

Name: Thomas Garber
Age: 14
Order in Family: 6
Sex: Male
Race: White
Birth Place: Va.
Attended School in Past Year: yes
Can Read: no
Can Write: no

Location

County: Augusta
District: North Subdiv.

Census Record Information

Page Number: 965
Dwelling Number: 1020
Family Number: 1025

FIGURE 5.A.3 ▶ Individual census record for Thomas Garber

The record provides a good opening for a discussion about the validity of the data found within the census data, especially since two years later Thomas is writing high-quality letters for the time. Searching the census data allows for a great instructional opportunity. These searches allow the teacher to show students that historical inquiry is not easy and the answer is rarely served up in a single Google search. I typically make purposeful mistakes in the search process and talk through the thinking and process being employed while searching. For example, I will search for Thomas in the Franklin County records only to find he is not there, but typically a student will remind me that Franklin County is in Pennsylvania. Students then tell me that I need to search in the Augusta County, Virginia, database. We then go back and conduct a search for the Garber family name in Augusta County, using the "family number" found within Thomas's "Personal Information" record to look at other family members, occupations, and levels of literacy, as well as other statistics. One could even go back to the 1850 Census records (http://us-census.org/pub/usgenweb/census/va/augusta/1850/pg0295a.txt) to further this discussion. After a thorough examination of the census data records, the students read and analyze a series of letters related to the life of Thomas Garber and his involvement in the American Civil War. Depending upon the student population, time, and available resources, students may either analyze the sources on computers or may be provided printed versions of the ten letters written by Thomas Garber. Letters written by others are also on the site. I will often create groups of four or five students and give them an opportunity to examine a single letter meticulously. Each group will be assigned one letter from the larger set to examine to extract as much information as possible related to Thomas's life, perspectives on the war, family dynamics, and so forth. The small group discussion gives each student a chance to test hypotheses, take into account the ideas of peers, and more fully understand the letter. The discussion should also enable each student in each small group, regardless of ability, to consider the information and understandings gained with other students who have not had the opportunity to review the letter.

Then, I will create new groups so that only one of the experts on a particular letter is in a group with one expert from each of the other groups; this allows a chance for each of the letters to be discussed within the new groups by an "expert" of that letter. Throughout the process, students are expected to write down details that interest them and to answer the questions that they posed at the beginning of the inquiry. Some of the letters I commonly use are the following:

Asher Harman (Thomas's cousin) to Albert Garber (Thomas's father and Asher's uncle), September 24, 1862
(http://valley.lib.virginia.edu/papers/A0808)

Thomas Garber to Albert Garber, September 25, 1862
(http://valley.lib.virginia.edu/papers/A0809)

Thomas Garber to Addie Garber (Thomas's sister), December 6, 1862
(http://etext.lib.virginia.edu/etcbin/civwarlett-browse?id=A0811)

Thomas Garber to Addie Garber, May 29, 1863
(http://etext.lib.virginia.edu/etcbin/civwarlett-browse?id=A0812)

At this point, most students feel an affinity to Thomas and begin to see that real individuals like him have historic agency and affect the course of history. I like to check in and see how many questions have been answered and provide additional sources that may be helpful in finding answers. I remind the students that historical inquiry is not perfect and sometimes, depending upon the available sources, questions go unanswered. This is a good point in time to share a letter (http://etext.lib.virginia.edu/etcbin/civwarlett-browse?id=A0814) from M. G. Harman (Thomas's cousin) to Albert Garber (Thomas' father), dated June 20, 1863 (Figure 5.A.4).

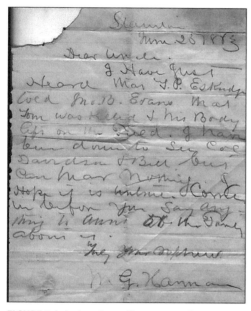

FIGURE 5.A.4 ▶ Copy of letter written by M. G. Harman to Albert Garber

Following is the entirety of the letter:

Staunton June 20, 1863

Dear Uncle,

I have just Heard Maj T.P. Eskridge told Mr. B. Evans that Tom was killed & his body left on the Field. I have been down to see Col Davidson & Bill but can hear nothing. I Hope it is untrue. Come in before you say anything to Aunt or the Family about it.

Truly your nephew

MG Harman

Students immediately respond with emotional comments about him being dead. I typically let the conversation go until a student reminds his or her fellow students that this is just one letter and that we should corroborate this with other sources. Often, a student will think to search the 1870 U.S. Population Census (http://valley.lib.virginia.edu/population_census) to determine if he was alive following the war. If this does not naturally occur, I will move the discussion in that direction. When the search is initiated for Thomas Garber and Augusta County, the resulting page provides an error message that this record could not be found.

Immediately, students respond that he is dead. Either a classmate of theirs or I will remind them of other possibilities, such as he moved, the census data is flawed, or the family number is different. We then search for his father, Albert, or another family member, and we find that the family number (1,025 in 1860) has changed to 686. Additionally, we see that Albert lost a considerable amount of land, which can begin a tremendous discussion about how society and life changed from the beginning of the war to the years that followed it. The search can now resume with a family name search (Garber) and a look at just the individuals with the same family number as Albert. Such searches can be done by choosing the option that lists results by "family unit." We find that Thomas is not included within these either (Figure 5.A.5).

676	1	Garber	Eli	44	Male	White	Farmer
686	1	Garber	Albert J.	66	Male	White	No Occupation
686	2	Garber	Mary J.	58	Female	White	Housekeeping
686	3	Garber	Kate M.	20	Female	White	No Occupation
686	4	Garber	Jane E.	18	Female	White	School
686	5	Garber	Helen	25	Female	Black	Domestic
779	5	Garber	Jacob	18	Male	White	

FIGURE 5.A.5 ▶ Thomas Garber's family unit data in 1870

The examination and conversation about the census data can create a good discussion, especially as students see the changes in the family dynamics and number of family members. The discussion often includes queries about the addition of a twenty-five-year-old woman named Helen; she was not listed in 1860 but is listed in 1870 as a black domestic. This questioning allows for a further dialogue about slavery and the differences between life, statistics, and so forth of this era and the present. Figure 5.A.6 depicts the letter from Lewis Harman (Thomas' cousin) to Addie Garber (Thomas' sister—the same one who received the initial letter) on July 20, 1863 (http://etext.lib.virginia.edu/etcbin/civwarlett-browse?id=A0816). This is an informational letter that discusses how Thomas's belongings will be sent home following his death.

The letter solidifies Garber's death for the students, but I will then tell them that we can search the newspapers from this time to find further corroborating sources. Through a search of the newspapers, we find a note in the Staunton Vindicator from July 3, 1863 (http://valley.lib.virginia. edu/news/rv1863/va.au.rv.1863.07.03.xml) that states that "Thomas Garber of Augusta County was wounded in fighting in Upperville and has since died." Another newspaper announcement about Thomas Garber is found in the Staunton Vindicator on May 11, 1866: (http://valley.lib.virginia. edu/news/rv1866/va.au.rv.1866.05.11.xml#03). When the date is pointed out and the students realize that the entry is from 1866, this instigates a discussion about why there is a note in the newspaper about Thomas three years after his death. The entry answers some of the questions:

> The remains of our gallant young townsman, Thos. M. Garber, youngest son of Albert J. Garber, Esq., color bearer of the 12th Virginia Cavalry, who fell mortally wounded in a cavalry engagement near Upperville, Va., were brought to Staunton on Tuesday week and re-interred in Thornrose Cemetery.

This discussion can conclude with an examination of why he would be reinterred, what type of families could afford to do this, and the lucrative opportunities available for the individuals reinterring soldiers buried in places other than the family cemetery.

Hd. Qrs. 12th Va Cavalry
Ripon Jeff Co. July 20, 1863

Dear Addie,

Your letter of the 15th has just been received & as I expect we will be marching soon I will answer it at once. I started dear Tom's knapsack home on the 17th inst in the care of Fred [illegible] who took Uncle [illegible] baggage home after his sad accident which I suppose you have heard of before this. I have also poor Tom's knife & testament which I failed to send by Fred on the 17. I will take good care of both & send them home to you by first opportunity. Unfortunately I did not see dear Tom on the morning after he died, as we moved forward at dawn in pursuit of the enemy; when I had gotten back in the evening he had been buried by a party of his Company who had been sent to bury the dear fellow. The poor fellow suffered very little dear Cousin, & I am sure he died as I wish to die, & all other brave soldiers fighting in our most ~~[illegible]~~ just cause. When I see you which I hope will not be a very long time from this, I will tell you all I know. You must excuse this short note, as I have not the heart to write after my late misfortune in losing my dear Uncle. Good by love to all.

Yr Affectionate Cousin
Lewis

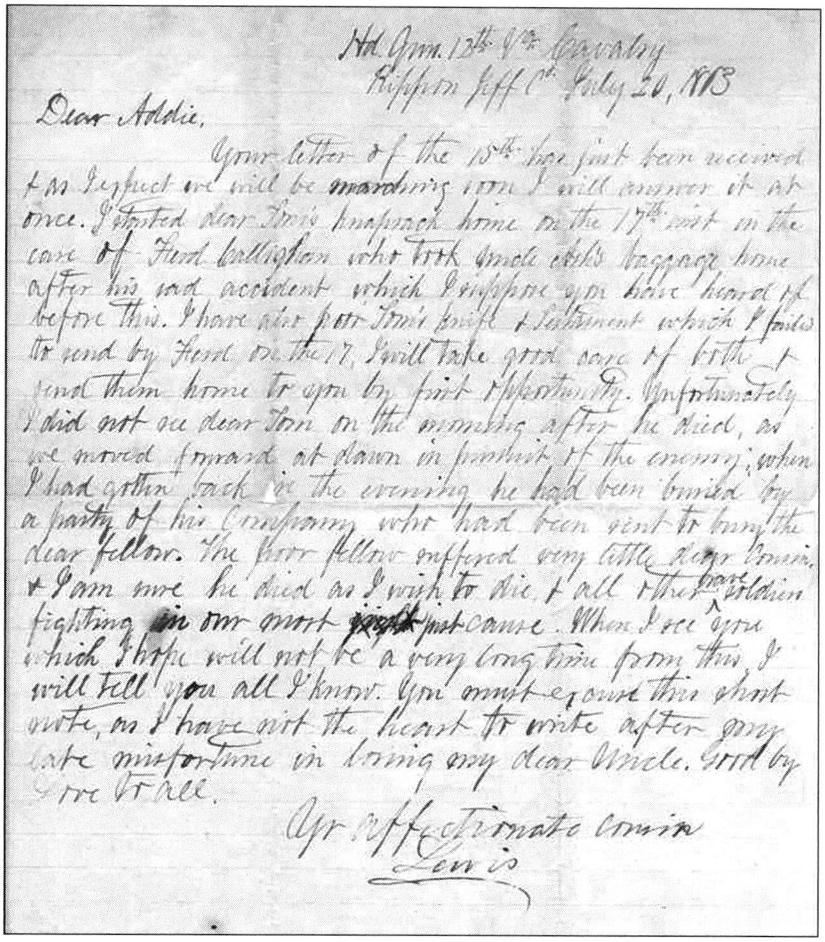

FIGURE 5.A.6 ▶ 1863 letter discussing how Thomas's belongings will be sent home

If time permits, I allow students to continue their searches on their own to find what they can about Thomas Garber on the Valley of the Shadow website and also through other means, such as a Google search. Students often find Upperville battle summaries, such as the one found through the National Parks Service website (www.nps.gov/hps/abpp/battles/va038.htm), battlefield maps of Upperville (www.civilwar.org/battlefields/middleburg/middleburg-history/civil-war-in-loudoun-county.pdf), or Virginia (http://americancivilwar.com/statepic/va63.html). Some find and appreciate seeing current images of the battlefield (www.johnsmilitaryhistory.com/aldie4. html) and (www.civilwarfieldtrips.com/stuart/pages/23farmfield.html), especially those who have not visited northern Virginia and/or live in geographic areas that differ greatly from the area around Upperville.

If students don't find some of the related sources that I think are valuable, and there is time, I will introduce these sources so that students will have a more well-rounded understanding of Thomas and his experiences during the American Civil War era. One of the best websites I have encountered for teaching about the Civil War era is one that provides issues of *Harper's Weekly* (www.sonofthesouth.net). The issue from July 11, 1863 includes a sketch (Figure 5.A.7) from renowned Civil War era artist Alfred Waud of the Battle of Upperville.

FIGURE 5.A.7 ▶ Alfred Waud's Sketch of the Battle of Upperville

Accompanying the sketch is a caption (www.sonofthesouth.net/leefoundation/civil-war/1863/july/ upperville-battle.htm) that described the sketch:

> On page 445 we reproduce a sketch by Mr. A. R. Waud, illustrating THE BATTLE NEAR UPPERVILLE, Ashby's Gap in the distance. The square inclosure is called the vineyard; on the right on the rise is a stone-wall; against this a charge was made, the men returning to form again a little to the left. On the extreme left five rebel regiments came out with their large flags to charge our men before they could form, but the First and Sixth regulars, sweeping round the hill, charged upon them while the band played Hail Columbia.

The description of the sketch always causes chills for me, as well as for most of the students, as it depicts the last moments of Thomas Garber's life from Waud's perspective. If it has not happened for a student up to this point, this is typically when history becomes real and is something that is constructed by people just like them. To take the impact a step farther, students are even able to view Thomas's tombstone in Thornrose Cemetery (Go to www.findagrave.com and search on Thomas Garber's name and date of death [June 21, 1863] to bring up the photo).

Typically, the last source I present is an autobiography by Charles Triplett O'Ferrall that can be found on Google Books (Go to http://books.google.com and enter the search term "Forty Years of Active Service"; Figure 5.A.8).

Forty years of active service

Charles Triplett O'Ferrall

FIGURE 5.A.8 ▶   Charles Triplett O'Ferrall's autobiography

Students often recall Thomas' first letter that they read as the hook. In it, Thomas notes, "You asked me what company I had joined, I have joined Capt. C. T. O'Ferrall's from Warren County, Va." In O'Ferrall's book, on pages 79 and 80, one can find a fairly brief but detailed description of Thomas' time in the Twelfth Virginia Cavalry:

> For some time prior to the battle of Upperville the color bearer of the Twelfth Cavalry was Tom Garber, a member of my company. It did not take me long to determine of what metal he was made. In a fight he was in his element, and the hotter it was the better he liked it. He was only seventeen years of age, yet he was over six feet in height, splendidly built, and much more mature every way than most boys of his age. He had been raised in the saddle and was a superb rider. A vacancy occurred in the color sergeancy of the regiment—how it occurred I do not now remember—and Tom applied for the position, and it was given him, and never in any war, on any field, were the colors of an army more grandly and heroically borne. He entered the charge at Upperville in the van, with his colors streaming in the breeze above his head as he charged down the field to the stone fence. There under the rain of lead he stood waving the stars and bars until just as I was shot, when he reeled in his saddle, and still clinging to his flag staff he fell to the ground dead. He was a brother of Major A. W. Garber, of Richmond, whose record as the commander of Garber's Battery is too-well known to require any encomiums from me. Of all the brave and intrepid boys whom it was my pleasure and privilege to observe during the four years of strife, I never saw one who was the superior of Tom Garber; and as brave and dashing as our

cavalrymen were generally I do not detract from them when I declare that I recall comparatively few who were his equals, taking them all in all. He rests in Thornrose Cemetery at Staunton beneath the sod of old Augusta, and while she can boast of many gallant sons, she has none more gallant than the young color-bearer of the Twelfth Cavalry, who yielded up his life at Upperville.

For many students, the entry in O'Ferrall's autobiography pulls it all together and is a fitting tribute to an amazing individual whose exemplary character is clearly displayed through the sources utilized throughout the investigation.

Events 5 and 6. Create Plausible Narratives and Complete Authentic Assessments

Once again, historical inquiry is about people and events and being able to create a plausible narrative that answers the original fundamental questions from different perspectives from various sources, so the answers are not mono-causal or mired in historical presentism. By this point, students are able to construct a detailed narrative about who Thomas Garber was and how he was involved in the American Civil War, including details focusing upon their individual questions that were posed at the beginning of the investigation. The narratives can be presented through verbal, symbolic, graphic, and/or visual means (i.e., a traditionally written narrative, website, museum-like exhibit, dramatic performance, letter written from a particular perspective, or multimedia documentary).

Event 7. Reflect on the Experience

The lesson can conclude with a discussion of the L (what they have learned) column of the KWL chart. Students can talk about what they learned and how they acquired the knowledge needed to create a plausible narrative. They can also think about what else it is that they want to know and where additional sources may be located to answer them. Through the historical inquiry process, students, often for the first time, may feel what it is like to conduct Authentic Historical Investigations and have a better appreciation of what it is that historians do. They may also develop critical [historical] thinking and creative problem-solving skills as they learn about citizenship and achieve national and state-specified social studies standards in an interesting and engaging manner.

Design and Delivery Issues

If you choose to apply the Authentic Historical Investigations strategy to enhance learning, there are several interrelated issues you should consider, including (a) facilitating key interactions online, (b) availability of various technologies, and (c) providing appropriate levels of scaffolding.

Facilitating Key Interactions Online

Authentic Historical Investigation can be conducted entirely online or in hybrid or conventional, face-to-face classrooms using printed versions of the sites. The Thomas Garber example represents a hybrid version of the strategy. Table 5.3 delineates the specific aspects of the lesson that were completed online and facilitated face-to-face.

TABLE 5.3 ▶ Online and face-to-face components of hybrid authentic investigation

EVENT	ONLINE LESSON COMPONENTS	FACE-TO-FACE LESSON COMPONENTS
Hook	Students examine the original and transcribed versions of the Thomas Garber letter on the Valley of the Shadow website.	
Fundamental Question(s)	Teacher posts initial thoughts about the letter to initiate dialogue using an online discussion forum. Students asked to start KWL chart by posting what they know and what they want to know about Thomas Garber. Teacher facilitates discussion resulting in a list of fundamental questions to be answered through the investigation.	
Primary and Secondary Sources	Students are given a list of specific sources that should be examined and are encouraged to find others. Students engage with primary and secondary sources found in repository. Students are encouraged and reminded to note questions that arise from their inquiries.	Teacher demonstrates process for locating relevant sources in online repositories, using prescribed checklist to talk through both physical and cognitive steps. Demonstration includes an examination of and discussion about each source, referring back and relating to fundamental questions. Demonstration includes both error-free searches and a few purposeful mistakes to illustrate key points. Throughout demonstration, students are asked what they think and what they would do, as well as what choices they would make and why. Students are divided into teams to analyze and discuss specific source(s). Teams are re-formed to discuss and share findings about specific sources.
Multiple Perspectives and Historic Causation	Students independently search for corroborating sources and additional information regarding Thomas Garber's life and death. Students are reminded to seek multiple perspectives and to avoid mono-causal explanations and historical presentism.	

(Continued)

TABLE 5.3 (Continued)

EVENT	ONLINE LESSON COMPONENTS	FACE-TO-FACE LESSON COMPONENTS
Plausible Narrative and Authentic Assessment	Students construct plausible narratives that answer fundamental questions from multiple perspectives using rubric to guide their efforts. (see Table 5.1)	Individuals or teams of students present their plausible narratives using a variety of formats and multimedia. Teacher assesses and provides constructive feedback on students' work using prescribed assessment rubric.
Reflection		Students participate in and teacher facilitates whole class discussion to wrap up lesson, reflect on experience and attend to remaining questions.

As you can see from Table 5.3, in the hybrid version of the lesson, you (as the teacher) are responsible for facilitating a number of substantive face-to-face interactions, particularly during the engagement with primary and secondary sources. You need to talk through and demonstrate key physical and mental steps in searching for and locating sources of relevant historical information, facilitate inquiry to illustrate how sources and information are related to the fundamental questions, ask students directed questions, and respond to students' questions to make sure they understand the process and are not missing any key points. You may also set up and promote various forms of small group discussions to facilitate interactions and the social development of meaning and knowledge.

Table 5.3 also highlights additional real-time, face-to-face interactions that are critical to the hybrid lesson. Specifically, you must consider and facilitate student presentations of their plausible narratives. You must also assess and provide students with feedback on their work using the prescribed assessment rubric as well as facilitate a lesson-ending discussion to have students reflect on their experiences, address remaining questions, and otherwise wrap up the lesson.

Converting the face-to-face components of the hybrid lesson to an online format is not easy. To transform the hybrid lesson into a totally online lesson, the teacher needs to plan all real-time interactions among students and between students and the teacher carefully. This requires the effective, efficient, and informed use of technology by the teacher and students.

Technology Access and Availability

The specific type and amount of technology that you want to use to facilitate Authentic Historical Investigations will depend on the teacher's and students' available time and resources, computer skills, and knowledge of historical investigations (along the novice to expert level continuum discussed earlier in the chapter). To facilitate the online portions of the sample hybrid lesson discussed earlier and depicted in Table 5.3, you and the students will need, at minimum, online access to and basic working knowledge of (a) digital repositories, (b) the Internet, and (c) an online discussion forum.

If you want to facilitate the same lesson totally online, you may need to integrate the use of additional technologies. Specifically, to facilitate engagement in primary and secondary sources, you and your students must have access to technology that allows you to (a) demonstrate and talk through the process of locating and analyzing relevant sources, (b) ask students what choices they would make and why throughout the process, and (c) provide students with constructive feedback on their choices and rationales. If you choose to group students and have them discuss their findings, you must also ensure access to technology that allows such teamwork. Then, to complete authentic assessments, technology must be available for students to present their plausible narratives as well as to reflect on and share their experiences with you and their classmates.

If the demonstrations and presentations are to be done synchronously, you may need to use a web conferencing application, such as Skype, ooVoo, or Join Me, so that teachers and students can see the demonstrations and presentations in real time and comment and provide feedback accordingly. If the interactions are to be asynchronous, you may provide access to and prepare students to use a presentation sharing tool (e.g., SlideShare, authorSTREAM) or other applications that allow users to post and share multimedia files (e.g., wikis, Dropbox, Google Storage). For a detailed discussion of pedagogical approaches and technology tools that may be used to facilitate a hybrid or a totally online course, particularly with a large number of students, refer to the third book in this series, *Online and Hybrid Learning Trends and Technologies,* Chapter 1, "Managing Large Online Courses: Pedagogical Approaches and Technological Tools," by Richard Hartshorne.

You may also readily implement Authentic Historical Investigations in conventional, face-to-face settings if you and your students have access to the Internet, digital repositories, and a presentation system in your class. All you would need to do is give students time in class to (a) examine the original letter, (b) discuss and formulate fundamental questions, (c) independently search for corroborating sources, and (d) construct plausible narratives. If you and/or your students do not have Internet access, you may still use Authentic Historical Investigations by using printouts and hard copies of the letters and other primary and secondary sources of history, as well as conducting all of the discussions and presentations as conventional, face-to-face interactions.

As you prepare and implement Authentic Historical Investigations (whether you do so in a conventional, hybrid, or totally online manner), you must consider the availability of technology and you should integrate its use in an authentic manner (like a historian would use it to conduct an investigation). Technologies should not be used just for the sake of using technology. You should also have alternative methods and sources available, such as paper-based copies of electronic sources, in case the technology fails.

Providing Appropriate Levels of Scaffolding

Conducting Authentic Historical Investigations can be a challenging task for teachers in any setting if proper scaffolds are not in place. It is essential that you find the zone of proximal development (Vygotsky, 1978) to engage and challenge students but not reach their points of total frustration. Teachers must provide multiple opportunities for students to engage in procedures that mirror those performed by historians. Early on, these investigations will begin with large amounts of scaffolding and structure, but as students progress along the novice-expert continuum and become more aware of the process and gain confidence, the scaffold may be minimized and eventually eliminated.

A scaffold is a temporary framework that is put up to support a process (e.g., learning of new concepts and skills) that may be beyond a person's capacity at any given point in time. Scaffolds may take many forms, such templates, outlines, advanced organizers, or simply a list of questions, steps, or recommendations. In the sample lesson plan for an Authentic Historical Investigation presented in this chapter, I used demonstrations, directed questions, and a checklist to scaffold the task of engaging in primary and secondary sources of history. I also guided students as they created individual KWL charts.

Students can readily search for, access, and read primary sources online. A simple checklist (either printed or posted) noting specific repositories and sources to find online may be sufficient to scaffold the task for students new to the process. However, many of the spontaneous, real-time interactions that help students interpret and later apply the information gained from the primary sources may be relatively difficult to duplicate and facilitate online. Plus, the ability to read students' facial expressions and body language as well as to ask questions and provide feedback based on students' actions and reactions in real time may be eliminated if the lesson is taught totally online.

Demonstrations, directed questions, and checklists are essential to facilitate teamwork, historical thinking, and the development of the six fundamental cognitive historical habits (i.e., questioning, connecting, sourcing, making inferences, considering alternate perspectives, and recognizing limits to one's knowledge) in conventional classroom settings. To facilitate the same processes online may require additional scaffolds. The skills and knowledge necessary to create and present plausible narratives and to reflect critically on their experiences may also require some scaffolding, particularly among novices. The key to remember here is that while good teachers can often scaffold learning through spontaneous, face-to-face interactions in conventional classroom settings, in totally online versions of Authentic Historical Investigations, such scaffolds must be even more carefully planned, developed and integrated.

Conclusion

To increase student enjoyment of history and content acquisition, it is vital that history teachers move away from the traditional, didactic methods found in the typical history classroom. Students must have opportunities to create authentic questions; utilize, scrutinize, determine the context of, and read a variety of sources; consider alternative perspectives; corroborate sources; and create plausible narratives (Waring, 2011). By conducting Authentic Historical Investigations, students will acquire the skills needed to inquire about the past and better navigate the present.

With the growing number of online primary source repositories, investigations like the one presented here become relatively easy to implement. It is amazing how many primary and secondary sources are readily available, typically at no cost. For example, the Library of Congress now has over 20 million digitized primary sources available for public consumption on its website. There is no rational reason to limit history students to reading chapters and answering questions at the back of the book when they could be conducting investigations of their own. Given the opportunity to conduct Authentic Historical Investigations, students will gain more knowledge of the past, a better understanding of the historical inquiry process, and greater skills to negotiate the present.

References

Allen, J. (1994). If this is history, why isn't it boring? In S. Steffey & W. J. Hood (Eds.), *If this is social studies, why isn't it boring?* (pp. 1–12). York, ME: Stenhouse.

Black, M. S., & Blake, M. E. (2001). Knitting local history together: Collaborating to construct curriculum. *The Social Studies, 92*(6), 243–247.

Bradley Commission on History in Schools. (1995). *Building a history curriculum: Guidelines for teaching history in schools* (p. 9). Westlake, OH: National Council for History Education. List available at www.nche.net/habitsofmind

Calder, L. (2006). Uncoverage: Toward a signature pedagogy for the history survey. *The Journal of American History, 92*(4), 1358–1370.

Chi, M. T. H. (1976). Short-term memory limitations in children: Capacity or processing deficits? *Memory and Cognition, 4,* 559–572.

Gardner, H. (1983). *Frames of mind: The theory of multiple intelligences.* New York, NY: Basic Books.

Gardner, H. (1993). *Multiple intelligences: The theory in practice.* New York, NY: Basic Books.

Gardner, H., & Hatch, T. (1989). Multiple intelligences go to school: Educational implications of the theory of multiple intelligences. *Educational Researcher, 18,* 4–10.

Hicks, D., Doolittle, P., & Ewing, E. (2004). The SCIM-C strategy: Expert historians, historical inquiry, and multimedia. *Social Education, 68*(3), 221–225.

Jensen, M. (2001). Bring the past to life. *The Writer, 114*(11), 30.

King, M., Newmann, F. M., & Carmichael, D. L. (2009). Authentic intellectual work: Common standards for teaching social studies. *Social Education, 73*(1), 43–49.

Levstik, L. S., & Barton, K. C. (2011). *Doing history: Investigating with children in elementary and middle school.* New York, NY: Erlbaum.

Mason, C. L., & Carter, A. (1999). The Garbers: Using digital history to recreate a 19th-century family. *Social Studies and the Young Learner,* 11–14.

Ogle, D. (1986). K-W-L: A teaching model that develops active reading of expository text. *The Reading Teacher, 39,* 564–570.

Scieszka, J. (1995). *The true story of the 3 little pigs.* New York, NY: Dutton Books.

Steffey, S., & Hood, W. J. (1994). *If this is social studies, why isn't it boring?* York, ME: Stenhouse.

Sternberg, R. J., & Horvath, J. A. (1995). A prototype view of expert teaching. *Educational Researcher, 24*(6), 9–17.

Vygotsky, L. S. (1978). *Mind and society: The development of higher mental processes.* Cambridge, MA: Harvard University Press.

Waring, S. M. (2011). *Preserving History: The construction of history in the K–16 classroom.* Charlotte, NC: Information Age.

Wiggins G., & McTighe J. (2005). *Understanding By Design.* Alexandria, VA: Association for Supervision and Curriculum Development.

Wineburg, S. (2001). *Historical thinking and other unnatural acts: Charting the future of teaching the past.* Philadelphia, PA: Temple University Press.

Wineburg, S. (2010). Thinking like a historian. *Teaching with Primary Sources Quarterly, 31*(Winter), 2–4. Retrieved from www.loc.gov/teachers/tps/quarterly/archive.html

Zhao, Y., & Hoge, J. D. (2005). What elementary students and teachers say about social studies. *The Social Studies, 96*(5), 216–221.

CHAPTER 6

Guided Experiential Learning

Focused Interactivity in Online and Hybrid Environments

Naomi Malone and Kendra Minor

Experience is, for me, the highest authority. The touchstone of validity is my own experience. No other person's ideas, and none of my own ideas, are as authoritative as my experience.

—Rogers, 1961, p. 23

IN THIS CHAPTER, WE ILLUSTRATE how an experiential learning strategy may be used to design totally online and hybrid learning environments. We begin with a brief historical and theoretical account of experiential learning to provide an understanding of its benefits and drawbacks. Such insights frame our subsequent discussion of Guided Experiential Learning (GEL), a specific experiential instructional strategy grounded in recent research on human cognition and instructional design. The GEL method is then applied in two example lesson plans to give you a road map for creating your own online or hybrid experiential learning environments. We conclude with recommendations for best practices in the application of experiential learning in K–12 settings.

P
sychologist and psychotherapist Carl Rogers (1983) suggests that significant learning can only be derived from learners' personal involvement on both the cognitive and affective levels, calling for a shift to student-centered learning with the educator taking a facilitative role. We agree with Rogers and others who have advocated experiential and student-centered forms of education as an alternative to traditional, teacher-directed instruction—particularly in online and hybrid learning environments that are designed to foster the development of higher-order thinking skills.

For this chapter, we focus on Richard Clark's (2005) guided experiential learning (GEL) instructional method to illustrate how experiential approaches to teaching and learning may be applied to facilitate e-learning. To begin, we review the historical and contemporary foundations of experiential learning theory to ground our discussion of GEL, an instructional method that integrates guidance and scaffolding with constructivist instruction to facilitate learning. We then present two lesson plans using the GEL method to provide road maps for creating online and hybrid experiential learning environments. We conclude by discussing issues that you may confront if you design and deliver online or hybrid instruction based on the GEL method.

Foundations of Experiential Learning Theory

In his book *Experience and Education,* John Dewey (1938) states, "I assume that amid all uncertainties, there is one permanent frame of reference: namely, the organic connection between education and personal experience; ..." Arguing that both teacher-centered and student-centered forms of education lacked a sound basis in educational theory, Dewey fashioned two central principles as a method for designing and evaluating effective educational experiences: (1) continuity, the idea that students learn from their developing, sound educational experiences, and (2) interaction, the notion that students' experiences are derived from their interactions with the environment and other individuals. However, Dewey was careful to make this distinction: "The belief that all genuine education comes about through experience does not mean that all experiences are genuinely or equally educative" (p. 25).

Besides influencing subsequent experiential learning theory, Dewey's work also spawned many different forms of instruction, such as "case-based instruction," "discovery learning," and "inquiry-based learning" (Clark, 2005), as well as "service learning" programs, such as the 4-H Youth Development Program (Carver & Enfield, 2006). David Kolb, arguably the most well-known contemporary supporter of experiential learning, built upon the work of Dewey to devise a descriptive model of experiential learning. As depicted in Figure 6.1, Kolb's continuous, cyclical process consists of four stages: (1) students' concrete experience through participation and involvement with people, places, and learning events; (2) reflective observation as students think about how their actions and consequences relate to their experiences; (3) abstract conceptualization when students formulate general principles that can guide future experiences; and (4) testing application of the principles as they react to situations where new learning can be applied (Kolb, 1984; Kolb & Fry, 1975).

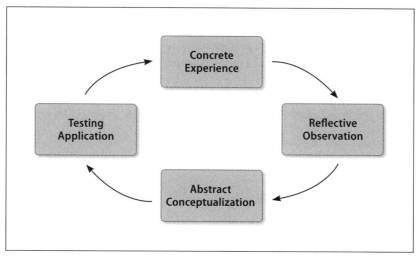

FIGURE 6.1 ▶ Kolb's experiential learning theory (ELT)

The apparent value of experiential learning has resulted in a number of recent models, including but not limited to those posited by Schank, Berman, and Macpherson (1999) and Clark (2005, 2008). To sort out various interpretations of ELT models, Lindsey and Berger (2009) synthesized published approaches, identifying four central tenets of experiential learning to help guide research and practice: Learning should (1) be student-centered rather than teacher-directed, (2) focus on real-world experiences, (3) include a high degree of self-direction for decision making, and (4) consist of feedback regarding decisions made by students. Additionally, Lindsay and Berger distilled three universal and sequential principles of experiential learning: (1) framing the experience, (2) activating the experience, and (3) reflecting on the experience (delineated further in Figure 6.2).

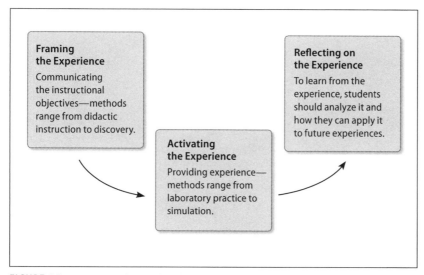

FIGURE 6.2 ▶ Universal principles of experiential learning

In general, it appears that current educational advocates of experiential learning agree with Lindsey and Berger's four central tenets (2009). However, the advocates differ regarding how much guidance teachers should give students while they are framing and activating their experiences, the first two universal and sequential principles. Specifically, a number of cognitive and educational psychologists argue against pure discovery elements of constructivist learning environments (see Clark, 2009; Mayer, 2004; Sweller, Kirschner, & Clark, 2007) while several constructivists support discovery learning methods (e.g., Hannafin, Land, & Oliver, 1999; Hmelo-Silver, Duncan, & Chinn, 2007).

Guided Experiential Learning

Although discovery-based educational approaches have gained popularity, some educators argue that approaches based on the assumption that students (alone or in teams) learn best if they are given a problem to solve or a task to perform with the goal of discovering a solution are fundamentally flawed (Sweller, Kirschner, & Clark, 2007). Citing a review of research on discovery learning (Mayer, 2004) and an analysis of discovery, experiential, inquiry, and problem-based learning (Kirschner, Sweller, & Clark, 2006), Clark, Yates, Early, and Moulton (2010) conclude that discovery-based approaches to teaching and learning are less effective than methods giving students a guided solution that includes a demonstration of the task's completion along with practice and feedback. Clark et al. believe novice learners with little or no previous knowledge of the subject matter need more guidance to overcome challenges. To provide such guidance within the context of experiential learning, Clark (2005) proposed an instructional strategy called "guided experiential learning."

Clark (2008) defined instructional guidance as, "providing students with accurate and complete procedural information (and related declarative knowledge) that they have not yet learned in a demonstration about how to perform the necessary sequence of actions and make the necessary decisions to accomplish a learning task and/or solve a problem" (p. 161). To go along with his definition, Clark (2009) suggests that:

▶ Guidance must provide an accurate and complete demonstration of how and when to perform a task or solve a problem.

▶ When transfer of knowledge to other tasks or problems is desired, guidance should also provide varied practice and declarative knowledge to help students adapt their learning to new situations.

▶ Guidance must require students to practice and accompany the practice with timely feedback.

GEL combines experiential learning with instructional guidance in the sequence of lesson-level instructional events listed in Table 6.1 (Clark, 2005, 2008).

TABLE 6.1   ▶   Events associated with the guided experiential learning (GEL) model

STEP	DESCRIPTION
1. Goals/Objectives	Skills, conditions, and standards that must be achieved in the lesson.
2. Reasons	Reasons for learning, advantages of learning, and risks of failure to learn and transfer.
3. Overview	To help students develop a mental model for the course, provide a course outline (and, when possible, display a visual model of how lessons are organized in the larger course) and then describe the instructional strategies that will be used in the lessons.
4. Conceptual Knowledge	Concepts, processes, and principles necessary to learn to perform a task or solve a problem with examples and analogies that support learning.
5. Demonstration	Demonstration of the procedure—a clear "how to" description for all elements of a task or solution.
6. Practice	Simpler problems should be given first, with more complex and varied problems given later in the exercise. Decrease guidance gradually as students develop more expertise.
7. Challenging, Competency-Based Assessments	Students receive feedback on their practice that focuses on (a) what they accomplished that was correct, and (if necessary), (b) how they need to adjust their procedure or strategy to complete their learning goals. Feedback about mistakes is focused on correcting the procedure used, not on the ability of the student.

Guided Experiential Learning Lesson Plans

To demonstrate the flexibility of guided experiential learning, we provide two lesson plans—Lesson A, Global Warming, for a hybrid lesson that combines both online and face-to-face classroom experiences and Lesson B, Say Hello to "Scratch," for a fully online lesson. In each lesson plan, we first discuss the lesson's objectives, educational standards, associated activities, and procedures we've used to develop the lesson. We then present each lesson with narratives describing every step of the GEL model along with screenshots to provide concrete examples of the related materials posted online.

Lesson Plan A

Global Warming *(Hybrid Lesson)*

Global Warming is a hybrid Grade 9–12 lesson that utilizes a wiki and interactive communications tools to facilitate both synchronous and asynchronous experiences. We refined the Global Warming lesson found on the PBS website (www.pbs.org/now/classroom/globalwarming.html) to show you how the GEL model may be applied to design and deliver a hybrid module.

The lesson focuses on helping students critically evaluate a controversial issue, global warming. Global warming refers to an increase in average temperatures around the world, believed to be caused by an increase in the greenhouse gases released into the atmosphere. The seven instructional events associated with the GEL model engage students in learning activities that require them to think deeply about the problems associated with global warming and engage in tasks to deepen their understanding, rather than simply memorizing information about the greenhouse effect, global climate change, and other facts.

The lesson is designed for social studies, debate, language arts, government/citizenship, and current events classes in Grades 9–12, addressing national standards in geography, science, health, world history, and language arts. The standards for the lesson plan come from "Content Knowledge," a compilation of content standards and benchmarks for K–12 curriculum by McRel (Mid-continent Research for Education and Learning; www.mcrel.org/standards-benchmarks/). As students begin to understand how the ecosystem has been altered by human actions, how the greenhouse effect may contribute to global warming, and how changes in the world's climate impact humans and the environment, they address the following National Geography Standards: Standard 8: *The characteristics and spatial distribution of ecosystems and biomes on Earth's surface;* Standard 14: *How human actions modify the physical environment;* Standard 15: *How physical systems affect human systems;* and Standard 18: *How to apply geography to interpret the present and plan for the future.*

What are the causes of global warming? Are the changes caused by human activity or is such thinking a myth? There are disagreements about global warming and climate change. This lesson is designed to help student's research and form reliable opinions on the issue. Before students can take a position on global warming, presentations of various arguments concerning global warming are used to demonstrate multiple viewpoints on the issue. After having seen different perspectives, students are tasked with completing a Venn diagram to record what people on both sides of the global warming debate argue regarding human responsibility for this issue. In addition to the National Geography Standards, this activity addresses McREL's Benchmarks for Language Arts, Standard 4 (Writing): *Gathers and uses information for research purposes;* Standard 7 (Reading): *Uses reading skills and strategies to understand and interpret a variety of informational texts;* Standard 8 (Listening and Speaking): *Uses listening and speaking strategies for different purposes;* Standard 9 (Viewing): *Uses viewing skills and strategies to understand and interpret visual media;* and Standard 10 (Media): *Understands the characteristics and components of the media.*

Once students have explored a variety of perspectives on global climate change, students are encouraged to incorporate their new knowledge by performing a part and whole task consisting of

(a) writing persuasive answers regarding their opinions on whether global warming is an imminent world threat and explaining why or why not and (b) writing their opinions on what actions they believe should be taken to address the global warming issue. Standards addressed by this last activity include the following: Life Skills, Thinking and Reasoning Standard 1: *Understands and applies the basic principles of presenting an argument;* Standard 2: *Understands and applies the basic principles of logic and reasoning;* Standard 3: *Effectively uses mental processes that are based on identifying similarities and differences;* and Standard 6: *Applies decision-making techniques.*

Traditionally the lesson is covered in five 50-minute in-class periods, plus time outside of class to complete the final project. For a hybrid approach, the lesson material was developed so some of the in-class activities could be completed online. The hybrid module follows the criteria for each strategy specified in the GEL model. The sequence of activities and assessments using the GEL model is shown in Figure 6.A.1.

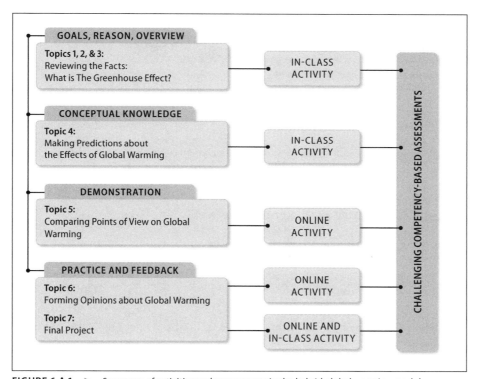

FIGURE 6.A.1 ▶ Sequence of activities and assessments in the hybrid global warming module

We used a combination of tools to create and enhance the learning environment for online and in-class activities. We chose to use a free website builder, offered by Wix (www.wix.com), to post the content for the lesson (Figure 6.A.2). Students can navigate through the website by clicking the tabs for each topic. A wiki was used for students to work collaboratively on group projects. Using the wiki made it easy to identify and track what each student contributed. Resources are available for creating a course wiki, such as Wikispaces (www.wikispaces.com) and PBworks (http://pbworks.com/education). Wiggio (http://wiggio.com) was used to share documents and for class discussion postings. Next, we detail each of the elements from the lesson with instructor notes and suggestions for integrating technology and creating a hybrid learning environment.

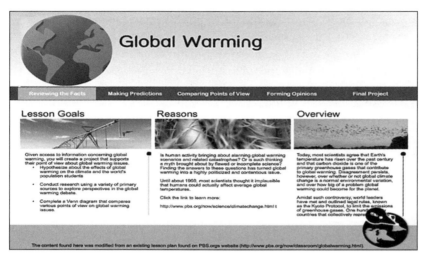

FIGURE 6.A.2 ▶ Screenshot from Global Warming lesson

Goal and Objectives

In the first event, students are introduced to the overall learning goals of the lesson that are posted on the class wiki, blog, or website:

> Given access to information concerning global warming, you will create a project that supports your point of view about global warming issues.

> ▶ Hypothesize about the effects of global warming on the climate and the world's population.

> ▶ Conduct research using a variety of primary sources to explore perspectives in the global warming debate.

> ▶ Complete a Venn diagram that compares various points of view on global warming issues.

> ▶ Take a position on global warming and support this viewpoint with reasons, facts, and examples gathered during lesson activities.

Discuss the learning goals with the class. Discuss how to access the course content (i.e., provide a link to the class website, blog, or wiki), and expectations for completing online activities.

Reasons

For the second event, students are given a rationale for learning about global warming. The activity asks students to view an interactive map and discuss what the markers on the map represent. The intent of the activity is to illustrate how widespread global warming indicators have become and how large the concentration of indicators in the United States is. The following explanation is posted as an introduction to the topic on the class wiki, blog, or website:

> Is human activity bringing about alarming global warming scenarios and related catastrophes? Or is such thinking a myth brought about by flawed or incomplete science? Finding the answers to these questions has turned global warming into a highly politicized and contentious issue. Until about 1960, most scientists thought it implausible that human activity could actually affect average global temperatures.

Then, ask students to view the "History of Global Warming" page (www.pbs.org/now/science/climatechange.html) to learn more about the topic. Discuss the importance of the topic and explain the ongoing debate surrounding it. Guide students to view the link on the history of global warming to provide additional context for the topic.

To learn the possible risks of global warming, direct students to go to the Union of Concerned Scientists' website (www.ucsusa.org/global_warming). Direct students to view the interactive Climate Hot Map (www.climatehotmap.org; depicted in Figure 6.A.3) and encourage them to explore the various markers on the map and explain what the markers indicate. Then, lead a class discussion on the additions of markers that have been made since the map was created.

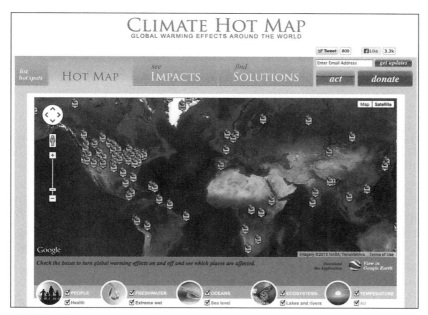

FIGURE 6.A.3 ▶ Interactive climate hot map

Overview

In the third event, students are given an overview of what they will be learning in the module. The following is posted on the class wiki, blog, or website:

> Today, most scientists agree that the Earth's temperature has risen over the past century and that carbon dioxide is one of the primary greenhouse gases that contributes to global warming. Disagreement persists, however, over whether or not global climate change is a normal environmental variation and over how big a problem global warming could become for the planet.
>
> Amid such controversy, world leaders have met and outlined legal rules, known as the Kyoto Protocol, to limit the emissions of greenhouse gases. One hundred forty countries that collectively represent 61.6% of greenhouse gas emissions worldwide have ratified the Kyoto Protocol.
>
> The United States does not support the Kyoto Protocol and disagrees with a number of its provisions. Instead, the United States is funding additional scientific research on the causes and effects of global warming, encouraging climate change technology research and development efforts, looking at how its own federal and state laws can regulate greenhouse gas emissions in the United States, backing the research and development of renewable energy sources, and pursuing other strategies that it believes will address global climate change without major upsets to the U.S. economy.

For the overview, students are also given a description of each of the tasks they will perform in the upcoming activities.

Conceptual Knowledge

For the fourth event, through reflective learning, students begin to explore the concepts, terminology, relationships, and principles needed to understand global warming. Before class begins, post the term "greenhouse effect" where students can see it. Then, to begin the class, ask students to think without talking about a definition for the greenhouse effect. Give students a minute to formulate their ideas and then have them write down and share their definitions. At the end of the allotted time, ask students to share their definitions with one or two other students sitting nearby and compare the similarities and differences in their definitions. Then, allow a few minutes for pairs or small groups of students to combine their definitions into one that they believe is the most accurate. Begin a class discussion by asking several pairs/groups to share their definitions of the greenhouse effect. Next, show students the Flash animation (found at the U.S. Environmental Protection Agency's website: www.epa.gov/climatechange/kids/basics/today/greenhouse-effect. html) that accurately describes the greenhouse effect and how it likely contributes to global warming (Figure 6.A.4).

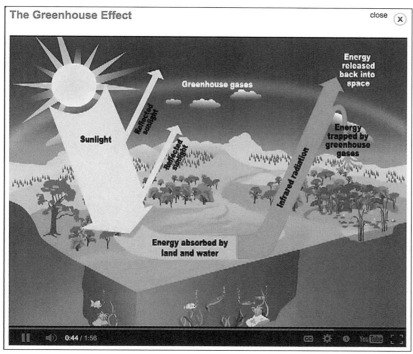

FIGURE 6.A.4 ▶ Screen shot of the greenhouse effect animation

Students correct their definitions based on what they've learned from the animation. Then, as a class, discuss the effects of greenhouse gases on the overall health of people worldwide by addressing questions such as these:

1. What types of illnesses/diseases can be attributed to greenhouse gas emissions?

2. How can changes in the world climate increase health risks for people worldwide?

With an understanding of the greenhouse effect and global climate change, students can now make predictions about the potential impact of global warming. Ask students to hypothesize about how the world's climate could change over the next one hundred years if humans do nothing to limit the levels of their greenhouse gas emissions. Also ask students to make predictions about the effects such climate changes could have on humans. Working in pairs, small groups, or as a class, students brainstorm a list of their ideas related to these questions. Each student should record a copy of the list to refer back to it later in the lesson.

Demonstration

For the fifth event, ask students to view video presentations that demonstrate how the issue of global warming is debated. Use broadcasts of some of the controversy surrounding global warming to demonstrate multiple viewpoints on the issue. The demonstrations provide ways for students to see both sides of the issue and to begin to form their own views.

Not everyone agrees about global warming and climate change. To illustrate some of the controversy surrounding global warming, have students view the following content from three Public Broadcasting Service (PBS) NOW broadcasts and videos:

▶ The Heat Over Global Warming: www.pbs.org/now/shows/304

▶ Climate Change and the Media Senate Hearings: www.pbs.org/now/shows/249/climate-change.html

▶ God and Global Warming: www.pbs.org/now/shows/343

To facilitate the demonstrations, teachers may do the following:

1. Post the Global Warming Venn Diagram (www.pbs.org/now/classroom/globalvenn.pdf) to the class wiki. Have students access it and review the directions for completing the diagram.

2. Have students answer the question on the discussion board, "Has human activity caused the world's climate to change over the past 100 years?"

3. Ask students to use the Venn diagram to record what people on both sides of the global warming debate say about human responsibility for this issue.

4. Post the Global Warming Venn Diagram resources list. Have students work in small groups and use the resources listed on the Global Warming Venn Diagram to access at least two of the "NOW Programs" and at least two of the "Other Global Warming Resources" for their research. The Global Warming Venn Diagram resources list can be found on pages 10–11 of the lesson plan (www-tc.pbs.org/now/classroom/global-warming-lesson-plan.pdf).

5. Have each group post its completed diagram to the discussion board on the web.

6. Have students respond to a discussion post from their peers.

7. Allow students to revise their responses for final grading.

Practice

For practice, use the sixth GEL event: Post the following directions and questions on the class wiki, blog, or website:

Now that you have explored a variety of perspectives on global climate change, take a position on the issue and support it with data from your previous research. Write two to three persuasive paragraphs to answer the following questions:

1. In your opinion, is global warming an imminent world threat? Why or why not?

2. In your opinion, what actions do you believe should be taken to address the global warming issue?

Support your opinions with specific information from the brainstorming lists and your completed Venn diagram.

Teachers may then do the following:

1. Review the self-evaluation and peer-evaluation rubrics with the students.

2. Have students post their responses to the discussion board on the web.

3. Have students respond to a discussion question from their peers and complete a self-evaluation and a peer-evaluation.

4. Allow students to revise their responses for final grading.

Challenging, Competency-Based Assessments

For the GEL seventh and final event (competency-based assessments), have students complete the final project by doing the following:

1. Choose a project from the Global Warming Project List handout (www-tc.pbs.org/ now/classroom/globalproject.pdf). Alternatively, students may design a project of their own with teacher approval. The goal of the project is for students to create something substantive that they can use to share their positions on global warming and to increase awareness about its related issues.

2. Allow students one class period to begin work on their projects, and then assign a completion date. When projects are completed, display student projects and/or have students present them to the class to demonstrate their points of view on global warming issues.

Throughout the lesson, evaluate students' participation in postings and discussions to assess their knowledge of the concepts covered throughout the lesson and in preparation for the final project.

For example, evaluate students on the quality of the postings and the degree that the postings or responses promote discussion with classmates.

1 point—Minimal response to the question

2 points—Posting or participation in class discussion in response to the question but does not stimulate further class discussion

3 points—Posting or participation in class discussion fully addresses the assignment and stimulates at least one substantial follow-up posting or more class discussion

At the end of the lesson, assess students on the final project in the following ways:

1. Give students completion grades for participating in class discussions and filling in the Venn diagram worksheet.

2. Use a scoring guide or a peer-evaluation rubric to provide students with feedback about the effectiveness of their persuasive writing responses to the questions posed in the lesson.

3. Use a scoring guide to evaluate students' projects and a self-evaluation rubric to have students evaluate their own work using criteria established prior to completion of the assignment.

4. Ask classmates to complete a peer-evaluation form that assesses the effectiveness of the project in terms of providing factual information to others.

TABLE 6.A.1 ▶ Venn Diagram Rubric *(4 = very strong, 1 = very weak)*

CATEGORY	4	3	2	1
Answer to the Question is Supported	Student's answer to the question "Has human activity caused the world's climate to change over the past 100 years?" is fully supported by the text.	Student's answer to the question "Has human activity caused the world's climate to change over the past 100 years?" has some support from the text.	Student's answer to the question "Has human activity caused the world's climate to change over the past 100 years?" has a little support from the text.	Students answer to the question "Has human activity caused the world's climate to change over the past 100 years?" has no support from the text.
Quality of Information	Venn diagram entries show advanced understanding of similarities and differences of what people on both sides of the global warming debate say about human responsibility for this issue.	Venn diagram entries show good understanding of similarities and differences of what people on both sides of the global warming debate say about human responsibility for this issue.	Venn diagram entries show basic understanding of similarities and differences of what people on both sides of the global warming debate say about human responsibility for this issue.	Venn diagram entries show little to no understanding of similarities and differences of what people on both sides of the global warming debate say about human responsibility for this issue.
Mechanics	All spelling, grammar, and mechanics are correct in the completed Venn diagram.	Most spelling, grammar, and mechanics are correct in the completed Venn diagram.	Some spelling, grammar, and mechanics are correct in the completed Venn diagram.	There is minimal use of appropriate spelling, grammar, and mechanics in the completed Venn diagram.
Design	Clean design; diagram has high visual appeal; color used effectively for emphasis.	Design is fairly clean, with a few exceptions; diagram has visual appeal; uses color effectively most of time.	Design meets requirements, but lacks visual appeal.	Cluttered design; low in visual appeal.

TABLE 6.A.2 ▶ Evaluation Rubric *(4 = very strong, 1 = very weak)*

CATEGORY	4	3	2	1
Attention Grabber	The introductory paragraph has a strong hook or attention grabber that is appropriate for the audience. This could be a strong statement, a relevant quotation, statistic, or question addressed to the reader.	The introductory paragraph has a hook or attention grabber, but it is weak, rambling, or inappropriate for the audience.	The author has an interesting introductory paragraph, but the connection to the topic is not clear.	The introductory paragraph is not interesting and it is not relevant to the topic.
Focus or Thesis Statement	The thesis statement names the topic of the essay and outlines the main points to be discussed.	The thesis statement names the topic of the essay.	The thesis statement outlines some or all of the main points to be discussed but does not name the topic.	The thesis statement does not name the topic and does not preview what will be discussed.
Evidence and Examples	All of the evidence and examples are specific, relevant; explanations are given that show how each piece of evidence supports the author's position.	Most of the evidence and examples are specific and relevant; explanations are given that show how each piece of evidence supports the author's position.	At least one of the pieces of evidence or examples is relevant and has an explanation that shows how that piece of evidence supports the author's position.	Evidence and examples are not relevant and/or not explained.
Transitions	A variety of thoughtful transitions are used. They clearly show how ideas are connected.	Transitions show how ideas are connected, but there is little variety	Some transitions work well, but some connections between ideas are fuzzy.	The transitions between ideas are unclear or nonexistent.
Closing paragraph	The conclusion is strong and leaves the reader solidly understanding the writer's position. Effective restatement of the position statement begins the closing paragraph.	The conclusion is recognizable. The author's position is restated within the first two sentences of the closing paragraph.	The author's position is restated within the closing paragraph, but not near the beginning.	There is no conclusion, the paper just ends.
Audience	Demonstrates a clear understanding of the potential reader and uses appropriate vocabulary and arguments. Anticipates readers' questions and provides thorough answers appropriate for that audience.	Demonstrates a general understanding of the potential reader and uses vocabulary and arguments appropriate for that audience.	Demonstrates some understanding of the potential reader and uses arguments appropriate for that audience.	It is not clear who the author is writing for.
Grammar and Spelling	Author makes no errors in grammar or spelling that distract the reader from the content.	Author makes 1–2 errors in grammar or spelling that distract the reader from the content.	Author makes 3–4 errors in grammar or spelling that distract the reader from the content.	Author makes more than 4 errors in grammar or spelling that distract the reader from the content.
Other Mechanics	Paper is typed, double-spaced, and five paragraphs long. The outline is included.	Paper is typed, but not double-spaced. The essay is four to five paragraphs long. The outline is included.	Paper is not typed, but is double-spaced. The essay is four to five paragraphs long. The outline may or may not be included.	Paper is not typed and not double-spaced. The essay is less than five paragraphs long and the outline may or may not be included.

The most important thing to work on to improve this essay is:

Lesson Plan B
Say Hello to "Scratch" *(Online Lesson)*

Scratch is a graphical programming language that is intended to make computer programming more engaging and accessible for children and teens by using building-block programming, media manipulation, and sharing and collaboration through the ScratchEd website (http://scratched.media.mit.edu). Scratch's online lesson with an introductory video introduces students to programming with Scratch using GEL. Students of all ages and levels of computer programming knowledge can learn computational concepts, such as iteration, conditionals, variables, data types, events, and processes, which will give them the foundation to transition into more traditional programming languages. The activities in this lesson are designed to explore computational concepts (e.g., sequence, loops, and events); practice (working iteratively and incrementally, testing and debugging, reusing and remixing, abstracting and modularizing); and review and reflect (expressing, connecting, questioning). Much of the material used to create this course can be found on the Scratch and ScratchEd websites. Their Creative Computing Curriculum Guide (http://scratched.media.mit.edu/sites/default/files/CurriculumGuide-v20110923.pdf) released under a Creative Commons license was especially useful. Lesson Plan B and its activities make use of two K–12 curriculum standards:

▶ Computer Science Teachers Association (CSTA) K–12 Computer Science Standards 2011 (http://csta.acm.org/Curriculum/sub/CurrFiles/CSTA_K-12_CSS.pdf). This course helps students master three of the five major strands addressed in the Level 2 standards, including: (a) Computational Thinking (algorithms, problem solving, abstraction, connections); (b) Collaboration (tools, endeavor); and, (c) Computing Practice and Programming (tools for creation, programming).

▶ ISTE's NETS for Students (www.iste.org/standards/nets-for-students), including: 1. Creativity and Innovation—students demonstrate creative thinking, construct knowledge, and develop innovative products and processes using technology; and 2. Communication and Collaboration—students use digital media and environments to communicate and work collaboratively, including at a distance, to support individual learning and contribute to the learning of others.

Table 6.B.1 lists the principles of experiential framework posited by Lindsey and Berger (2009) and describes the components used in the lesson to address the principles and related curriculum standards.

TABLE 6.B.1 ▶ GEL Course Components—Connections to Level 2 Standards

EXPERIENTIAL LEARNING PRINCIPLES	COMPONENTS	DESCRIPTION	STANDARDS ADDRESSED
Framing the Experience: Goals, Reasons, Overview, Concepts, & Demonstration	Sequence	Identifying a series of steps for a task	CSTA: Computational thinking
	Loops	Running the same sequence multiple times	CSTA: Computational thinking
	Events	One thing causing another thing to happen	CSTA: Computational thinking
Activating the Experience: Practice	Being iterative and incremental	Developing a little bit, then trying it out, then developing some more	CSTA: Practice & Programming
	Testing and debugging	Making sure that things work—and fixing mistakes	CSTA: Practice & Programming
	Reusing and remixing	Making something by building on what others—or you—have done	CSTA: Practice & Programming ISTE: Creativity & Innovation
	Abstracting and modularizing	Building something large by putting together a collection of smaller parts	CSTA: Practice & Programming ISTE: Creativity & Innovation
Reflecting on Experience: Challenging Competency-Based Assessments	Questioning	"How is a program like a recipe?"	CSTA: Computational Thinking; Collaboration ISTE: Communication & Collaboration
	Evaluating	Comparing and contrasting programs and sharing the evaluations with others	CSTA: Collaboration ISTE: Communication & Collaboration

Goals/Objectives

Figure 6.B.1 illustrates how the lesson's goals and objectives are presented to students online. Students will learn how to:

▶ Memorize and recite the main parts of the Scratch interface (Video review of interface within an introductory video)

▶ Explain how a computer program is similar to a recipe

▶ Apply the concept of a recipe in a particular situation (Assignment 1: Get the cat to move in a square with solution provided)

▶ Put together scripts to form a whole to create a new program (Assignment 2: Create a new program with no solution provided)

▶ Compare and contrast two programs that perform the same task to evaluate which one is better and why (Students upload their projects)

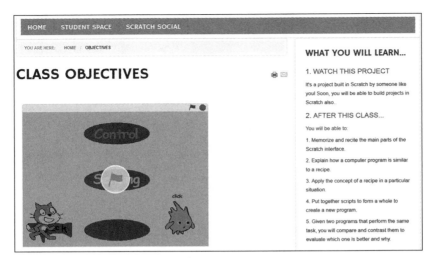

FIGURE 6.B.1 ▶ Scratch class page objectives.

Overview

Students watch videos that introduce them to Scratch and the history of Scratch. They see how the program helps them to be creative and critical thinkers and why that is important. The video also shows students how easy it is to use Scratch and lets them see that it is like other programs they already use. The video provides a walk-through of the Scratch user interface, giving names to each specific area that students will be using in subsequent lessons, including:

▶ Block Categories

▶ Editor (Scripts, Costumes, Sounds)

▶ Sprites

▶ Stage (where the action happens)

▶ Blocks

Conceptual Knowledge

The section called Scratch Basics, consisting of six videos, teaches students the concept of Sprites and their costumes (the Scratch cat and other objects in the students' programs are called Sprites). Each program can have multiple scripts, one or more for each Sprite students want to control. Students also learn what it means to write programs in a procedural language. In procedural programming languages like Scratch, one thing happens right after the other. Students are asked to think of writing a program like a recipe in which things must be done in a specific order. Figure 6.B.2 provides a screenshot of the videos that present students with the conceptual knowledge covered in the lesson.

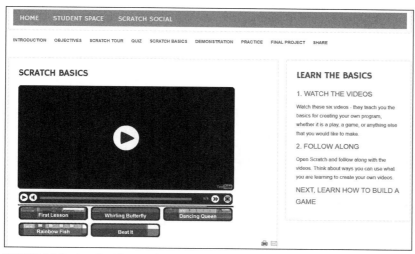

FIGURE 6.B.2 ▶ Six videos teaching Scratch Basics to learn how to start programming

Demonstration

A complete demonstration of how to create a project from beginning to end is provided in this unit. Figure 6.B.3. shows the five demonstration videos that guide students through the process of creating a breakout game in Scratch.

FIGURE 6.B.3 ▶ Five demonstration videos show how to create a breakout game in Scratch

Practice

After students have gotten an idea of how to create a project from beginning to end, they are given a chance to practice. The Practice page (Figure 6.B.4.) provides a set of Scratch Cards that can be downloaded and followed step-by-step to create mini-programs that reinforce the concepts learned in the Scratch Basics section.

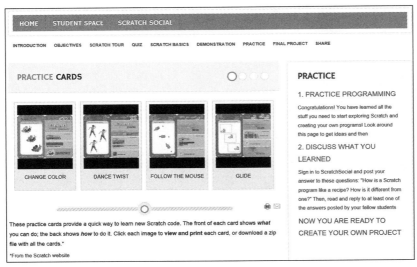

FIGURE 6.B.4 ▶ Practice section of the course

Challenging, Competency-Based Assessments

Assessments, including a quiz, a discussion question, a final project, and a collaborative reflection, are designed to enhance students' learning experiences. To make sure students know the function of each major component of the Scratch interface, they are shown the interface with each section labeled and described, and then they are given a quiz created in Scratch to test their knowledge.

To complete course activities online, students set up two accounts: one on the Scratch website to upload and present their projects and the other on the course website to assess other students' work. They set up their course accounts at the beginning of the course and their Scratch accounts after they finish their projects. A video shows them how to create an account and upload projects directly from the Scratch program.

To reinforce computational thinking, students discuss the question, "How is programming like a recipe?" in the website's social space, called ScratchSocial, depicted in Figure 6.B.5.

To assess students' ability to integrate everything they have learned, they are then asked to create a project and upload it to the Scratch website. The Final Project page, illustrated in Figure 6.B.6, provides resources that help students brainstorm ideas.

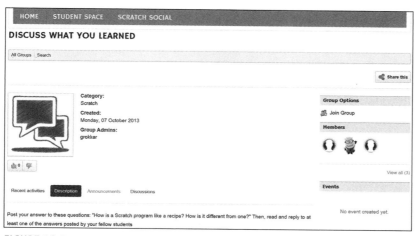

FIGURE 6.B.5 ▶ The discussion section of Scratch Social

FIGURE 6.B.6 ▶ Sample projects on the Scratch Final Project page

In keeping with the social and interactive elements that are integral to designing in Scratch, students participate in a final peer assessment activity. They are asked to share a link to their uploaded project on Scratch Social. They then select another student's project to provide reflective feedback, using the Final Project Assessment Rubric (Table 6.B.2.).

TABLE 6.B.2 ▶ Final Project Assessment Rubric

TRAIT	EXCEPTIONAL	ACCEPTABLE	AMATEUR	UNSATISFACTORY
Specifications	The program works and meets all specified criteria.	The program works and meets most of the specifications.	The program does what it is supposed to do, but some parts produce incorrect results, and/or several specifications are not met.	The program does not work and/or most specifications are not met.
Readability	The blocks are exceptionally well organized and very easy to follow.	The blocks are organized and fairly easy to follow.	The organization of blocks is understandable only by someone who knows what it is supposed to be doing.	The blocks are poorly organized, and the logic is hard to follow.
Documentation	The documentation is well written and clearly explains the procedure used to accomplish the program's objective.	The documentation provides some explanation of each separate procedure.	The documentation provides a barebones overview.	There is little to no documentation, or the documentation does not explain the process well.

Finally, students are asked to reflect on what they learned in the course, discussing how and why it is relevant to their goals at school, at home, and in their future plans (Figure 6.B.7).

FIGURE 6.B.7 ▶ Share your Projects page on Scratch Social

Design and Delivery Issues

In this section, we discuss some of the potential challenges inherent in applying guided experimental learning, primarily focusing on the use of technology to design and deliver the sample lessons. We also offer suggestions for best practices, based on lessons learned during the design and delivery of the sample lessons.

The key factor in designing learning experiences is not technology but the instructional events (i.e., goals; reasons; overview; conceptual knowledge; demonstration; practice and feedback; and challenging, competency-based assessments) designed to achieve specified educational outcomes. As noted by Hirumi in Chapter 2, "Applying Grounded Strategies to Design and Sequence e-Learning Interactions," of the first book in this series, *Online and Hybrid Learning Design Fundamentals,* instructors should first select and apply grounded instructional strategies to design and sequence key instructional events, and then they can choose the appropriate tools to facilitate each event.

However, creating a hybrid or fully online lesson does require you to become comfortable using different tools to support lesson objectives, instructional strategies, and student assessments. A few considerations for integrating technology include your level of comfort in the use of the technology, students' access to the Internet, and institutional requirements. Additional factors include ease of integration with existing technologies, as well as assessing any hidden costs for upgrading, adding extra features, or getting technical support.

While GEL provides many benefits, using a guided experiential approach may be challenging for teachers and students, particularly in online or hybrid learning environments. Although access to technology has increased in many schools, teachers' technology skills and knowledge remain a challenge. Using GEL to create a hybrid or fully online lesson may present difficulties if you have not been trained to use the necessary technology, do not understand how to implement technology, have limited access to technology resources, are unwilling or unmotivated to use these resources, or are resistant to altering your teaching practices.

To become familiar with how to facilitate learning in an online environment, you need to plan for the possibility of managing large class sizes, as discussed by Hartshorne in Chapter 1, "Managing Large Online Courses: Pedagogical Approaches and Technological Tools," of the third book in this series, *Online and Hybrid Learning Trends and Technologies.* You need to create online activities that guide learners in making decisions from multiple perspectives, provide timely guidance and feedback, and create online assessments. In addition, you need to consider students with special needs, as discussed by Straub and McKinney in Chapter 6, "Designing e-Learning Environments for Students with Special Needs," in the first book in this series, *Online and Hybrid Learning Design Fundamentals,* to provide multiple pathways to demonstrate mastery. For example, the Venn diagram exercise to compare and contrast multiple perspectives on global warming in our chapter might be replaced with a drag and drop computer exercise in which the special needs student is given a list of perspectives and asked to drag and drop each perspective into the correct "basket."

In this chapter, we were able to support and enhance the guided experiential learning activities for both hybrid and online learning using various types of technology. The two sample lessons use only a few of the myriad technologies that you may choose to deliver instruction. For example, like many schools, you may use Blackboard or Moodle as a platform for facilitating e-learning. However, less technological, more accessible, and easier to manage tools, such as blogs, free website builders, and wikis can also be used. For the more technologically adept, there are numerous open-source applications and software programs, some with extensive developer support systems (e.g., MediaWiki, Drupal, Joomla, Audacity, and Freemind) that can be used to create innovative lessons and units at a low cost. For a discussion on the use of specific technologies to facilitate online learning, refer to Chapter 4, "The Promise of Web 2.0 Technologies" in the first book in this series, *Online and Hybrid Learning Design Fundamentals,* as well as Chapter 2, "Using WebQuests to Implement Inquiry-Based Learning," and Chapter 7, "Designing Inter*PLAY* Learning Landscapes to Evoke Emotions, Spark the Imagination, and Promote Creative Problem Solving," in this book.

Although it may appear time-consuming and expensive to create content and activities such as the demonstrations suggested by GEL, creating a hybrid or online learning environment does not mean that you have to go out and learn the newest technologies. There are many free, accessible educational resources that can be used to support these learning events. For example, PBS.org, along with a number of additional websites and repositories discussed in Chapter 3, "Reusing Educational Resources," in the first book in this series, *Online and Hybrid Learning Design Fundamentals,* provide an array of resources, including videos and podcasts as well as reusable stills and animated graphics.

In addition to teachers preparing themselves to use technology for instruction and learning, teachers need to prepare their students. While students in the 21st century are much more technologically savvy and confident about using these new tools than earlier generations, teachers must prepare them to function and collaborate in team environments because these skills are becoming increasingly important in the workplace. Students will also have to be guided on how to access and, in some cases, navigate the different resources they are expected to use. For a discussion on preparing students, see Chapter 5, "Preparing Students for e-Learning Success," in the first book in this series, *Online and Hybrid Learning Design Fundamentals.*

Each lesson presented in our chapter was created using a variety of instructional media to support collaborative and interactive learning. The tools we chose to use were adaptable, accessible, and easy for learners to modify. For example, the hybrid Global Warming lesson used Wix (www.wix.com), a free website builder and Wiggio (http://wiggio.com), a wiki, to facilitate the online portions of the hybrid lesson. The wiki was chosen because of its availability, ease of navigation, facility for collaboration, and its design, which encourages students to engage in discussion and create and display individual and group projects. Using the wiki made it easy to identify and track what each student contributed and to assess what material each student could or could not understand or edit. Several related resources are available to teachers, including Wikispaces (www.wikispaces.com/content/teacher) and PBworks (http://pbworks.com).

The Scratch lesson was hosted on a Joomla (www.joomla.org) website and enhanced with several free, low-cost components to make it interactive and collaborative. Unlike some free, hosted websites, such as Wikispaces, if teachers use Joomla, they must find a way to install it on a server, through their institutions or on their own websites. Joomla also has a steeper learning curve than wikis; for example, although knowing HTML and/or programming is not necessary, teachers who have these skills will be able to build better, more full-featured learning environments.

For the Global Warming course, the downside to using the wiki was the lack of real-time communication. To resolve this issue, Wiggio was used to host virtual meetings and provide a place for students to chat and discuss class projects. Wiggio is a web toolkit that includes (a) a shared calendar that allows participants to manage group events; (b) a folder that can be used to upload and share files, edit documents and spreadsheets, view videos and photos, and listen to audio files; (c) meeting spaces that allow students and teachers to meet virtually via conference calls and chat rooms; (d) polls to get quick responses from group members; (e) facilities for sending and receiving messages through text, email, or voice note; and (f) a linking tool for placement of shared links. Using Wiggio, students are able participate in online class discussions with the instructor or with their team members.

Several alternative resources are available for you and your students to videoconference, including HotChalk (www.hotchalk.com), Skype (www.skype.com), and Google Apps for Education (www.google.com/enterprise/apps/education). Additional tools used to enhance the learning environment can be included, such as an interactive map and videos from PBS.org. The collaborative technology installed to facilitate the Scratch lesson was JomSocial (www.jomsocial.com), a Facebook clone that can be customized to create a members-only or Facebook-integrated community network. It incorporates all of the familiar Facebook functions, including the chat toolbar that shows who is online. Several features we missed by using a wiki, as compared to a content management system like Moodle (https://moodle.org), were the facilities to deliver quizzes and tests, take surveys, record grades, and give and review assignments within the system. Because the Global Warming course was hybrid, the assessments were designed to be face-to-face and graded manually. In contrast, the Scratch lesson used JomSocial to create most of the assessments as they were primarily driven by collaborative discussion activities. We gave one quiz, which was developed by modifying an uploaded Scratch project. The Scratch lesson does not currently integrate a grading system, although it has capabilities for integration with Moodle, Blackboard (https://blackboard.utk.edu), and other third-party learning management systems.

Creating an online or hybrid course and integrating different software applications provides a greater degree of flexibility. The Global Warming lesson used a website to present students with text, video, pictures, and links to some external sites and a wiki for students to post and share their work. In contrast, the Scratch lesson was hosted on a Joomla website and used several software applications to repurpose existing instructional Scratch videos and to facilitate the collaborative aspects of the lesson. There are, however, countless possibilities for creating hybrid or online courses using guided experiential learning. Teachers may simply use a website or a learning management system to facilitate an online course or the online portions of a course applying GEL. Or a variety of software applications and platforms may be used to design and deliver online and hybrid lessons applying GEL. Just remember, using multiple platforms and applications can make a course harder to maintain and manage over time.

Conclusion

Experiential approaches to teaching and learning in general and guided experiential learning specifically provide opportunities for students to use their critical thinking skills, which is an important component of each of the lessons. The tools and methods used in the GEL method provide students with different ways to think logically about and reflect on the issues in each lesson and make up their own minds about their positions. Lesson Plan A helps students gain knowledge about global warming, and Lesson Plan B helps students develop some skills needed for computer programming through research, discussion, demonstration, and inquiry. GEL provides opportunities for students to engage in learning that transcends rote memorization, requiring them to think about concepts and issues and apply them to real-world situations. The activities for each lesson introduce goals and provide opportunities for students to reflect on issues and demonstrate skills in an online or hybrid course. We have seen the advantages for students when they are guided in an experiential learning environment, and we encourage teachers to implement GEL in their classrooms.

References

Carver, R. L., & Enfield, R. P. (2006). John Dewey's philosophy of education is alive and well. *Education and Culture, 22.1*, 55–67. Retrieved from https://muse.jhu.edu/journals/education_and_culture/v022/22.1carver.html

Clark, R. (2005). *Guided experiential learning: Training design and evaluation*. Redondo Beach, CA: Center for Cognitive Technology, Rossier School of Education, University of Southern California. Retrieved from www.cogtech.usc.edu/publications/clark_gel_workshop_tradoc_05.pdf

Clark, R. (2008, January). *Design document for a guided experiential learning course*. Contract DAAD 19-99-D-0046–0004 from TRADOC. Retrieved from www.cogtech.usc.edu/publications/gel_design_document.pdf

Clark, R. E. (2009). How much and what type of guidance is optimal for learning from instruction? In S. Tobias & T. M. Duffy (Eds.), *Constructivist theory applied to instruction: Success or failure?* (pp. 158–183). New York, NY: Routledge, Taylor and Francis.

Clark, R. E., Yates, K., Early, S., & Moulton, K. (2010). An analysis of the failure of electronic media and discovery-based learning: Evidence for the performance benefits of guided training methods. In K. H. Silber, & R. Foshay, (Eds.), *Handbook of training and improving workplace performance.* (Vol. I, pp. 263–297). Washington, DC: International Society for Performance Improvement. Retrieved from www.cogtech.usc.edu/publications/clark_etal_2009_analysis_of_the_failure_of_electronic_media.pdf

Dewey, J. (1938). *Experience and education.* New York, NY: Macmillan.

Hannafin, M., Land, S., & Oliver, K. (1999). Open learning environments: Foundation, methods, and models. In C. M. Reigeluth (Ed.), *Instructional-design theories and models: A new paradigm of instructional theory* (Vol. II, pp. 115–140). Mahwah, NJ: Lawrence Erlbaum.

Hmelo-Silver, C. E., Duncan, R. G., Chinn, C. A. (2007). Scaffolding and achievement in problem-based and inquiry learning: A response to Kirschner, Sweller, and Clark (2006). *Educational Psychologist, 42*(2), 99–107.

Kirschner, P. A., Sweller, J., & Clark, R. E. (2006). Why minimal guidance during instruction does not work: An analysis of the failure of constructivist, discovery, problem-based, experiential, and inquiry-based teaching. *Educational Psychologist, 41*(2), 75–86.

Kolb, D. A. (1984). *Experiential learning: Experience as the source of learning and development.* Englewood Cliffs, NJ: Prentice-Hall.

Kolb. D. A., & Fry, R. (1975). Toward an applied theory of experiential learning. In C. Cooper (Ed.), *Theories of group process* (pp. 33–57). London, UK: John Wiley.

Lindsey, L., & Berger, N. (2009). Experiential approach to instruction. In C. Reigeluth and A. Carr-Chellman (Eds.), *Instructional-Design Theories and Models.* (Vol. 3, pp. 117–142). New York, NY: Routledge.

Mayer, R. E. (2004). Should there be a three-strikes rule against pure discovery learning? The case for guided methods of instruction. *American Psychologist, 59*(1), 14–19.

Rogers, C. R. (1961). *On becoming a person: A therapist's view of psychotherapy.* London, UK: Constable.

Rogers, C. R. (1983). *Freedom to learn for the 80's* (2nd rev. ed). Columbus, OH: Charles Merrill.

Schank, R. C., Berman, T. R., & Macpherson, K. A. (1999). Learning by doing. In C. M. Reigeluth (Ed.), *Instructional-design theories and models: A new paradigm of instructional theory* (Vol. II, pp. 161–81). Mahwah, NJ: Lawrence Erlbaum.

ScratchEd. (2011). Creative computing: A design-based introduction to computational thinking. Retrieved from http://scratched.media.mit.edu/resources/scratch-curriculum-guide-draft

Sweller, J., Kirschner, P. A., & Clark, R. E. (2007). Why minimally guided teaching techniques do not work: A reply to commentaries. *Educational Psychologist, 42*(2), 115–121.

CHAPTER 7

Designing Inter*PLAY* Learning Landscapes
to Evoke Emotions, Spark the Imagination, and Promote Creative Problem Solving

Christopher Stapleton and Atsusi "2c" Hirumi

TO PREPARE THE NEXT GENERATION for life in a rapidly changing and highly competitive global economy, we must advance the innovative thinking and creative problem-solving abilities of our students across disciplines and grade levels. Igniting students' imaginations, creativity, and passions are keys to success that are not often used or embraced in traditional, teacher-directed, test-driven, educational settings. Inter*PLAY* is a learner-centered approach for fostering innovative thinking and creative problem solving based on experiential learning theory. Like other experiential approaches, it assumes that children, adolescents, and adults learn best when presented with relevant, meaningful, and interesting goals. It also fosters skill development and the learning of facts, concepts, procedures, and principles in the contexts of how they will be used. However, like education in general, experiential approaches to teaching and learning neither explicitly nor adequately address the role of human emotions and imagination during the learning process; thus, they do not fully utilize the capabilities of emerging technologies to facilitate individual and group learning. The Inter*PLAY* instructional theory builds on existing experiential theories by integrating three primary conventions of interactive entertainment (story, play, and game) with the basic elements of instruction (objectives, assessments, and instructional strategies) to evoke emotions, spark imagination, and foster creativity and innovative thinking.

The notion that people learn best from real life experiences is not new. The *Oxford Dictionary of Scientific Quotations* (2005) recognizes Aristotle as stating, "For the things we have to learn before we can do them, we learn by doing them" (p. 9). As early as the 19th century, Dewey (1897) began to advocate experiential education that combines direct experience with the environment and content to enhance learning. Since then, many have taken up the call for experiential approaches to teaching and learning, including but certainly not limited to the influential works of Kolb (1984), Piaget (1962), and Lewin (1943).

Experiential learning theories assume that adults, adolescents, and children learn best when they are presented with relevant, meaningful, and engaging challenges. Advocates of experiential learning also believe that facts, concepts, procedures, and principles are best learned when presented in the contexts of how they will be used (Shank, Berman, & Macpherson, 1992). However, we believe that experiential approaches to teaching and learning, like other instructional theories and strategies, do not adequately address the role of human emotions, creativity, and imagination during the learning process and thus, do not fully utilize the capabilities of emerging technologies to engage learners and facilitate individual and group learning.

Most of us recognize that our emotions and imaginations have a direct impact on how and why we learn and make decisions. We tend to remember events that have significant impacts, whether positive or negative, on our emotions. We are also attracted to and repeat behaviors that give us pleasure and avoid tasks that anger or overly frustrate us and make us unhappy. What's more, we don't just react to the world; we imagine what could be and plan ways to make our thoughts become a reality. We remember past events and predict possible outcomes of our actions before we make decisions. Pondering the past, the present, and the future along with the consequences of our decisions have one thing in common: all require our imaginations. Recognized approaches to teaching and learning, however, often do not address the role of human emotions and imaginations during the learning process.

The InterPLAY instructional theory builds on existing experiential theories and strategies by integrating three primary conventions of interactive entertainment (story, play, and game) with three basic elements of instruction (objectives, assessments, and instructional strategies) to evoke emotions, spark the imagination and promote creative problem solving. To help you design engaging and memorable online and hybrid learning experiences, we (1) define three basic conventions of interactive entertainment, (2) posit our InterPLAY instructional strategy that integrates the three conventions with instruction to evoke emotions and spark the imagination, (3) present two K–12 lessons to illustrate the application of the InterPLAY instructional strategy, and (4) discuss key issues in designing and delivering InterPLAY-based learning experiences.

InterPLAY Conventions

Interactive entertainment consists of the interplay of three basic conventions: story, play, and game (Stapleton & Hirumi, 2011; Stapleton & Hughes, 2005). Each convention is further driven by basic elements that are distinguished to facilitate the analysis and design of instruction. Story elements focus on characters, worlds, and events (or plot) to incite an emotional investment (pathos). Play elements are made up of repeated cycles of stimuli, responses, and consequences to invite participation. Game elements consist of rules, tools, and goals (procedure) to escalate challenges that lead to achievement(s). The conventions of interactive entertainment and their elements are integrated with the three basic elements of experiential learning (objectives, assessments, and instructional strategies) to evoke emotions, spark the imagination, and promote creative problem solving. Figure 7.1 depicts the key conventions and elements of the InterPLAY instructional theory.

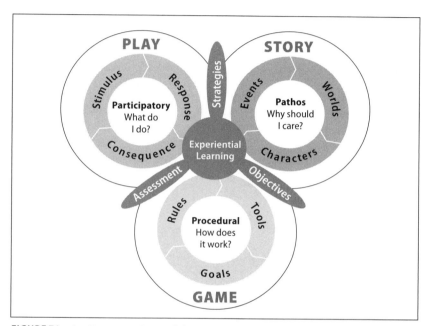

FIGURE 7.1 ▶ Key conventions and elements of the InterPLAY Instructional Theory

Story Elements

Entertainment starts with stories that evoke compassion (pathos) and capture the empathy of individuals in the audience by answering the basic question, "Why should I care?" Compelling books, movies, and television shows incite and seal an emotional bond with members of the audience that keeps them engaged throughout the experience (and helps sell related promotional items). The elements of story establish the motivation and emotional connection with the subject matter for learning and/or amusement. The characters draw empathy from the audience by being someone that viewers can identify with in some way. Even if the characters are total fantasies, people should be able to identify with the characters on an emotional level. Once there is an emotional attachment, the author can propel the action forward with various characters' interactions. Story events become consequence generators that are embedded with dilemmas, challenges, or conflicts that enable the characters' transformations from ordinary to extraordinary.

Stories can spark students' imaginations and encourage an investment in learning through emotional attachment. Given an author with an expressive imagination, any topic—famous figures, inanimate phenomena, or even abstract theories—can be taught in the form of a compelling story. When the learners' imaginations are stimulated within a virtual scenario, this gives context and relevance to the subject matter and to students' lives, allowing students to build a relationship with the material. This is what we call "painting with the audience's imagination" (Stapleton & Davies, 2011).

Stories without emotions are merely narrations. Narrations consist of a list of facts that may or may not be related within a series of events. This dry, isolated list is unlikely to compel learners to internalize information or understand it in a larger or more personal context. For example, consider the *Lord of the Rings* series. As an audience member, just knowing that the hobbit Frodo lives in the Shire isn't of much interest by itself. But when I find out that he is a little guy facing impossible odds (as many of us feel in life), my empathy makes me care about Frodo, I put myself in his (metaphorical) shoes, and I feel what Frodo feels.

Authors engage each person in the audience by answering the question, "Why should I care?" To establish a compelling story premise, authors need to weave together the story elements by answering key questions that illuminate each element:

> *Story Questions.* Why should I care about the characters, worlds, and events?

- **Characters.** Whom do I identify with? Who am I as a participant/protagonist in the narrative?

- **Worlds.** In what context does the story's world provide meaning and relevance?

- **Events.** What happens and when to propel the action forward and stimulate a desire to know more?

Play Elements

Central to the physiological and psychological interactivity of entertainment is play's participatory role in engaging the mind and body. Play stimulates the physical and mental interactions among real, virtual, and imaginary realities. While the story can be passive, playing (like learning) is active and cannot be passive. Play invites us to take action through trial and error and answers the core question, "What do we do?" By answering the question, play illustrates the relationship among stimulus, response, and consequence with no punitive consequences. Like a playground, this invitation should be filled with intuitive clues and engaging activities that invite the learners' imaginations to fill in details not provided in the story. Opportunities to make mistakes without fear of failure motivate and invite learners to inquire and discover and, later, create and experiment. I do it again, I get better, but then the circumstances change, and I do it again. Play also provides immediate gratification. As entertainment, play and repeating the play process are fun. In a driving simulator, I turn the wheel, the car responds, and the consequence is that I stay on the road and avoid other objects, or I lose ground or crash. Play can be as simple as catching and throwing a ball to as complex as building an entire virtual world.

As learners *inquire* and *discover* through play, they should be acquiring the basic domain-specific knowledge necessary to feed creativity in the next InterPLAY event. The nature of the feedback is critical here and must be presented in a constructive manner to help learners become aware of the consequences of their choices. The feedback must not simply state whether the learners' inquiries or discoveries were either right or wrong. Corrective feedback must be given to promote further inquiry and discovery if necessary or to facilitate the transition to the next Inter*PLAY* stage and motivate learners to *create* and *experiment*. Where there can be more than one appropriate answer, depending upon the objective, it is important to provide learners with options to better understand the dynamics of the domain, relevant cause and effect relationships, and to come to their own conclusions by using feedback to inform corrective behavior.

Similar to the notion of playing the child's game of "Hot or Cold," feedback to players can be "warmer" or "cooler" and "hotter" and "colder." This type of constructive feedback does not reprimand the player, but it provides the learner with enough data to understand the consequences of his or her actions and continue pursuing opportunities to get it "just right." Depending on the objective (i.e., to avoid or collide with the target), "hot" and "cold" are neither right nor wrong. Providing information in less absolute terms yet in a constructive manner allows the feedback to be more of a critique than a judgment.

In fact, students may learn more from making mistakes and making less appropriate choices than by getting the "right answer" right away. This is when the concept of *play* is so important: Students must be allowed to make mistakes with no punitive consequences in order to facilitate learning. In other words, it is important to "make losing fun" so learners will test the limits of their knowledge and explore all possible choices to obtain the domain-specific knowledge necessary to be creative. To facilitate the process, authors need to answer the following play questions:

> *Play Questions.* What do I do?

- **Stimulus.** What invites me to participate? Let me try...

- **Response.** How do I respond to the stimulus? If I do this, then it will...

- **Consequence.** What happens as a result of my response(s)? Because I did this, that happened…. If I decide to do something else, what would happen?

Game Elements

Game elements (or game mechanics) answer the question, "How does it work?" Game elements interweave goals, rules, and tools to monitor behavior, measure performance, and manage resources to build the players' investments in the experience. The investment of personal time and effort further motivates learners to overcome difficult challenges where they risk losing or take a chance at winning. Game elements distinguish the use of entertainment as a means versus as an end. Where entertainment can be consumed to pass time, education needs to be challenging enough to foster a sense of achievement. Entertainment as a "means versus an end" in education uses the power of entertainment to "sweeten the medicine." It motivates students to create and experiment. Like play, game elements also allow students to make mistakes, and when they do, they want to try again (Hirumi, 2010).

In sports, we play games to win or lose; in education and entertainment, losing needs to be fun so that participants are encouraged to try again. In experiential learning, we learn through our mistakes. Mistakes are not failures. Failure is when we give up and do not learn from our mistakes or make mistakes again and again because we did not learn from them. Educational games should encourage a fearless drive to risk, try, make mistakes, and try again with new insights. If learners do not make mistakes, the challenge is too easy, or they are not trying hard enough to achieve beyond their present capabilities. A learning experience that makes the learner avoid risk discourages growth. Failure to make losing fun or otherwise engaging can be the shortcoming of unsuccessful interactive entertainment and is viewed as one of the problems with education. In education, the negative consequences associated with failure discourage risk taking. Unless students have very high self-esteem and an exceptionally strong sense of self-worth, they will not persist after failure, let alone repeated failures. Winning and success have their own payoffs; more time and energy need to be spent in education and instructional design on how to make losing fun and insightful or engaging by pushing our students' and our own abilities further.

Game elements establish and amplify rules of engagement between the real and the virtual or imagined players. The nature of the game establishes a goal with measurable outcomes where you can either win or lose on multiple levels. The rules govern the players' expectations, actions, and use of tools (e.g., weapons, resources, data, or special powers) that may impact the results of their choices, strategic thinking, and problem solving. Authors need to answer the following game questions:

> *Game Questions.* How do I win? How do I "game the system"? How well are my insights, strategies, and problem-solving skills rewarded? Does the game meet my expectations? Are there enough options and choices to form a unique strategy?

- **Goals.** What for? What is the object of desire?
- **Tools.** With what? What resources, powers, and choices do I have?
- **Rules.** Why not? What are my limits, conditions, or choices?

InterPLAY Instructional Strategy

Interactive entertainment utilizes the conventions of play, story, and game in distinct ways to engage participants and spark their imaginations. In education, the power of interactive entertainment is used to engage and motivate learners' cognition through: (a) the story's ability to spark passion in the subject matter; (b) the play's ability to invite physical as well as social participation; and (c) the game's procedural mechanics to structure complex tasks that encourage strategic planning, risk taking, and creativity, and that make failure fun. The InterPLAY instructional strategy utilizes the core interplay conventions found in interactive entertainment to facilitate learning. To apply InterPLAY, we recommend that you create a learning environment that facilitates the six instructional events depicted in Figure 7.2: (1) expose, (2) inquire, (3) discover, (4) create, (5) experiment, and (6) share.

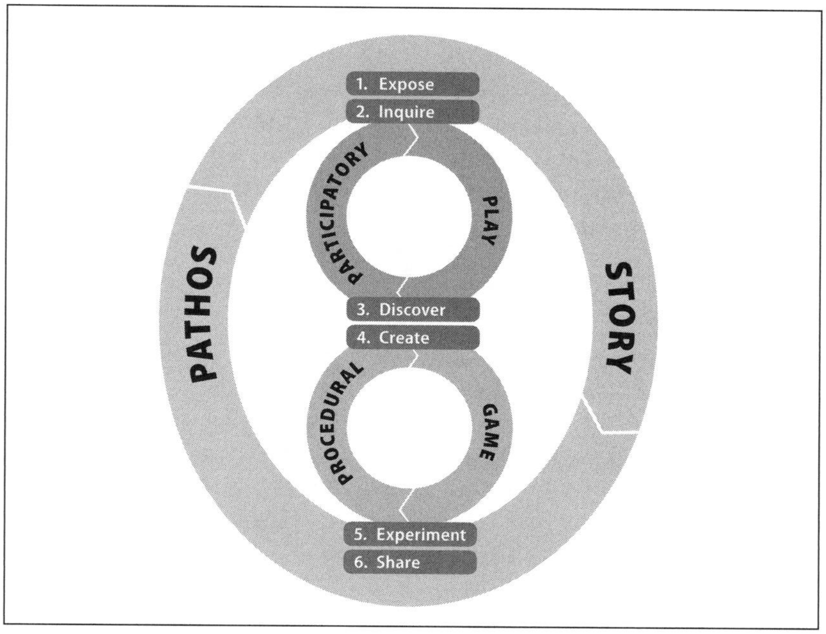

FIGURE 7.2 ▶ Application of InterPLAY conventions to form the InterPLAY strategy

Story Events

The *Story* events focus on the pathos (evoking compassion or sadness) or other emotions that are critical to sparking an entertaining educational journey and finding a cathartic closure to the learning experience. These outcomes inform both the first and sixth (last) events of *Expose* and *Share* and provide a cyclical or spiraling pattern to the designed experience. Story focuses on establishing instructional relevance for students, assuming they may have little to no interest in the instructional topic from the beginning. The motivation sparked by the story that stokes emotions, plays out until the last event and continually escalates the investment of the player to go further, play harder, and risk more. In answering the key story question, "Why should I care?" we tap into a personal experience (either real or fictional) that the students can identify with as an archetypal "everyman" or "everywoman." The story uses information about students' demographics, needs, and interests to formulate characters who gain empathy (and other emotions) from them before introducing any concepts or challenges. We start by enlisting a character to reveal or demonstrate either most students' background stories or experiences. The character and participants' journeys and reactions are shared at the end from the students' perspective to establish relevance and gain closure to the sequence of events. The character's point of view can be a subject-matter expert, a fictional character, or the students themselves. In good storytelling form, the character's perspective needs to expose the students within an appropriate learning environment to propel the learners' interest and stimulate inquiry within the story and the subject matter. The other story event, *Share*, is used last in the sequence to establish the transformation of the students from novices to experts in applying the lessons learned. Many learning experiences are not completely absorbed until learners teach or share with others. Thus, sequence comes full circle with the students becoming the teacher.

Event 1: Expose. This event provides not only the backstory to inspire empathy for the character or player, but also orients the audience to the same reference point or point of view. In entertainment, exposure may be accomplished through different story devices. A movie may use an establishing shot to set the context and provide the lay of the land. A video game may use a cinematic cut (or scene) in the form of a mission briefing, a theme park may use a "preshow" to engage people waiting for the ride, and a playground may feature colorful, climbable structures.

For learning, exposure provides context for an instructional unit and learning objectives and sparks the motivation to learn. The initial event should expose students to the objectives in a meaningful way, inviting them to engage and to achieve the challenges to be set before them. From the point of view of the learner, what makes the subject matter real and relevant? Instructors need to examine the lives of their target learners to understand what excites and challenges them, such as particular activities, media, aspirations or dreams. Being a hero? Taking on a dangerous adventure? Becoming rich and famous? What spectacular defeats and disasters could be set up to create an exciting drama? While entertainment can be passive, education should be an active experience that the students can reflect on during the entire course (this point will be explored further in the next section). Exposure becomes the common experience that can be leveraged as a reference point throughout the class. Successful exposure is achieved when it prompts the desire for inquiry (event 2). The elements of story (characters, worlds, and events) allow us to construct this instructional event as well as the final event.

Event 6: Share. What experiences and outcomes can we create that will motivate learners to compare results, brag on achievements, and inquire about what went wrong with one choice and right with the other? What dramatic action could we participate in that makes us want to tell others about it? It is hard not to share our feelings after watching good movie or having an exciting adventure. Education should be designed to have similar effects. The sharing of personal experiences and feelings becomes the sixth story event, facilitated at the end of the lesson or unit to seal memories of the learning experience and to facilitate the transfer of learned skills and knowledge to the next unit. The process of sharing compels learners to reflect on their experience and put lessons learned into their own as well as others' perspectives. Individual reflection draws out the personal value and meaning of the learning experience that cannot be taught, yet reflection is critical for the experience to be remembered or related. The collective sharing becomes the body of knowledge that students will take to heart and remember over time—knowledge that will be readily transferable to other applications. If sharing activities are constructed appropriately, teachers will learn from students, and students will learn from each other. This is where the expectations of the teacher for the students and the students' expectations of the experience are evaluated and assessed to inform the next journey. Success is achieved with InterPLAY when students express the desire to share their experiences.

Play Events

Play events engage learners with the material and inform the second and third events of *Inquire* and *Discover*.

Play provides learners with an open-ended environment with no pressures or expectations of winning or losing or having the right or wrong answer. Play invites low-risk, high-fun participation to gain understanding and familiarity with the material. Play focuses on inviting and building engagement with the subject matter by providing constant, satisfying feedback. Though we can pique students' interest within the emotional context of good story elements, we now need them to interact with the dynamic elements of the subject matter. The jump from story to play is facilitated through the elements of play, including stimulus, response, and consequence to illustrate the relationship between cause and effect through trial and error. Exposure (the first event associated with story) will not and should not necessarily satiate the students' interest, but instill the desire to seek the objectives of the unit. In fact, exposure to the story should leave them wanting more, prompting inquiry, much like how a movie trailer can be entertaining, yet is not a complete story. The trailer becomes a teaser to motivate people to pay for a ticket and attend the screening when the movie is released. Exposure sets up the motivation to inquire and discover by setting a common context, point of view, and reasoning.

The engagement of play is set up by the two interdependent events; inquiry sparks the curiosity to discover what is to be revealed. The interaction between inquiry and discovery invites safe and tantalizing physical participation to satiate that curiosity. The purpose is to uncover dynamic forces and elements within the subject matter that will later be tested with the game elements of InterPLAY.

The object of play is the toy, and the context of play is the playground. These two aspects of interactive entertainment (toy and playground) are helpful in designing the Inquire and Discover instructional events. Toys and playgrounds immediately spark interest in participation, yet in a nonthreatening consequence that is free of expectations or competition, which come later with game elements. Playing without expectations and competition is not superfluous to learning but central. The tools of work become the toys for play. Constructive play relates the joy of engagement with the importance of learning skills. The playground extends the play dynamic to the context of learners' surroundings or workplace (school). The playground provides the response to the toy's stimulus that plays out the consequence of action in a compelling and immersive context. Together, Inquire and Discover provide experiences, familiarity, and confidence in understanding the nuances of the subject's tools and functions.

Event 2: Inquire. If the first event (Expose) properly sets up the desire to learn, then student inquiry should be automatic. The inherent objective of inquiry is to validate the success of the previous event. Inquiry should provide a response to students' curiosity with something to do that showcases different skills and knowledge and various cause and effect relationships related to the subject matter. What are the questions we want the students to ask that define the subject matter and the professional experience, that is, what are the questions that a professional in this field would ask? How can we use the elements of the next event (Discover) to spark these questions, using the elements from the first event? How do we invite and encourage students' interactive engagement with the subject matter? Their curiosity evolves from an intellectual inquiry into a physical inquiry, using interactive devices and interfaces. Such exchanges transform students from "vessels," passively waiting for knowledge to come to them, to "sparks," who proactively seek knowledge by engaging the subject matter. Interactions with playful cause and effect devices (toys/tools) should culminate in some form of consequence that provides useful feedback and prompts students to discover the value and relationships among the different aspects of the subject matter in fuller context during the next instructional event.

For instance, playing with a ball needs no instructions. The shape and properties of the ball (toy) inform its purpose and use to throw, bounce, spin, and so on. When we see the ball in action (stimulus), we naturally want to possess and control it and explore its properties and discover our skills. When we hit, throw, or bounce the ball (responses), we also risk losing control or possession of it (consequence). Through this interaction, we better understand the different properties and responses in relationship with the toy and each other in the context of the learning environment. The consequences result in altering our dexterity, speed, aim, and technique to evolve our ability to react to the environment, such as the surface of the court, obstacles, or other players. Once we start to apply predetermined expectations, scoring, or competition, we transform play into a game. The opportunity to play openly with each element outside the strict context of competition or the rules and confines of the court allows us to understand the properties of the separate elements without any fear of failure. The opportunity to play openly also demonstrates the nuances of students' performances by testing their limitations by themselves and in relationship with each other that lead to discovery. Successful inquiry leads to discovery.

Event 3: Discover. Not every example of inquiry and discovery is as straightforward as a bouncing a ball. However, utilizing tools as toys (in other words, playing with tools to imagine and understand cause and effect relationships with no particular rules or goals, except maybe having some fun playing with them) during instruction can help translate the learning objective into playful inquiry and discovery (the third event). What aspects of the subject matter, when discovered, would spark and fascinate the learner? How do most people or professionals respond to subject-specific stimuli in the real world? What are the consequences of doing things right or wrong or doing nothing at all? The answers to such questions enable you to set up and plant consequence generators in the learning landscape to spark curiosity, fun, and engagement. The translation of learning into playful forms of inquiry and discovery creates the "fun factor" to inspire repeat play and extend the exploration that is needed to achieve a discovery. Where playful, active inquiry produces the satisfaction of continual exploration, it is discovery that provides the personal reward, the achievement, and the "aha" moment. The consequences of discovery, whether negative or positive, provide feedback to inspire further creation and experimentation.

Discovery is successful when learners start to apply what they learned in unique combinations to solve a problem or realize an opportunity in a creative manner.

Game Events

Game events heighten the personal challenge of the subject matter's material by asking students to create a novel solution to an authentic problem and to test their creation through experimentation. Game focuses on evaluating the students' mastery of concepts after they have understood the nature and properties of the subject matter through open-ended, playful discovery. The dynamics of simply playing with a ball can transform drastically with the added element of competition, whether against themselves, other players, or a computer. With explicit goals, fair rules, and empowering tools, game design rapidly becomes the testing ground (or assessment) for both the student and the instruction. However, without playful interactions, the game's elements may discourage, overwhelm, and negatively impact the learning experience.

The initial three events associated with the Inter*PLAY* strategy provide experience, familiarity, and confidence in understanding the basic facts, concepts, and principles associated with the subject matter. The fourth event, Create, sets up opportunities for students to apply what they've learned in novel ways and to internalize their understandings made through discovery. And then the Experiment (event five) challenges students to take personal risks with their confidence in the material by testing their skills, approaches, strategies, or techniques developed in the previous event.

Event 4: Create. The act of creating is a pivotal point in the learning and entertainment process. It transforms the experience from being merely reactive to truly interactive. Instead of responding to cues, the learner contributes to the content by applying elements of the subject matter in novel ways. What unique solution can we create that hasn't been created before that we can call our own? What can we learn by making mistakes? How do we reward risk taking? What can we learn from taking risks and making mistakes that make such results more successful? Following a predetermined path, which is prescriptive rather than strategic in nature, or reaching a predictable conclusion, which represents an external rather than an internal goal, is counter-intuitive to creativity. To create not only increases the personal investment level, thus increasing the entertainment value, it also brings an intrinsic understanding to a new level of sophistication, where knowledge is internalized, which adds to the learners' confidence level. Creating is critical in setting up the experiment phase, where knowledge is tested and performance is evaluated. Success of the Create event is demonstrated by the learners' desire to test their creation—whether it is an object, a plan, or a strategy.

Event 5: Experiment. How do we measure success? What activities can test the solutions we created? An experiment provides an opportunity to assess student learning and provide feedback while removing the stigma of losing or winning. Like true scientific experimentation, the goal is less about the hypothesis being right or wrong than about setting up the elements of the subject matter so that new data points (knowledge) and insights (feedback) can be gained. Entertainment is set up in a similar way, so that the best games make losing almost as fun as winning. By viewing making mistakes as part of the fun, what might have been students' frustration turns into challenges, and learners are encouraged to get up and try again. Mistakes or miscalculations made by the learner provide valuable feedback and input from the students' point of view, especially when their interests are high but their understanding may be lacking. How do we show results that are not right or wrong, but insightful, making us think, go back, and create another solution? What feedback can help inspire new approaches? The experiments, whether they fail or succeed, provide new data points and insights to the body of knowledge for the whole class, especially if shared. Sharing mistakes can earn more points if the whole class can learn, which can reward risks and encourage teamwork.

As discussed earlier in this section, the final instructional event (Event 6: Share) brings students back to the story to increase their collective knowledge and reinforce, reflect upon, and assess the lessons learned. Students' abilities to synthesize data and articulate their findings through successful storytelling empower them with confidence in themselves, in their peers, and in their teacher. This confidence stokes a desire to continue learning outside of class.

Table 7.1 provides a checklist to help you assess your application of the Inter*PLAY* strategy.

TABLE 7.1 ▶ Checklist for applying the InterPLAY instructional strategy and creating experiential learning landscapes

KEY CHARACTERISTICS	ANSWER TO QUESTION		SUGGESTIONS FOR IMPROVEMENT
	Yes	No	
Event 1: Expose. Does exposure to physical artifacts and/or psychological stimuli, along with story, hook the learner and prompt eager inquiry?			
Event 2: Inquiry. Does the landscape provide sufficient resources and stimuli to prompt questions and invite further interactivity and discovery?			
Event 3: Discover. Does the landscape provide optional paths to reveal and demonstrate vital facts, concepts, rules, and principles through trial and error with no punitive consequences?			
Event 4: Create. Does the landscape provide enough valid options and components for learners to formulate unique associations and combinations, follow novel approaches, and create unique solutions to overcome challenges, solve problems, and/or realize opportunities?			
Event 5: Experiment. Does the landscape provide opportunities for learners to test their creation(s) and obtain constructive feedback to formulate corrective actions and results?			
Event 6: Share. Do the landscape and experimental results inspire the sharing of findings, insights, reflections, and revelations?			
Events 1–6. Can the application of the strategy and the landscape be improved to inspire the next level of learning beyond the unit?			

InterPLAY Learning Landscape

Just as every story has its stage, every play has its playground, and every game has its field or game board, every instructor has constructed his or her own learning environment to help guide, inform, stimulate and motivate learning. This is especially true in preschool, where the learning landscape is as important as the learning curriculum. Popular expert on early childhood learning, Bev Bos (1990) suggests rather than trying to get children ready for school, we should get schools ready for children. Accordingly, to prepare the learning environment for InterPLAY, you should create a learning landscape that integrates physical, virtual, and imagined realities to spark emotions, engage the body and challenge the mind using story, play, and game.

Mixing Realities and Melting Boundaries: Real, Virtual, and Imagined

The real world, virtual world, and imaginary world all contribute to InterPLAY by stimulating the learner's hands, head, and heart (Figure 7.3). Playful stimulus and interfaces engage the body (hands) as part of the learner's real world. Games challenge the mind (head) as part of the learner's virtual world and tests the learner's ability to apply lessons learned from the experience. Stories are used to spark emotions (heart) and paint a picture in the learner's imaginary world. If InterPLAY does not engage the hands, head, and heart, the InterPLAY instructional events cannot be fully experienced.

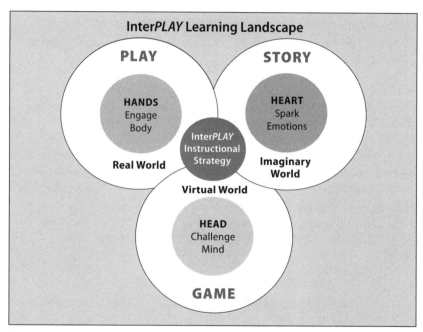

FIGURE 7.3 ▶ The InterPLAY instructional strategy and events set within the context of an InterPLAY Learning Landscape

Several learning resources and interactions are pervasive components of InterPLAY learning landscapes. Like the activation of a learner's hands, heart, and mind, these learning resources and interactions are vital to InterPLAY.

InterPLAY Resources: Content Information, Tools, and Demonstrations

Access to critical learning resources is important and should be provided throughout the learning experiences. Critical resources include content information, tools, and demonstrations. Development and testing of InterPLAY indicates that learners should be able to have access to resources when they desire or need them. Presenting content information, tools, and demonstrations in sequential fashion or forcing learners to review and otherwise use resources when learners may not need or want them may disengage learners from the learning experience. Providing just-in-time access to resources helps ensure that learners attend to each resource when necessary and that each resource is used in a personally relevant and meaningful manner.

Content Information. To master a topic and develop skills, learners typically need access to content information. Learners must be able to encode, consolidate, and recall verbal information, concepts, rules, and principles to demonstrate procedures, solve problems, and make important decisions. However, forcing content information onto learners can undermine the dramatic flow of story and disrupt the playful interactions of games that make interactive entertainment engaging (Egenfeldt-Nielsen, 2006; Hirumi & Hall, 2010; Hirumi & Stapleton, 2008). The importance and depth of content information, in turn, may be overlooked, oversimplified, or trivialized while attempting to keep players entertained (Clark, 2003; Hirumi & Hall, 2010; Mitchell & Savill-Smith, 2004). Clearly, content information needs to be organized and presented to learners in effective and efficient ways to facilitate learning.

To facilitate InterPLAY and reinforce the relevance of its learning experiences, instructors should allow learners to access small chunks of content information when they want and need it. You should also consider limiting learners' access and guiding learners to inquire about specific content early in the learning process to make sure they are not overwhelmed with information, eventually reducing and even eliminating such support as learners acquire content expertise. Access to content information may be also integrated into the learning experience in a variety of ways. For example, learners may use personal devices, such as cell phones, iPods, and tablets, to access content information. Environmental devices, such as radios, billboards, computers, and books embedded within the virtual learning environment may also be used to communicate audio and text information. For details and illustrations of a dozen techniques that may be used to convey content information and facilitate learning that do not break the dramatic flow of story or the playful interactions of game play, see Hirumi and Hall (2010).

Tools. Tools may vary by learning environment, based on both learners' and instructional needs. Tools may include telecommunication technologies and social media, such as text messaging, electronic bulletin boards, blogs, and wikis to facilitate social interaction among learners and between learners and the instructor. Tools may also include general productivity tools, such as word processors and spreadsheets, as well as multimedia development tools, such as Adobe Photoshop and Windows Movie Maker to enable learners to create their own content. Links within the learning environment may be provided, or learners may be encouraged to keep such applications readily accessible during InterPLAY. The key is to analyze both learners' and instructional needs to identify tools that may help learners communicate as well as progress through and complete the InterPLAY experience.

Demonstrations. Based on a critical analysis of learner-centered instructional strategies, Kirchner, Sweller, and Clark (2006) concluded that inquiry, discovery, and problem-based methods are often fatally flawed because they do not show learners how they are supposed to put pieces together and apply what they have (supposedly) learned. In other words, novices need to see how experts perform and do things in order for them to apply and transfer newly acquired skills and knowledge successfully. Access to demonstrations is thought to be particularly important as learners start to create and experiment during Inter*PLAY*, especially if you are teaching students some form of intellectual or psychomotor skill. However, simple demonstrations of people playing (to inquire and discover) may also facilitate Inter*PLAY* and help learners overcome challenges if they find themselves stuck and in the need of guidance.

InterPLAY Interactions: Assessment and Feedback

Assessment and feedback are essential interactions that should be integrated throughout the Inter*PLAY* learning experience. All Inter*PLAY* events need some form of assessment and feedback to maintain context, timing, and relevance. Without assessment, teachers cannot determine whether students have discovered the basic concepts, rules, and principles necessary to create and experiment. Without feedback, students are unable to determine the effectiveness of their creations. Assessment and feedback are also essential for learners to monitor their progress and facilitate achievement of specified learning outcomes.

The ways that story, play, and game (the three primary conventions of interactive entertainment) unfold and flow are crucial aspects of building intensity, engagement, and enjoyment for learners. So, these enjoyable experiences cannot be interrupted by formal assessments and feedback. Breaking the flow of Inter*PLAY* may dissipate excitement. Learners' engagement may need to be reignited if such obtrusive instructional event(s) interrupt their engagement. Instructors must integrate assessments and feedback into Inter*PLAY* events in a seamless manner—to become explicitly aware of students' performance while managing learning and associating performance directly with learning—without breaking the flow of story, play, and game. Instructors' over-arching role is to integrate story, play, and game with the basic elements of instruction: objectives, assessments, and strategies.

Constant assessment and feedback may be accomplished by incorporating sensing and triggering devices into the learning landscape. Such devices detect the learners' choices and actions and, in so doing, reveal their skills, knowledge, attitudes, and abilities. The development and use of sensing and triggering devices in interactive learning environments requires additional research. However, the use of such devices to measure learners' understanding and their ability to apply, analyze, evaluate, and create provides a much broader range of assessment methods beyond multiple-choice testing. Multiple tracking of learner actions provides new levels of assessment that are being leveraged by research and development. The following lessons have been created by applying the Inter*PLAY* instructional strategy and are being tested to inform the continued development of the lessons, as well as the continuous improvement of the Inter*PLAY* instructional theory, tools, and techniques.

InterPLAY in Action

We present two lessons to illustrate the application of the Inter*PLAY* experiential learning strategy. The lesson on robotics (Lesson Plan A) is a hybrid lesson, designed to be delivered both online and face-to-face in a conventional middle school science classroom to prepare for high school. The lesson on maintaining health and wellness on a lunar colony (Lesson Plan B) is conducted totally online. Both lessons are parts of a series of lessons on space exploration called *Mission: LEAP* that address space science, technology, engineering, and math (STEM) by challenging students to establish a virtual, lunar colony by formulating, testing, and sharing viable solutions for overcoming challenges with living off-world.

The Inter*PLAY* instructional events correlate entertainment heuristics with experiential theories of learning. Inter*PLAY* also corresponds with the scientific process, which is at the core of most science standards. The congruence between Inter*PLAY* and scientific inquiry, illustrated in Table 7.2, is fundamental to integrating entertainment and learning science so they do not compete with or dilute each other. The Inter*PLAY* instructional events follow a natural and logical progression with each event stimulating the next step, allowing you address the scientific inquiry skills as well as knowledge-based objectives.

TABLE 7.2 ▶ The relationship between Inter*PLAY* instructional events and the scientific inquiry method

INTER*PLAY* INSTRUCTIONAL EVENTS	SCIENTIFIC INQUIRY METHOD
1. Expose	1. Ask questions
2. Inquire	2. Do background research
3. Discover	3. Construct hypotheses
4. Create	4. Test hypotheses
5. Experiment	5. Analyze data and draw conclusions
6. Share	6. Communicate results

These lessons show examples of how you may use the Inter*PLAY* strategy to create or adapt your own curriculum. Lesson Plan A, Robotics—Extending Human Performance in Lunar Colonies, illustrates how the Inter*PLAY* strategy may be used to create a hybrid lesson using existing NASA assets and educational guides (www.nasa.gov/audience/foreducators/topnav/materials/listbytype/Lunar_Nautics_Designing_a_Mission.html). Lesson Plan B, Sustaining Health and Wellness on a Lunar Colony, illustrates how Inter*PLAY* may be applied to develop a completely online learning game.

Lesson Plan A

Robotics—Extending Human Performance in Lunar Colonies (Hybrid Lesson)

This hybrid lesson on robotics is designed to teach learners how robotics can extend human performance and how robots are essential for establishing and maintaining life in colonies on the moon. Events 1–3 of the InterPLAY instructional strategy (Expose, Inquire, and Discover) and event 6 (Share) are completed online. Events 4–5 (Create and Experiment) are facilitated in class. Resources are made available both online and in class. The terminal and enabling objectives for the lesson are listed in Figure 7.A.1, along with correlations to national science standards, required prerequisites, and resources.

Terminal Objective

Given specific lunar environmental challenges, learners will demonstrate how robotics can extend human performance by successfully completing a series of predefined tasks.

Enabling Objectives

When asked to design a robot to overcome challenges, learners will

- examine human needs and activities necessary to build a city on Earth;
- distinguish between Earth and lunar environments;
- recognize how robots have been used in lunar colonies;
- discriminate among requirements for navigating different terrain;
- discriminate among requirements for operating different tools;
- build a robot to successfully navigate terrain, operate tools, and complete specified tasks;
- test the robots and evaluate their design;
- develop teamwork, collaboration, coordination, and communication skills; and
- develop innovative thinking and creative problem-solving skills.

National Science Education Standards

NS.9–12.1 Science as Inquiry
- Abilities necessary to do scientific inquiry
- Understandings about scientific inquiry

NS.9–12.2 Physical Science
- Structure and properties of matter
- Motions and forces

NS.9–12.4 Earth and Space Science
- Energy in the earth system (and as applied to the lunar environment)

NS.9–12.5 Science and Technology
- Abilities of technological design
- Understandings about science and technology

Required Resources

Prerequisites: None

Materials: Access to a computer with an Internet connection

Time Requirements: 60 minutes; challenges are episodic and can be played multiple times.

FIGURE 7.A.1 ▶ Robotics lesson objectives, related standards, and requirements

Designing instruction from an entertainment perspective starts with asking, "What will most excite learners about the objectives and requirements?" Then instructors apply this premise to the overarching learning experience. We define robots as integrated technology designed to extend, replace, and enhance human functions with varying degrees of automation. In the case of the lunar colony, robots help us ward off a hostile environment to facilitate human survival. The premise of warding off hostile elements to survive sets the stage for a heroic adventure, an ideal starting point for InterPLAY. With limited biological life support, robots are the arms and legs of the colony. While demonstrating the different aspects of knowledge about robotics, learners are encouraged to feel the importance of becoming future engineers by practicing soft skills related to being roboticists. With particular references to NASA and space exploration, we aim to instill innovative thinking and other skills that professionals working in space will need, such as creative problem solving, communications, and teamwork. To illustrate how the InterPLAY instructional strategy may be applied to facilitate achievement of specified objectives, we describe how each event was designed to facilitate achievement of this Robotics lesson and present figures that illustrate how the events look to learners online.

Figure 7.A.2 illustrates the home page for the robotics lesson and depicts the major components of the InterPLAY experiential learning landscape. By going to Team Challenges, and selecting Missions, learners enter the landscape and are exposed to the story.

FIGURE 7.A.2 ▶ Mission: LEAP homepage, providing access to major components of the Robotics InterPLAY Learning Landscape

Event 1. Expose

Initially, learners enter the lunar colony complex via a virtual spaceship dock that is welcoming home a shuttle just returning from another lunar colony. Learners are invited to the virtual environment as novice engineers. Learners begin to become acquainted with their mission and related topics through conversations with the astronauts from the returning shuttle. Learners/novice engineers are soon presented with the challenge of creating a new colony on another part of the moon. Realizing this will have to be done by creating robots that can assist the student engineers in performing the tasks that humans cannot accomplish, due to the unique challenges of the lunar environment, the novice engineers quickly begin to see what challenges lie ahead. Throughout, expert characters provide the novices with the necessary information to prepare them for their mission.

FIGURE 7.A.3 ▶ Prototype for online Mission: LEAP robotics expedition *(© 2011 Simiosys)*

Students assess their understanding of robotics and lunar habitation through prompted activities as they learn from the many online and in-class activities already created on the NASA.gov website (Figure 7A.3). The learning of domain knowledge is determined by requiring students to choose correct responses to reflect their understanding. Later, students will be invited to participate in existing online discussions with NASA experts about how to build an off-world colony and how robots might solve challenges that may be seen on the lunar terrain.

The three main purposes of the Expose event are to:

1. Show learners what the topic is and stimulate interest in a lunar colony.

2. Stimulate their curiosity in how a lunar colony could be built by encouraging them to ask questions at the outset of the lesson, just as scientists do as an essential part of following the scientific method.

3. Stimulate their desire to participate in scientific challenges.

The Expose event achieves these purposes through the telling of dramatic stories by veteran astronauts who demonstrate the challenges and consequences of their venture. These stories about their hopes, fears, successes, and failures will motivate learners to inquire about the type of world they will be colonizing and what will make robots successful in order to transform their role from novice to expert.

Events 2 and 3. Inquire and Discover

Figure 7.A.4 illustrates how students navigate through the InterPLAY events and access NASA assets repurposed to support the lesson. Inquiry helps translate learning objectives into "playful discovery" of what is possible. Through character interactions and examples, students are further motivated to inquire and discover key concepts, possibilities, and abilities related to the use of robots.

FIGURE 7.A.4 ▶ NASA learning assets linked from Mission: LEAP robotics expedition to support InterPLAY instructional events.

During initial inquiry, students will play with a web-based robotic simulation that explores mechanical engineering, navigation, rover operation, robot assembly, and other techniques necessary to build an experimental colony in an extreme environment on Earth. Figure 7.A.5, for example, includes a screen shot of a freely accessible online simulation created by NASA that allows students to play with the design of virtual rovers and see how they work in extreme desert conditions (NASA Desert RATS experiments accessible at www.nasa.gov/audience/foreducators/robotics/home/ROVER.html).

During the inquiry/discovery phase, students are also given the opportunity to play with different robotic components (e.g., different types of robotic arms and locomotion). Through dialogue with "expert characters" in a virtual world environment, learners are able to inquire and discover how different robotic components, such as cylindrical and spherical arms, and wheeled and walking locomotion, work (or don't work) to complete different tasks under varying gravitational, atmospheric, and terrain conditions. Through additional resources made accessible in the learning landscape, such as experiment logs, learners can also search and discover how robots have been used within other contexts. For example, the Mars Rover, Robonaut, and Canadarm have been used to explore the Martian surface, looking for signs of life. Through triggered responses from "experts," learners are presented with lessons learned about how robots have been previously used in different space environments to extend human performance.

FIGURE 7.A.5 ▶ NASA learning assets linked from Mission: LEAP robotics expedition to explore the Desert Rat Experimentation Camp

During inquiry/discovery, learners may also advance their knowledge of robotics at an assembly workbench. Here, they can build and play with robots to complete assorted tasks that are made evident in the area. Learners may test different uses and functions of robots with different robotic components and discover the limits of those components by manipulating the environmental conditions or operations. Learners avoid obstacles and operational problems by selecting appropriate components to assemble their robot, based on the needs of the task, indicating an understanding of robotic intent and abilities. If the right components are used, the robots will perform better. If not, robots will perform poorly or fail. When learners are able to reach a predetermined performance level (set by the instructor), they can proceed to the next step in the process. If not, learners can choose different locations and tasks and try again. Data and character interactions provide feedback about the potential performance of the robot and encourage learners to continue. In this manner, story flow and dialogue are not interrupted by formal assessments; rather they are supported by performance data that is tracked and measured in time, errors, creative attempts, and use of resources. Dialogues and demonstrations show learners the consequences of certain selections that can lead to not completing upcoming tasks successfully. The play segment of the InterPLAY strategy prompts learners to investigate the value of robotics in greater detail, paying closer attention to tasks and how they can begin to help solve challenges through creative alternatives and experimentation.

Events 4 and 5. Create and Experiment

The game events of Create and Experiment are implemented in the classroom in this lesson to provide an opportunity for the teacher to gather insights on students' performances and allow the teacher to emphasize additional learning opportunities as a larger group exercise. The social aspects of the classroom also provide entertainment value and additional opportunities to immerse learners in and excite them about the lesson, as they ask questions. Teachers can encourage students to keep track of their own and others' questions in notebooks or on their computers in a special file. As questions are answered, students may record these answers and later, when reflecting during the culminating learning event, they may share their discoveries, mistakes, and insights verbally, as well as on the Mission: LEAP social network page. Teachers can also utilize existing online tools and lessons provided by NASA in class to instruct or inspire learners to access these assets beyond the lesson.

Teachers can prompt creation and experimentation by providing an overarching mission, where students are challenged with an emergency scenario that has severe real-time consequences. Skills, knowledge, attitudes, and resources discovered previously during play contribute to the challenge as students compete with the clock. Having students compete against each other or against previously set standards adds an additional level of engagement. Teachers can also enrich the learning environment by having students pretend that the classroom is the lunar colony and different parts of the school grounds are parts of the lunar terrain: lunar surface (playground), craters (ditches), terraformed land (grassy courtyard), and so forth. The classroom can be stocked with recycled materials (tubes, paper, plastic containers), supplies (paper, rubber bands, string) and tools (scissors, rulers, etc.) to construct their robots. The classroom should also be set up to facilitate achievement of the overall mission. For example, you may set up the classroom with several stations, each with its own challenge, information, and materials, as outlined in the following example.

To start the lesson, teachers should present students with some backstory, a mission, and tasks for completing the mission. For example, teachers may tell students this story

> *A meteor just hit a remote part of the moon. The meteor was small, but it caused an avalanche that has trapped four of your fellow colonists who were exploring the area. The robot used by these colonists was destroyed by the avalanche. The situation is urgent. You will be divided up into teams. Each team must build a robot to go to the location, clear the debris, and bring your friends and associates back to base. There are five stations around the room. At each station, you must select a specific robotic component (arms, power source, legs, programming, or communication) and then place the component on a body that will be assigned to each team. I've given each of you a team number. Now, go find your teammates and complete the mission. Keep in mind, there's time for only one attempt, so be sure to test and make sure your robot is fully operational before bringing it to me for final approval and deployment. Hurry, before it's too late!*

At each station, students may find recommendations and different design options for varying environmental conditions. All options have advantages and disadvantages and students must speculate and decide which option is best for each component, based on the mission and given environmental conditions. With recommendations and available data in hand, students select parts, attach them to their robot see if the parts work. Each mission may require a different configuration of robotic components. For example, if a challenge demands overcoming obstacles, learners should select legs that are large enough to overcome obstacles (such as rocks and rough terrain) versus wheels that may be better on flatter surfaces. Students make and test similar choices for each component until the entire robot is complete.

After creating their robots, students test the utility of their creations. Students can compete against each other to see which robot best completes the challenge. Teachers may also want to have the students critique each robot. Tracking the number of times learners had to override their robots manually to complete tasks will assess their robots' levels of autonomy. Assessments of successful completion of tasks and success of the overall mission may be based on a points system. For example, the robot may need to do a mobilization task involving a leg component. If the most advantageous type of leg is chosen, the performance takes less time, with fewer errors, and less need for manual overrides. However, if a less efficient type of leg is chosen, more time and manual overrides will be needed and more errors will be made, decreasing the accumulation of points. Depending on how it would affect the number of points, students may choose to switch out the leg component mid-task. Doing so would cost negative points in performance but gain positive points for succeeding in the task. The instructor should make clear to students that mistakes are positive aspects of the learning experience. Regardless of individuals' scores, the whole class can learn from everybody's mistakes, and successes can increase the lesson's learning value and impacts.

By creating and experimenting, learners glean why certain components and types of robots work better than others under varying conditions and for certain kinds of tasks. They also learn how the extension of human performance by robotics has many challenges, providing numerous lessons learned through compounded problems and cascading cause and effect consequences.

Event 6. Share

Students who successfully complete their mission experience the journey from novice to expert/ hero by overcoming challenges associated with living in hostile, off-world environments and building lunar colonies. After completing their experiments, students compare their results and experiences with others through three primary means: (1) by configuring visual graphs of performance; measuring tasks, time, errors, and use of resources; (2) by developing a post-mission summary report, using prescribed checklists and rubrics to assess their performances; and (3) by posting their experiences on the Mission: LEAP social network page. Learners receive recognition from mentors and team members by sharing their experiences. By learning from one another, there are no losers in this hybrid approach, only risk-taking explorers willing to take chances to learn more.

Lesson Plan B

Sustaining Health and Wellness on a Lunar Colony
(Online Lesson)

This totally online lesson explores requirements for sustaining physical and mental health in a simulated lunar colony. The lesson is designed as a virtual game that teaches students how medical and life support systems can extend human survival throughout a lunar colony. As medical assistants in the colony, students help the resident expert regulate the health and wellness of a Lunar Rover expedition team, using available tools to analyze data, diagnose physical and mental problems, and formulate solutions. Figure 7.B.1 lists the terminal and enabling objectives for the lesson, along with related national science education standards and required resources. The lesson and its objectives cross over with the Robotics lesson to illustrate the interdependencies of different applications of STEM to the larger picture of off-world habitation.

Again, in developing instruction from the entertainment perspective, we emphasize, "What premise will most excite the learner?" Lunar Rover expeditions involving high-stakes survival scenarios in extreme environmental conditions set up the mission. The student's role is to monitor the team's health and wellness, observe symptoms, diagnose problems, and engage appropriate emergency responses. The activity is meant to inspire further questions outside of gameplay, such as: What cool tools will help us understand the inner workings of our bodies in the future? How does the life support system help us stay alive, and how can we determine whether the system is causing any negative symptoms? How do we read data and graphs to diagnose problems early, respond appropriately to minimize damage to human life, and accomplish the mission's objectives? To demonstrate how the InterPLAY instructional strategy was applied to facilitate achievement of this lesson's objectives, we describe the design of each event and present figures that illustrate how the events look to students online.

Event 1. Expose

After selecting the Lunar Colony Life Support game from the Mission: LEAP website, students are greeted by name (from their log-ins), told that they are expected on Colony Artemis, and asked to board the next shuttle to the colony. Visuals display their launch. Onboard, they are greeted by a fellow passenger: "Welcome [Name]! Keeping everyone healthy is a big job. We appreciate your help. I remember the last time I was on Colony Artemis …" Visuals flash back to when the passenger helped out on the colony as a health officer. The flashback demonstrates the use of a diagnostic tool, the wrist-o-meter, which measures temperature, blood pressure, and heart rate. Graphical examples of results are displayed, including both normal and abnormal readings. Visuals display landing on the colony. Upon touchdown, students exit the vehicle and experience the lunar colony for the first time!

Terminal (TO) and Enabling (EO) Objectives

TO 1.0 Given a graphical interface, as the medical assistant, the learner will be able to analyze health metrics data.

EO 1.1 Monitor instrumental output using the onscreen displays.

EO 1.2 Use the graphical indicators of instrumental output to identify when abnormal health conditions prevail.

TO 2.0 Given symptoms and available resources, as the medical assistant, the learner will be able to determine causes of abnormal health with at least 90% accuracy.

EO 2.1 Use symptoms, diagnostic tools, health data, and personal records to identify a problem.

EO 2.2 Use the symptoms and the available health-care guide to distinguish a physical problem from a mental/behavioral one.

EO 2.3 Given a physical problem, use the diagnostic tools available, personal records, and the health-care guide to identify the cause of the physical problem.

EO 2.4 Given a mental and/or behavioral problem, use the diagnostic tools available, personal records, and the health-care guide to identify the cause of the mental/behavioral problem.

TO 3.0 Given problems and available resources, as the medical assistant, the learner will be able to formulate solutions to alleviate the problem with at least 90% accuracy.

EO 3.1 Use the health-care guide to determine if the physical cause is individual or system based.

EO 3.2 Given a physical cause for an individual problem, use the health-care guide to identify a solution.

EO 3.3 Given a physical cause for a system-based problem, use the health-care guide to identify a solution.

EO 3.4 Use the health-care guide to determine if the cause for a mental/behavioral problem is individual or system-based.

EO 3.5 Given a cause for a mental/behavioral individual problem, use the health-care guide to identify a solution.

EO 3.6 Given a cause for a mental/behavioral system-based problem, use the health-care guide to identify a solution.

EO 3.7 Develop teamwork, collaboration, coordination, and communication skills.

EO 3.8 Develop innovative thinking and creative problem-solving skills.

National Science Education Standards

NS.9–12.1 SCIENCE AS INQUIRY

- Abilities necessary to do scientific inquiry
- Understandings about scientific inquiry

NS.9–12.3 LIFE SCIENCE

- Matter, energy, and organization in living systems
- Behavior of organisms

NS.9–12.5 SCIENCE AND TECHNOLOGY

- Abilities of technological design
- Understandings about science and technology

Required Resources

Prerequisites: None

Materials: Access to a computer with an Internet connection.

Time Requirements: 60 minutes; challenges are episodic and can be played multiple times.

FIGURE 7.B.1 ▶ Health and wellness lesson objectives and requirements

Students see a door marked "Health & Wellness." They go through the door and see a digital health officer examining a patient's medical condition. Upon entry, students are asked "Do you have the knowledge and equipment necessary to fill the role of medical assistant on the expedition?" If they select "yes," students receive a message indicating that they have been stricken with a disorder that cannot be detected without the wrist-o-meter, which puts their life in danger. They are then given the opportunity to restart and re-enter the health and wellness facility. If learners select "no" or "I don't know," they are given further instruction on how to use the wrist-o-meter to detect early symptoms of health problems and also an electronic manual with instructions on how to save lives in various emergency situations. The yes/no consequences reward those who do not rush through activities. Such dramatic consequences may also inspire future active inquiry and demonstrate the importance of discovering new information and tools.

Events 2 and 3. Inquire and Discover

To inquire and discover key concepts necessary to sustain physical and mental health in off-world conditions, students use the five cool tools listed below to examine and diagnose patients, and make recommendations.

1. **Wrist-o-Meter.** An instrument for checking temperature, blood pressure, and heart rate (depicted in Figure 7.B.2);

2. **MicroPen.** A microscope in the shape of a pen (e.g., click and drag to "slides" to display a video of blood cells);

3. **X-Ray wand.** As the wand is held over parts of a patient's body, an x-ray image of that body part appears on the computer/tablet screen;

4. **Nutri-Meter.** Shaped in the form of a Popsicle, the instrument is placed into the patient's mouth to see whether the person has any nutritional deficiency; and

5. **Communicator.** For health monitor alerts, this two-way communication device flashes and beeps for incoming health alerts and enables health and wellness experts to send messages to colonists.

One challenge in the health and wellness center has medical assistants examine prospective team members to recommend those healthy enough to join the expedition. Students are given the opportunity to perform three medical imaging tests to examine each prospective team member. On each instrument, they can see a display of results and are prompted: "What is your assessment?" When an appropriate assessment is made, the expert responds positively; an incorrect assessment triggers corrective feedback from the expert. The results of each test indicate the patient's condition with one or more patients showing symptoms of a problem.

After the tests and assessments have been completed, students are asked to make a recommendation or they may conduct further exams with available tools or consult research resources (such as medical journals, manuals, and logbooks) before making a recommendation. Students then receive feedback on their recommendation. They are given praise from the health expert and prospective team member for appropriate recommendations, and corrective feedback and a graphic description of potential negative consequences for recommending someone who is not healthy enough for the expedition from the expert.

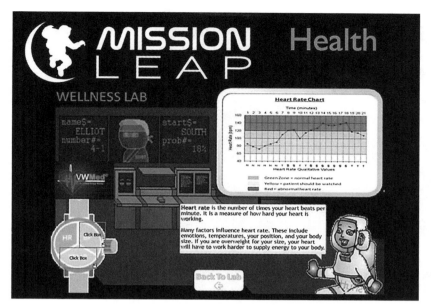

FIGURE 7.B.2 ▶ Prototype for Mission: LEAP online health and wellness expedition referencing simulated medical tools *(copyright © 2011 Simiosys/MOSI)*

At the end of each student/patient interaction, the symptoms are entered into a logbook (tab 1). On tab 2, the health officer demonstrates how to use the logbook to link symptoms to illnesses. On tab 3, the health officer demonstrates how to use the logbook to match possible solutions to an illness. Students may also review previous digital logbooks from previous fictional characters to see successful and unsuccessful medical efforts. This promotes the ability to learn from other character's mistakes.

Events 4 and 5. Create and Experiment

Using available tools and data, students now choose an expedition from a list of options to begin their extreme off-world medical training. Students are then tasked with selecting appropriate team members for the expedition from a roster of astronauts, and providing proper notes to monitor team members' health and wellness (as depicted in Figure 7.B.3). The challenge is for students to pick the best teams for particular expeditions to ensure the fewest risks to the expedition and the health of team members. These goals may be in conflict. Participants need to understand individuals' previous medical conditions to fully understand the risks of choosing team members.

Each type of expedition has specific health requirements and risks. Each potential team member has different health issues (some minor, some potentially serious). The participants' goals are to use their health monitoring tools to assess each candidate for the expedition and then to choose appropriate astronauts for the team. The number of candidates varies to challenge the player. In some cases, an expedition may need to be canceled based on a need for constant monitoring. During the expedition, some astronauts may need to be provided with one of three levels of medical response: (1) remain working with the monitoring team, (2) cease working and receive treatment, or (3) undergo an emergency evacuation.

FIGURE 7.B.3 ▶ Prototype for Mission: LEAP online health and wellness expedition, tasking students to create and experiment with the best methods for crew selection *(copyright © 2011 Simiosys)*

A scenario for the expedition is generated, depending on which team members are chosen. For example, as the expedition team drives the rover to the first station, a team member gets nauseous and asks that the vehicle be stopped. Students are able to use their diagnostic tools and an online logbook to note symptoms and research possible solutions. Students need to make decisions concerning their patients such as whether they should continue the mission or return to base. In this example, the illness is space sickness, similar to seasickness, and symptoms can be reduced using pills from the medical kit, so the mission can be continued.

As soon as the students successfully identify and treat the problem, the team can continue to the first stop of their expedition. The task here is to collect samples. Learners will notice that one member of the team does not participate. When asked, this team member reports being extremely tired. Using the nutri-meter will identify the problem—a calorie deficiency. The team member further reports that he was so excited that he didn't eat the last few meals. Consuming sufficient calories can be a problem in extreme environments where the choices are limited and repetitious. The treatment is a protein bar, included in the medical kit.

As the team moves through additional tasks, different health issues appear. In the crisis scenario, students are contacted through their communicators and directed to meet another team at their rover. When the students arrive, the team members are slumped over in the vehicle. Students may use the wrist-o-meter to find that all the patients have low heart rates, combined with low body temperatures. The logbook will have a solution, but the ill team members need to be driven back to base immediately to survive. Students must decide whether to take both vehicles back or to continue the mission with a reduced team. When the expedition is over, data is produced to show the levels of performance and risk that were taken. Students can choose to repeat the same expedition to better their scores or choose another expedition and apply the lessons they learned from this, as well as any previous expeditions.

Students' success as they work with the Create and Experiment events is assessed by how well they use and assimilate the domain's knowledge, as they perform the Inquire and Discover events—making appropriate decisions by considering varying factors that will impact the mission's end results. The conditions vary each time, so students can create different solutions, based on data gathered from the tools, peers, or the instructor. As students experiment, they test the validity of their solutions. They learn from the feedback of their successes and failures, and through this process develop strategic and innovative thinking skills.

Event 6. Share

Assessment of a mission is based on responses to health and wellness issues, use of tools, correct identification of symptoms and causes, implementation of solutions, and total time taken to accomplish the mission. Scores and awards appear in the logbook, and students are encouraged to share their experiences on the website's Facebook page. For best learning results, students need to participate in an after-action review with peers and/or the instructor. This critical period of sharing shows students that they can learn more from their mistakes and others' mistakes and experiences than they could have learned from getting everything right on their own.

Design and Delivery Issues

If you choose to apply the InterPLAY instructional strategy, you need to be aware of key issues and common mistakes that can undermine the entertainment or educational value of the learning experience. Even though, from your perspective, education may be the primary purpose for applying the InterPLAY instructional theory, it is designed for having fun with learning from students' perspectives. Having fun while putting this theory into practice, however, is not about combining educational objectives with superficially entertaining packages or sprinkling educational tidbits into entertainment. The InterPLAY experiential learning theory is based upon entertainment heuristics that couple directly with an instructional strategy grounded in research and theory. Education and entertainment serve and support each other; one never overwhelms the other. When you immerse yourself with the theory, InterPLAY can be used as an impromptu technique for learning exchanges between the instructor and students, as well as via detailed instructional designs, such as this mission.

We are all expert consumers of entertainment and education, but few of us are expert creators of both entertainment and education. An entertainment expert can transform a boring educational experience into a fun experience; however, an expert educator can destroy students' fun by using traditional instructional methods and designs. What looks fun on paper can fall flat in play. And what may seem boring in design can come alive during implementation. Teachers can transform their students' online and hybrid experiences into engaging learning landscapes by using four key tools from entertainment to help ensure that students have fun while learning: observations, focus groups, play tests, and expert reviews.

Observations. What stories interest your students? What stories do they tell their friends? What games do they play? How do they play? To apply the Inter*PLAY* instructional strategy properly and design effective Inter*PLAY* experiential learning landscapes, it's critical to understand how your students relate to the basic conventions of story, play, and game. Observe students as they are engaged in education and in entertainment. Visit a playground and see what games children play and how they interact with each other. Observe students playing with toys, and note their actions and reactions. Go to a theme park and sit in one spot; observe a variety of people and groups engaged in the same or similar activities. Watch and listen; gain an understanding of what attracts kids' attention, increases their engagement, and makes them smile. At school, take opportunities to stand outside your classroom and watch your students interacting, or observe students in class as they work through a group activity. Listen to the stories they tell, and watch how they interact with each other. Take notes, and relate what you see and hear to story, play, and game. To write stories and design game play that engage your students, you must know what types of stories and games and forms of play interest and excite them. You also need to understand the interplay among story, game, and play.

Focus Groups. Once you have basic knowledge of your students' preferred stories and styles of play and game, consider conducting a focus group to gain a better understanding of their needs, interests, and opinions. Pull together a small group of students, and ask them open-ended questions (not leading questions) about their fears and fantasies. What were some of their most exciting life and learning experiences? Where were they at these times? Who were they with? Why were their experiences exciting? What were their most boring life and learning experiences? Why? Listen carefully and take notes or record the conversation. Don't forget to ask students about the content matter you're teaching to determine their interest in the subject. Are the skills and knowledge to be covered in class relevant to their needs? Are they confident in their ability to succeed? What is it about the subject matter that might gain and sustain their interests? A rich and deep understanding of your students' stories, the games they like to play, how they relate to each other as they play, and how story, play, and game interrelate in your students' daily lives will give you the fuel you need to apply the Inter*PLAY* instructional strategy and create engaging Inter*PLAY* learning landscapes.

Play Tests. When you have an idea, you need to test it early and test it often. If the design process is just a theoretical or intellectual exercise, Inter*PLAY* will not work. Don't try to avoid mistakes or failure during play tests. Fail often to succeed sooner. Try as hard as you can to succeed, but take chances. That is when you will gain the most valuable insights and seize opportunities to generate exciting and engaging ideas for learning. Take an existing game and change its theme to one from your subject matter. Create a paper prototype of your game, and play it with students. Sit down with your students and have them attempt to design a game about the subject matter. Play testing is exploratory, open-ended, subjective, and qualitative. Make sure somebody is working to make the play test fun and somebody is observing and collecting data. Plant a colleague or friend in the group play test to record his or her own in situ observations. After the experience, gather them around to have a group discussion to express their reactions to and feelings about the game. Let them speak openly and do not direct their answers. Rather, use one answer to inquire deeper into your students' memories and experiences. What was the most interesting aspect of the experience? Why? Who had a different response? Why? Why do you think the responses were different? What was the most frustrating experience? Why? Is that good or bad?

Don't assume negative responses are bad; they are clues to discover surprising revelations about novel approaches. Play testing is not a judgment, but an informative critique.

Expert Reviews. Conduct expert reviews when you are to the point of presenting a preliminary and/or a final Inter*Play* design. Experts may range from subject matter experts, to experts on your student population, to expert storytellers and writers, to experts in play and game design. Ask experts about their reactions, considering their particular areas of expertise. An expert's reaction is not a judgment as much as it is an insight. Also keep in mind that experts may provide more insights by the questions they ask than the opinions they share. Why did you select this character? Why is the user allowed to let the patient die? The key is not to defend your work or rationalize your choices, but to engage in the dialogue with experts to take your design to the next level.

Concluding Thoughts

In education "done is often good," but with entertainment, "it is not done until it is good." Two stages are critical to development: Rapid development of the first version of the design leads to achieving the objectives (done). However, time to develop multiple iterations to refine the design makes the experience satisfying (good). The lessons included in this chapter were designed by instructional design students as their first effort with the Inter*PLAY* theory. This chapter is meant to show how one would start to utilize the theory. For practice, consider both of these lessons along with what you have learned about Inter*PLAY*, and explore how you could make them better with a little more entertainment or education value. Self-critique and reinventing your teaching methods can take more time, yet by doing them, you'll be taking the best path toward designing successful, entertaining, and engaging learning experiences. When you think your plans are *good* and *done*, make one more effort to take your program "over the top" to being *great* and *fun*. Try this with the two lessons presented in this chapter; there is always room for improvement. Take turns with colleagues to practice critiquing each other's work, and you'll all develop your own abilities to self-critique—the most important aspect of designing any creative product.

The authors would like to acknowledge and thank Kimberly Bates, Kamalkoli Bhattacharya, Christopher Chapman, Katrise Richard Dillion, Roger Hadley, Gregory Igel, April Forcier, Araceli Matos, Elizabeth Szgeti, Amanda Newton, and John Walker for their help and contributions to development of the Mission: LEAP lessons.

References

"Aristotle." (2005). In W. F. Bynum & R. Porter (Eds.). *Oxford Dictionary of Scientific Quotations* (21:9). Oxford, UK: Oxford University Press.

Bos, B. (1990). *Together we're better: Establishing coactive learning environments for young children.* Roseville, CA: Turn the Page Press.

Dewey, J. (1897). My pedagogic creed. *School Journal, 54,* 77–80.

Dewey, J. (1916). *Democracy and education:* An introduction to the philosophy of education. New York, NY: Macmillan. Retrieved from www.gutenberg.org/files/852/852-h/852-h.htm

Dewey, J. (1938). Experience and education. New York, NY: Macmillan. Retrieved from www.schoolofeducators.com/wp-content/uploads/2011/12/EXPERIENCE-EDUCATION-JOHN-DEWEY.pdf

Hirumi, A. (Ed.). (2010). *Playing games in school: Using simulations and videogames for primary and secondary education.* Eugene, OR: International Society for Technology in Education.

Hirumi, A., & Hall, R. (2010). Presenting content information and facilitating instruction: Design techniques for advancing game flow. In M. S. Khine (Ed.), *Learning to play: Exploring the future of education with video games* (pp. 55–78). New York, NY: Peter Lang.

Kirschner, P. A., Sweller, J., and Clark, R. E. (2006). Why minimal guidance during instruction does not work: An analysis of the failure of constructivist, discovery, problem-based, experiential, and inquiry-based teaching. *Educational Psychologist, 41*(2), 75–86. Retrieved from http://igitur-archive.library.uu.nl/fss/2006-1214-211848/kirschner_06_minimal_guidance.pdf

Kolb, D. A. (1984). *Experiential learning: Experience as the source of learning and development.* Englewood Cliffs, NJ: Prentice-Hall.

Lewin, K. (1943). Defining the "field at a given time." *Psychological Review, 50*(3), 292–310.

Mitchell, A., & Savill-Smith, C. (2004). The use of computer games for learning. Retrieved July 23, 2007 from www.m-learning.org/archive/docs/The%20use%20of%20computer%20and%20video%20games%20for%20learning.pdf

Piaget, J. (1962). *Play, dreams, and imitation in childhood.* New York, NY: Norton.

Shank, R. C., Berman, T. R., & Macpherson, K. A. (1992). Learning by doing. In C. M. Reigeluth (Ed), *Instructional design theories and models: A new paradigm of instructional theory* (pp. 161–179). Hillsdale, NJ: Lawrence Erlbaum.

Stapleton, C. B., & Davies, J. (2011, October). Imagination: The third reality to the mixed reality continuum presented at the 10th IEEE International Symposium on Mixed and Augmented Reality, Basel, Switzerland.

Stapleton, C. B., & Hirumi, A. (2011). Inter*PLAY* instructional strategy: Learning by engaging interactive entertainment conventions. In M. Shaughnessy & S. Fulgham (Eds), *Pedagogical models: The discipline of online teaching* (pp. 183–211). Hauppauge, NY: Nova Science.

Stapleton, C. B., & Hughes, C. E. (2005, January). Mixed reality and experiential movie trailers: Combining emotions and immersion to innovate entertainment marketing. In *Proceedings of the 2005 International Conference on Human-Computer Interface Advances in Modeling and Simulation,* New Orleans, LA (pp. 40–48).

Applying Game and Brain-Based Learning Principles to Enhance e-Learning and Education

Matthew Laurence

IN THIS CHAPTER, WE DISCUSS how educators can use the principles of brain-based learning and game design and development techniques to increase student engagement in classroom material. Key challenges and considerations unique to game-based courses are reviewed and advice to mitigate and even eliminate these issues is offered. Real-world examples of various means by which digital, hybrid, and classroom game-based learning platforms have met with success are provided as additional support for the concept. Additionally, a short set of game design steps incorporating the lessons from this chapter is provided to help propel teachers into constructing their own game-based lessons. The chapter concludes by noting the similarities between gaming and pedagogical design, encouraging educators to consider that gameplay in school isn't a threat to education—not when games and education can become one and the same.

Everywhere we look, the walls are tumbling down. Education as an online initiative is a foregone conclusion. Day by day, we find more researchers who delight in pointing out economic trends and technology statistics, all with the same basic outcome: Our schools are going digital at a shocking rate (Christensen, 2008). What is more interesting is that the increasing prevalence of online instruction is only a herald of things to come; soon we will see widespread proliferation of hybrid and completely digital learning models. The real questions, then, are not in terms of if or even *when* this revolution is coming (after all, in many ways, it's already here), but rather *how*. What will these new systems look like, and how can we ensure they are going to be effective replacements for brick-and-mortar, paper-and-pencil institutions?

One way to answer these questions is to look at what is driving this digital revolution. The rise of social networks, multiplayer gaming environments, and the Internet itself have all played a role in determining the direction of education—not because they are pedagogically sound but because they have changed the way we think and learn (Carr, 2010). The patterns that have shaped the Internet may be the same patterns that will shape online education, and with that basic concept in place, we can start getting our answers.

At this point, let's turn to games. From board games to intricate online affairs, like *World of Warcraft,* the entire game industry is built around the concept of engagement. The underpinnings of game design have been used to make social media darlings like Farmville and, at the same time, have been modernized and inspired by advances in technology and the Internet. Just as today's digital natives must know what all their friends are doing and keep them updated on their own activities, so, too, must today's gamers share their achievements with their peers. The thinning barrier between entertainment software and social media suggests that the world we live in and the relationships we are compelled to monitor can be leveraged for the purposes of engagement. Here, then, we come to the perfect intersection between today's technological wonders and education. We have already seen how game development techniques may become pervasive across online environments, and this vast field now encompasses education as well.

Using methods of engagement from entertainment software and social media can help us ensure that learning in the digital world is just as effective—if not more so—than physical environments. Even better, these techniques can be used to improve brick-and-mortar and hybrid classrooms. Simply pointing out methods of engagement used in games cannot do this; a more applicable pedagogical model must be found, and, to that end, brain-based learning theory may accomplish this goal. The reason for this choice is simple: the tenets of brain-based learning parallel the methods of entertainment design with remarkable congruence (Atkinson & Hirumi, 2010).

This chapter illustrates how brain-based learning principles can be and have been used to deliver engaging hybrid and online game-based courses that have aided in student interest and retention. This chapter focuses on what brain-based learning represents in this increasingly digital and interconnected age: a pedagogical paradigm that can be used to construct engaging lessons and courses with the same underlying principles as the best games and movies. Brain-based learning tracks exceedingly well to the fundamental theories of entertainment design, and using these techniques, especially in this wired age, can allow savvy instructors to reap vast gains in student engagement and content retention. In a review of game-based technologies and brain-based learning in educational environments today, one can find fully digital and do-it-yourself

K–12 lessons that teachers can adopt immediately, as well as key design and delivery issues such endeavors may encounter.

Brain-Based Learning

Before we get too involved with the potential applications of this theory, a short refresher is in order. When we talk about brain-based learning, what we're discussing are the theories developed at the Caine Institute. Based on neurological and biochemical studies of human learning and the brain, the 12 principles of brain-based learning developed by Caine and Caine (1997) provide an excellent foundation for the development of engaging lessons. In short, they are a series of basic rules for understanding the apprehension of events and experiences by the brain.

By addressing the 12 principles, educators can create three conditions that are thought to be fundamental to higher-order thinking and complex learning (Caine, Caine, McClintic, & Klimek, 2005). In turn, the three conditions may be used to craft interest and retention in entertainment as well as education. The three fundamental conditions are the following:

1. **Relaxed Alertness.** A state of mind where perceived threats are minimal and the level of challenge is high allows individuals to be ready to learn, motivated, attentive, and able to tackle a diverse set of obstacles without fear of failure.

2. **Orchestrated Immersion.** A learning environment that provides orchestrated immersion brings its material to life; students know they have a wealth of options for understanding content; they are receptive to authentic experiences that are rich with meaning and detail.

3. **Active Processing.** This is what we want to see from our students—the organization and integration of information in a manner that is meaningful to them. To invoke active processing of a concept is to put the learner on the path to understanding, not just memorization. It is an emotional as much as an intellectual state of being.

You may already see some similarities between the three basic conditions and the basics of game design, and that's no accident. The goals of game developers and educators are basically the same—they want their players or students to remember the lessons they have to teach, to be drawn into the world they've created, and to be engaged by the material within. Now let's touch on key examples of how games manage to do this and how the principles of their construction can be used to enhance your own classroom lessons.

No Classes, Just Games

Teachers must be forgiven if their first reaction upon hearing the phrase "game-based course" is to assume a video game simply could not become a viable lesson on its own. At some point, don't we need to stop playing around to get down to the serious business of teaching and learning? Not so. In fact, the notion of stopping play and breaking students' immersion in it before a lesson can begin is a poisonous concept for any course, game-based or not. The best classes are those that truly engage the learner, placing them in a world that makes sense in the context of the material and refusing to break that spell right up until the moment the bell rings and they step outside. A game-based course, that is, a class fully presented through a game, with no teacher directly present at any time, is more than possible; it's already been done.

Conspiracy Code, a series of game-based courses designed and developed by 360Ed in partnership with Florida Virtual School, is the ultimate expression of this concept. Even better, its efficacy isn't hopeful, pie-in-the-sky prediction—the courses themselves have, in some cases, performed better than their counterparts in standard learning environments (Farr, 2010).

There are currently two versions of *Conspiracy Code* available: one intended to teach a full course of high school-level American history and one a course of intensive reading. Each is a self-contained adventure, played out in 3-D environments wherein students control the characters Eddie Flash and Libby Whitetree. These protagonists are working to protect the near-future city of Coverton from the efforts of Conspiracy Incorporated, a shadowy organization bent on world domination. Over the course of the game, students will find and collect clues, avoiding enemy agents and well-meaning security guards as they recover these important pieces of information. Each clue is a webpage, displayed inside the game's client as soon as the student recovers it, and represents a single article in the course. Students must collect clues (articles) to progress, which often include small assessments. At the end of every mission (a total of 10 for the game), students encounter a larger, culminating assessment of high-order thinking that requires them to use their creativity and the knowledge they've gained to construct something related to both the subject matter and the game.

Relevance to both the subject and the game is one of the primary ways *Conspiracy Code* engages learners, tying all of their assignments and tasks back into the game's storyline and setting. Basically, for every question, logbook entry, and essay students must write, they are given a plausible reason why Eddie and Libby must accomplish this task to further their goals and defeat Conspiracy Incorporated. Even teachers are incorporated in this manner, as they are given the role of students' contact within an underground resistance movement. By interacting with students through the game and its associated learning management system—SiTi (student interface/teacher interface)—teachers can monitor students' progress and provide feedback behind the scenes without breaking the sense of immersion. When Eddie and Libby debrief their contacts on what they've accomplished during a mission, for instance, students are essentially telling their instructor what they've learned.

However, there is only so much one can expect a teacher to accomplish within the constraints of the classroom environment. Most teachers certainly will have neither the budget, nor the team of game developers on hand to produce a high-end video game. So while it's good to discuss how products like *Conspiracy Code* engage learners with intriguing gameplay and brain-based learning designs, some aspects of video games are not as easily applied in a classroom setting. Teachers typically do not have access to artists who specialize in three-dimensional designs, animators, professional voice actors, and so on, but what they *can* do is tweak how the material is framed. Justifying educational content doesn't require a full video game. What is truly needed is an instructor who knows how to present a course in a way that the subject matter *sticks* in students' imaginations and knowledge bases. This is perhaps the greatest takeaway for the average instructor in terms of the *Conspiracy Code* series. *Conspiracy Code* has shown that by demonstrating to students why it's important to understand a given piece of material, the chances that they will internalize and remember that knowledge increase dramatically. Students are frequently bored by traditional teaching and learning methods—so snap them out of it! Promote your course's content with ideas and scenarios that capture their imaginations and give them reasons to learn. The best part is, the justification you choose only needs to be tangentially related to the topic at hand; the true requirement is that students *care* about what they are learning.

To see a working instance of students being encouraged to learn for reasons that are not directly related to the content, we turn to our next set of examples of brain-based learning and games. While *Conspiracy Code* shows us how brain-based learning principles can be applied in a fully digital setting, the work of Scott Laidlaw provides the perfect example of how game-based instruction can be accomplished in the classroom without a single computer.

Pencils, Books, and Board Games

Engagement is not the goal—it's just a means to an end. As we move into perhaps the most practical section of this chapter, I want to make this point clear. One should never mistake entertaining and engaging with educating. The former must always be subservient to the latter. The rather dim view many have of games in terms of their educational value is in large part due to developers forgetting this simple relationship.

Scott Laidlaw is an instructor who has never made the mistake of putting entertainment before education. Through years of trial and error, he has been able to teach middle school mathematics via extensive, customized board games. Laidlaw began with a thematic approach, using props, such as an enormous map of the world, and putting his students in the shoes of global pirates during the Renaissance. From here, he moved on to a medieval kingdom-building exercise. Each time, these games were beset with disasters as often as successes, and each time students played a game, Laidlaw learned from his mistakes and built anew. His third game, played on hand-painted deer hides, chronicled the coming-of-age journey of a young, prehistoric tribal girl named Ko; with this game and an integrated curriculum to help fifth grade students use what they had learned on standardized tests, Laidlaw doubled the average state test score in mathematics and helped increase students' math proficiency rate from 28% to 80% (Los Alamos National Lab, 2011). More games followed, and Laidlaw managed to maintain his students' attention even through situations where a game turn could not be completed unless an eight-step algebraic equation was correctly solved.

The wonderful thing about Laidlaw's example is that his method requires no fancy technology— just an understanding administrator, the desire to engage students, and perhaps most important, the drive to soldier on in the face of adversity. We can take away three major lessons from Laidlaw's efforts to combine board games and mathematics. These lessons are described broadly enough that they can be applied to any course.

Lesson 1. The right theme can capture the imagination

Pirates. Medieval fiefdoms. Shamanistic rites of passage. These are the sorts of things that put images in the heads of your students and make them wonder what comes next. Problems involving the circumference of a pizza or cars traveling in different directions may never be interesting, no matter how many times they are posed. By providing students with an intriguing premise—an exciting new layer on top of the standard course material—you can hook them. Any time students ask themselves a question about the course's content, they are interested, even if it's something simple, like, "How does *this* fit into building a pirate empire?" Getting students to engage with content is the key to long-term learning, and the right theme can do this.

Lesson 2. Create a goal to work toward

Now that your students actually have a setting to be curious about, we need to give them a goal. Here is where a lot of classroom lesson plans fail. Telling students that the knowledge you're supplying will be useful someday may do little to nothing to engage their interest. Simply teaching subject matter because "it will be on the test" is even worse. Instead, giving students a reason to continue engaging—a tangible, compact, easy-to-understand goal they can achieve— means giving them a reason to keep learning. For Laidlaw, engaging students was illustrated by any number of accomplishments, such as turning a pitiful hamlet into a powerful fiefdom. And the game *Conspiracy Code* presents students with the goal of stopping a nefarious conspiracy. In both cases, the material the students learned became the necessary means to reach an end—and infinitely more interesting as a result.

Lesson 3. Never assume you'll get it right the first time

Laidlaw iterated constantly and faced numerous problems along the way. For every game you create at first, from simple pen-and-paper creations to full-scale digital developments, you will design some elements incorrectly. Obtaining feedback, testing early, and being flexible are the keys to success. If you plan on using games to teach in your classroom, then prepare to change your designs in the face of issues you never could have foreseen. This may be the most nebulous bit of advice, but I've included it here because everyone seems to assume that the great successes of education and entertainment alike sprung into being fully formed. This is, unfortunately, not the case; game development of any sort comes with its unique blend of crushing frustrations. Just as good games can be used to focus students' attention on a concept and crystallize key ideas, failed game designs can feel terribly disappointing to the creator. Do not get discouraged— setbacks afford opportunities to improve what you've done, nothing more. Besides, if you don't make mistakes, you probably aren't creating something significant. With experience and feed-back, your chances of outright failure will diminish, and the end result will be an engaging game that teaches course material better than you could have imagined.

Of Course, There Are Issues

It should be clear by now that there are definite hurdles to overcome when attempting to integrate brain-based learning principles through game-based learning models. These problems can be general as well as determined by the type of game model you choose to employ. In this section, I will try to lay out potential problematical issues you might encounter when trying to create an educational game, as well as offer suggestions on how to avoid and bounce back from them.

To begin with, not all games will appeal to all students. No magic bullet for game designs guarantees that every player will be enraptured. This is to be expected. The point of designing learning games is not to solve all the educational world's problems at once—rather, it is to *improve* engagement in learning for as many students as possible. With that in mind, let us look at a subset of this problem: Gender appeal. This is not an issue to be ignored. Girls are often left on the sidelines when it comes to games, and designers must think of a theme and goals that appeal to all students. This is due in part to media treatment of the subject and the prevalence of violent video games on the market, to which boys are simply more attracted than girls (Lemmens & Bushman, 2006). Strong female and male protagonists, interesting interpersonal relationships, and mechanics that focus on characters' growth and self-improvement can all help to bridge the gender gap, but really, the main thing you need to overcome is the stigma that games are built for boys. Your job is becoming easier every day, as games are becoming more and more widespread, but it is important to keep in mind that you not only need to convince your students that your game is an appropriate method to use for your subject matter, but also their parents and your administrators.

On that note, let us turn to the next possibly contentious issue—everyone's a critic. If you are already convinced that games can teach, great! If your students are on board, even better! The problem here is that a significant part of your job is not yet done. You may also need to prove to uneasy parents and budget-minded, risk-averse administrators that game-based education is not only in the best interests of your pupils, but also doable and effective. In your defense, a wealth of studies and meta-analyses have been performed that consistently show "that games promote learning and/or reduce instructional time across multiple disciplines and ages" (Van Eck, 2006). Games have been found to be valuable instruments for teaching a variety of concepts, and many educational researchers and educators have agreed that using games in schools "could help address one of the nation's most pressing needs—strengthening our system of education and preparing workers for 21st-century jobs" (Charles & McAlister, 2004; Federation of American Scientists, 2006; Holland, Jenkins, & Squire, 2002; Sheffield, 2005). But perhaps research is not enough. In this case, you must communicate. Show naysayers your ideas and walk them through your game's basic ideas, sharing how you plan to engage your students. If you have put a great deal of thought into your design, your ideas may be enough to convince them. If not, then perhaps you should consider these conversations your first round of feedback—gleaning elements that will improve your game and help you interest others in playing it, not bury it forever.

Naturally, issues of grading will come up among administrators and students. Sometimes, games don't lend themselves well to quantifiable scales, and that's a problem. How do you relate Timmy's acquisition of 10 cows for his hamlet to his actual course grade? In addition, many school systems require instructors to teach to the test or at least to prepare your students to achieve a series of predefined state standards, both of which may seem inimical to spending time on an immersive game world that will nab students' attention. The truth here, however, is that these expectations only become problems if you allow them to control your course's curriculum. Look at them as the useful constraints that they are—these are the minimal boundaries within which you must work. A clear understanding of these measurable course outcomes will actually make your job easier. By having constraints, you can exercise your creativity far more effectively than by seating yourself in front of a blank computer or notepad and hoping you come up with something compelling. Does your game need to produce some sort of real grade? Does it need to cover benzene rings? These are your starting points. Don't try to make a do-everything *uber*-game; focus instead on what is truly necessary. In the case of state-mandated tests and standards, don't panic; remember that the game is merely a different way of presenting information, and nothing will be lost in translation if you don't want it to be. Build your game around the standards, so that all aspects of the game—before, during, and after students use it—touch on what is required. Make certain that every point in those sprawling, itemized, state-mandated lists is addressed by your game's mechanics, and if for some reason you can't include something on the list, take it out and make a note to teach it separately. When you begin designing the game with your goals (matching state standards) at the forefront of your mind, you'll realize that the standards make a more solid foundation than freewheeling, directionless brainstorming ever could. By ensuring that your game's activities and content areas fulfill the standards (and most likely surpass them), you'll also set administrators' and parents' minds at ease.

When it comes to the types of games you use, the problems can vary. Digital games are great, but only if students have access to computers that can run them. Hardware concerns can ground your ideas before they even get beyond the planning stage. This problem increases in severity if the game needs to be played at home as well as at school, because every student must have a computer that will play the game (and likely an Internet connection). Championing digital games can easily mean opening oneself up to defeat by attrition, as hardware and software incompatibilities chip away at your student base. The solution here, however, is simple. Plan ahead, check system requirements, and make sure students and parents alike are on the same page when it comes to getting things installed and activated. The next issue you may face is one of privacy. A digital game will almost certainly use the Internet, especially if it reproduces an entire course. Students will need a place to submit assignments, and they may even need to do research outside your course. What's an instructor to do? The key here is that a digital course can be safe—the right one will make students' activities transparent to educators and guardians, all communications will be recorded and archived, and the bulk of the course will be confined to "safe" places, known quantities in an admittedly scary world. In all honesty, the problems you will find in this regard will more often than not be confined to the perceptions of others, not any real privacy threat. The Internet can often seem like a seething cauldron of predators and viruses, especially to those parents and administrators who aren't tech-savvy. The solution here is the same as before: Communicate, placate, and persevere. Finally, a word of warning if you plan on making your own digital game for your classes' use, rather than purchasing a pre-made course: Software development is incredibly difficult, and building a game that teaches a full course's worth of material could take hundreds of thousands of dollars and a full team of artists, producers, designers, and programmers. Be extremely careful if this is a course of action you plan on taking. Start designing games on a modest scale and allow your successes to encourage you to create more comprehensive games as your skills improve. Like Scott Laidlaw, you could begin by designing a board game as a means of teaching a unit and consider feedback from it when creating new iterations of the game. Once you're satisfied with the non-digital game, you might feel ready to create a digital game for a different unit of study, using your board game's features as a model.

For board games and similarly non-digital initiatives, of course, the problems of intensive software development go away, making them the most practical examples of game-based education. By tailoring a game to your classroom, a casual back-and-forth dialogue is constructed with your students. This dialogue will, in turn, help you tweak and tune your board game into a compelling diversion that actually educates your students. The potentially negative issues you will face in the nondigital setting are far more personal. A malicious student may find a way to break your game and wreck the experience for others. You may listen to students, parents, or administrators complain about certain game features they deem unfair or too advantageous for a given student or group of students. Actual imbalances need to be addressed, or they can undermine the educational value at hand. And, as with any traditional lesson, your theme and storyline may not prove compelling from one class to the next.

Essentially, because of a game's innovative features and students' interest in it, your worth as an educator could soon be tied to the game mechanics you design—something that is, if you take a moment to think about it, a wild concept.

The solution here (beyond employing a strong sense of willpower and perseverance) is to take all these issues as feedback and criticism. Your game—and, by extension, your course—is only as good as your ability to adapt, tweak, and improve it. You will never build the perfect game. It doesn't exist. What you will do is encounter problems and setbacks aplenty, so expect them and use them. You can let your ideas lie fallow, or you can turn all those problems into fertilizer and grow something really special.

Practice Makes Perfect

Lesson planning through game design is not an easy task. Though I've discussed a number of approaches and identified key points for building a game-based course (as well as given advice for avoiding or mitigating various obstacles), no clear roadmaps have been laid down to help interested instructors get started. As every subject will have different requirements, simply providing one or two sample game designs may not get you very far. So instead, in this section I've presented a process you can take to develop any game-based course. Consider the following as a rough guide to help you jumpstart your plans—in just 10 easy steps, of course.

Step 1. Gather your constraints

What are your limitations? Do you have to teach to a test? Are you trying to reach a specific demographic? What will your students' parents say? Do you have an administration to convince? Here is where you compile everything you know about what your game must be—what it will need to teach and who it will need to please. These limitations and considerations will form the backbone of your game because they spell out the minimum requirements for what you must accomplish.

Example. Let's say we're building a game to teach geometry. I'm sure you can easily visualize concerns from parents and administrators as well as the sorts of standardized benchmarks you'll need to hit, so instead of delving into these specifics, let's talk about how this first step can tie into our understanding of brain-based learning. Our desire to achieve a state of relaxed alertness means that our game must be challenging but not frustrating. We need a difficulty curve that keeps our students engaged without feeling threatened. In terms of geometry, a good way to accomplish this might be to have each phase of the game incorporate elements of future chapters that students can take advantage of but don't need to use in order to win (such as instances where knowing the formula for computing the areas of new geometric shapes would be useful but not required). Utilizing orchestrated immersion is a task for Step 2, but we can also start with active processing here by making sure your game is well-balanced and coherent, with logical progressions of knowledge and skill required from your students. Basically, you will need to organize the path your students will take through the game in a manner that makes sense in terms of the game's rules and the course material they'll need to learn through the entire game experience.

Step 2. Define your design

Now that you know what you have to incorporate into your game, it's time to figure out what sort of game you're actually creating. What will allow you to accomplish all the goals and sidestep all the problems you've formulated in Step 1 and still ensure that the game will be fun? Well, we're not quite to fun just yet—instead, ask yourself what sort of game you'd like to make. Is it a new video game or a modification to an existing one? A card game? Perhaps a board game, like Laidlaw created? Once you've chosen your medium, you need to define what kind of game it will be—what sort of genre and play-style will your game have? It could be a strategy game, where students build empires, or an action game where they must make quick decisions and react in real time. Maybe a puzzle game, where they need to complete riddles and use clues to advance, or maybe a story-based adventure game, where interesting characters, plot elements, and settings form the backbone of your students' engagement. Regardless of what you choose, here is where you define the basics of your design and the type of game you'll be making.

Example. For our geometry game, let's say we want to make a card game with a focus on battles—students will try to build a board position by putting down strong cards and using them to attack their opponent's setup. Perhaps you already see a problem—"battles" are an inherently masculine activity. Do we not risk alienating our female students with this format? This is absolutely a potential pitfall, but one that can be incorporated into the design to ultimately improve it. Perhaps the routes to victory are varied, with students able to win not just by attacking their opponents, but by building up their own assets to a state of unassailable renown. Many strategy games allow for cultural, technological, and diplomatic victories alongside military ones—why not yours? Being all-inclusive doesn't necessarily have to dilute your efforts. Instead, it can provide additional depth and engagement. Now, to continue, there may be some light fiction to explain why your students are dueling, but the basic concept will focus on using the competitive nature of the game to increase orchestrated immersion. The cards they collect can teach the concepts of the game in different ways (such as explaining how to find the area of a circle with multiple cards, each with various effects on the game). How the students build their decks and use their knowledge of geometry to battle their opponents should serve to bring the material to life and give the students multiple paths to understanding.

Step 3. Conceptualize your mechanics

How will your game play? What sort of mechanics will it have? Mechanics are the rules of your game—the nuts and bolts of how it's played. Will students roll dice to determine the outcomes of certain events, or will they put numbers into a spreadsheet you've prepared? Will they move pieces on a board and, if so, will they do it as a result of successfully solving a problem, random chance, or simply because it's their turn (and they get two moves per turn)? Basically, how is the game played? Here is where you will create those answers and use them to form the framework of your game.

Example. Our geometry game is a card game—a dueling game. Let's say that students can put down cards by solving geometric problems. The more difficult the problem, the stronger the card. Certain types of cards may require them to solve certain types of problems (monsters require knowledge of area, spells require knowledge of angles, etc.) So in order to build a well-rounded deck, they will need to know a lot of different geometric concepts. Once their deck is constructed, they will draw a hand of cards and then play one card per turn, solving problems you provide in order to charge their spells and summon their creatures. Once in play, these cards can have various effects on the game and may alter the rules in various ways according to their texts. Once a victory condition is met—such as reducing an opponent's "life" to zero or emptying the opponent's deck or something similar—the game is over. As students will need to build a strong deck to be successful and will likely favor more powerful cards, they will need to expand their knowledge of the material to have the best chance of winning, touching most strongly on the tenets of active processing of and orchestrated immersion in the subject matter.

Step 4. Scattershot your ideas

Now it's time to think of various scenarios you'd like to see in your game. Here is where you begin brainstorming all sorts of things you want your students to be able to do, throwing out all kinds of blue-sky, gee-that-would-be-great ideas. Make a big list of everything you want your students to be able to experience—and enjoy—in your game. What are the "moments" you want to capture?

Example. For our geometry game, let's focus on ideas that touch on the core concepts of brain-based learning. Here are a few samples of neat things we could do. We want our game to be social, so let's include a leader board and tournaments with prizes in the form of "rare" cards. Let's also get our students involved by having them submit designs for their own cards. Let's have the game reward players not only for knowledge of geometry, but also strategy and tactics by making their board's position part of the gameplay—perhaps we can have the layout of the cards on the game's board correspond to certain bonuses they might receive. Creating geometric shapes with cards might empower them, but only if they adhere to principles outlined in class (putting cards in the shape of a right triangle will be effective only if their power ratings conform to the Pythagorean Theorem, for instance). Other interesting ideas can be including a campaign of sorts, with students teaming up to match their wits against "boss decks" of your own design. Maybe the teacher could have his or her own "power" deck that the whole class needs to team up to overcome, and victory would only be possible with full knowledge of the course. These are just some interesting examples of how you can expand on your initial concept and build out a really intriguing classroom experience.

Step 5. Distill your successes

By now, you should have a huge list of game ideas: strategies for how your game will be played, the mechanics you'd like to use, the genre and type of game you want to make, and the constraints you're going to need to work around. Now it's time to take the best (and most important) of these ideas and distill them into a working game design. Write out how your game will function to mitigate and address constraints, reach some of your brilliant moments, and work as a result of your mechanics.

Example. What we're going to need to write here is a list of rules. This is basically an expansion of Step 3, when we wrote our first mechanics. Now we're refining them into a playable set of instructions. This list will tell anyone who reads it how your game is meant to be played, and we hope it will incorporate some of those delightful ideas you dreamed up in Step 4. Here is a quick list of things you'll want to put into your rules:

- How do you win the game? What are your players striving to achieve? These could include defeating their opponents, acquiring a goal, making a lot of money, achieving something worthwhile, and so on.

- What can players do when they take their turns? What actions will the players take when they are "in the spotlight"? Do they roll dice, play cards, solve problems, write notes in a ledger, create star charts, or something else?

- How do they accomplish their goals? What are the tools players will have available to them? This question deals with the systems they'll use—or come into conflict with—as they play your game. For our geometry game, our players will solve geometry problems in order to play cards that will allow them to compete against their opponents. How those mechanics function is what you need to answer here.

Step 6. Construct your prototype

You have a design document—now it's time to turn it into a prototype of the game. If this is a small-scale, in-house board game or something similar, this stage won't be too demanding. Basically, what you're going to do is bring your idea to life; lay out the basic, untested, and raw steps of gameplay and see how they function. The end result should be something of a "vertical slice"—a perfect example of how your game works in a very small, all-encompassing dose. Someone should be able to play this slice for fifteen minutes and get an idea of how a semester's worth of gaming will feel.

Example. In the case of our geometry game, the vertical slice/prototype might be two decks' worth of cards, focusing on a small portion of the overall course. Playing it should give testers an idea of how the total course will play out, without you having to create hundreds of cards and distill dozens of lessons into them. A vertical slice is a way for you—and whoever is giving you feedback—to get an idea of how the full game will work before you spend the time making the full game.

Step 7. Field-test your vertical slice/prototype

Ask your friends, family, students, neighbors, coworkers … anyone and everyone who is willing, to give you feedback on what you've created. Lead them into a short test session with the goal of gathering feedback and tweaking your designs—and be prepared to revamp a lot of what you've created as other people begin mucking around in and making suggestions to improve your masterpiece.

Example. You need to go into your test knowing precisely what you want to discover, and it needs to be a lot more specific than asking, "Is it fun?" Some very important types of feedback to look for are the following:

> **Ease of Use.** How hard is your game to understand? Is it easy to pick up and play? Do your players get confused quickly, or do they jump right in?

> **Depth of Play.** Rather than asking if your game is fun, you might want to see if it requires *deep enough* thought processes to play. Do your players need to think in various ways to engage with it successfully? Can they see themselves spending more time with it and discovering new strategies? Do they want to get better at playing it? Chess is one of the ultimate examples here; easy to learn, a lifetime to master.

> **Effectiveness.** Does your game actually teach the subject? Do students who play it come away with knowledge of the material or, at the very least, an increased desire to learn the material?

> **Viability.** Can this become a full game as envisioned under your constraints? Is the amount of work too much for you? If there are changes to incorporate or original elements that didn't make it into this prototype, will not including them derail your project?

Step 8. Incorporate your feedback

Consult your list of all aspects of the game that didn't work right, all the ideas you scrapped because a few people didn't like them, and all the compliments and complaints that were voiced. This is where some original ideas you'd still like to use get blended into your designs. Tweak your documents, remake your mechanics, and rebalance your numbers now because these adjustments will be harder to make as time goes on.

Example. This step touches on just about everything that's come before—it's where you tie it all together and set down the blueprint for the final version of your game. You may end up reusing a lot of what you created for your prototype, or you may have to throw everything out, but the goal here is to make changes when it's easy. Having to go back and retool a finished game is always much harder than building in those tweaks and improvements from the start.

Step 9. Build your game

Time for the long haul. Now you need to build everything out—and make it enough to fill a semester. This is where you create the game in its entirety, write out your rules, your lesson plans, and your schedules. At the end of this step, you should have a working game inspired by your imagination and refined by feedback.

Example. There are hundreds of finished educational games out there beyond the ones described in this chapter. I highly recommend searching online for samples of educational games to compare against your own creation here—you will be astounded at the variety returned by a simple search for something like "great educational games." Most of the commercial products you'll find will be aimed at entertaining first and probably focusing on a very narrow subject, but the production values and wholeness of their products will be helpful to notice as you align your own goals. For a few quick examples, look at Peaceable Kingdom's board games, which attempt to teach cooperation to young children, the Nobel Prize organization's collection of educational video games, and *Lure of the Labyrinth,* by Learning Games to Go.

Step 10. Polish your product

Of course, we're not done yet. This is the step you may find yourself on for a very long time, because while your game is complete, it's probably still a little rough around the edges. You're going to need to work at it constantly, tweaking and tuning as time goes on and your students explore the systems you've created. They may find ways to "break" your mechanics (i.e., exploiting or otherwise undermining your systems to gain an unfair advantage, such as a student who figures out how to generate infinite gold with an unexpected combination of moves), or they may suggest incredible new features you feel you have to add. Modifying your game in response to such feedback will be an ongoing task, and this step is here to ensure that you are always open to new ideas and problems. Your game may be built, but there will always be room for improvements—rejoice in that fact, as it means you have built something students want to use and enhance!

And in the End...

It should be clear by now that game-based courses may be complicated endeavors, filled with potential snares and pitfalls to bring down the unwary. What I would like to leave you with, however, is the promise they represent for the future of education. In terms of totally online, hybrid, and traditional courses, games hold the potential to revolutionize your classroom. Video games won't always be around (Hirumi, 2010)—they'll transition to something bigger, brasher, and probably more controversial. Quality education, however, will always be needed, and the principles of game design and development, so closely linked to the principles of brain-based learning, remain timeless tools to be used in that regard.

All it takes is a moment of distance from the hubbub of the Internet and the more lurid spectacles of the video game industry to realize that the mechanisms at work in driving users' attention to these things aren't inextricably linked to the more unsavory stereotypes with which they are associated. Instead, games represent something we can learn from—something so primal and embedded in our psyches that the ideal techniques for building them are nearly note-perfect representations of what brain-based learning tells us we should do to keep kids engaged in their lessons.

We can learn a lot from games and, by the same token, so can our students.

References

Atkinson, T., & Hirumi, A. (2010). The game brain: What does the brain tell us about playing games in schools? In A. Hirumi (Ed.), *Playing games in school: Using simulations and videogames for primary and secondary education* (pp. 57–73). Eugene, OR: International Society for Technology in Education.

Caine, R., & Caine, G. (1997). *Unleashing the power of perceptual change: The potential of brain-based teaching.* Alexandria, VA: Association for Supervision and Curriculum Development.

Caine, R. N., Caine, G., McClintic, C., & Klimek, K. (2004). *12 Brain/mind learning principles in action: The field book for making connections, teaching, and the human brain.* Thousand Oaks, CA: Corwin .

Carr, N. (2010). *The Shallows: What the Internet is doing to our brains.* New York, NY: W. W. Norton.

Charles, D., & McAlister, M. (2004, September). Integrating ideas about invisible playgrounds from play theory into online educational digital games. In M. Rauterberg (Ed.), Lecture Notes in Computer Science: Vol. 3166. Entertainment Computing—ICEC 2004: Third International Conference, Eindhoven, The Netherlands, Proceedings. (pp. 598–601). Retrieved from http://books.google.com/books?id=BaUC776zbOoC&lpg

Christensen, C. (2008). *Disrupting class: How disruptive innovation will change the way the world learns.* New York, NY: McGraw-Hill.

Csikszentmihalyi, M. (1990). *Flow: The psychology of optimal experience.* New York, NY: HarperCollins.

Farr, R. (2010, November). A study of instructional effectiveness: Conspiracy code: Intensive reading. Bloomington, IN: Educational Research Institute of America. Retrieved from www.flvs.net/areas/aboutus/Documents/CCIR%20Efficacy%20Studies.pdf

Federation of American Scientists. (2006). Harnessing the power of video games for learning. The National Summit on Educational Games, October 25, 2005. Washington, DC: Author. Retrieved from www.fas.org/gamesummit/Resources/Summit%20on%20Educational%20Games.pdf

Hirumi, A. (Ed.). (2010). *Playing games in school: Video games and simulations for primary and secondary education.* Eugene, OR: International Society for Technology in Education.

Holland, W., Jenkins, H., & Squire, K. (2003). Theory by design. In M. J. P. Wolf & B. Perron (Eds.), *The video game theory reader* (pp. 25–46). New York, NY: Routledge.

Jenkins, H., & Squire, K. (2003). Understanding Civilization (III). *Computer Games Magazine, 154*(September). Retrieved from www.educationarcade.org/node/113

Lemmens, J. S., Bushman, B. J., & Konijn, E. A. (2006). The appeal of violent video games to lower educated aggressive adolescent boys from two countries. *CyberPsychology & Behavior, 9*(5), 638–641.

Los Alamos National Lab. (2011, July). Imagine Education recognized for innovative approach to math education [Press release]. Retrieved from www.lanl.gov/newsroom/news-releases/2011/July/07.20-imagine-education.php

Sheffield, B. (2005). What games have to teach us: An interview with James Paul Gee. *Game Developer, 12*(10), 4.

Sousa, D. A. (2001). *How the brain learns: A classroom teacher's guide* (2nd ed.). Thousand Oaks, CA: Corwin.

Van Eck, R. (2006). Digital game-based learning: It's not just the digital natives who are restless. EDUCAUSE *Review, 41*(2), 16–30. Retrieved from http://net.educause.edu/ir/library/pdf/erm0620

APPENDIX

ISTE's National Educational Technology Standards

ISTE's NETS for Students (NETS·S)

All K–12 students should be prepared to meet the following standards and performance indicators.

1. **Creativity and Innovation**

   Students demonstrate creative thinking, construct knowledge, and develop innovative products and processes using technology. Students:

   a. apply existing knowledge to generate new ideas, products, or processes

   b. create original works as a means of personal or group expression

   c. use models and simulations to explore complex systems and issues

   d. identify trends and forecast possibilities

2. **Communication and Collaboration**

   Students use digital media and environments to communicate and work collaboratively, including at a distance, to support individual learning and contribute to the learning of others. Students:

   a. interact, collaborate, and publish with peers, experts, or others employing a variety of digital environments and media

   b. communicate information and ideas effectively to multiple audiences using a variety of media and formats

   c. develop cultural understanding and global awareness by engaging with learners of other cultures

   d. contribute to project teams to produce original works or solve problems

3. **Research and Information Fluency**

   Students apply digital tools to gather, evaluate, and use information. Students:

   a. plan strategies to guide inquiry

   b. locate, organize, analyze, evaluate, synthesize, and ethically use information from a variety of sources and media

   c. evaluate and select information sources and digital tools based on the appropriateness to specific tasks

   d. process data and report results

4. **Critical Thinking, Problem Solving, and Decision Making**

   Students use critical-thinking skills to plan and conduct research, manage projects, solve problems, and make informed decisions using appropriate digital tools and resources. Students:

   a. identify and define authentic problems and significant questions for investigation

   b. plan and manage activities to develop a solution or complete a project

   c. collect and analyze data to identify solutions and make informed decisions

   d. use multiple processes and diverse perspectives to explore alternative solutions

5. **Digital Citizenship**

   Students understand human, cultural, and societal issues related to technology and practice legal and ethical behavior. Students:

   a. advocate and practice the safe, legal, and responsible use of information and technology

   b. exhibit a positive attitude toward using technology that supports collaboration, learning, and productivity

   c. demonstrate personal responsibility for lifelong learning

   d. exhibit leadership for digital citizenship

6. **Technology Operations and Concepts**

   Students demonstrate a sound understanding of technology concepts, systems, and operations. Students:

   a. understand and use technology systems

   b. select and use applications effectively and productively

   c. troubleshoot systems and applications

   d. transfer current knowledge to the learning of new technologies

© 2007 International Society for Technology in Education (ISTE), www.iste.org. All rights reserved.

ISTE's NETS for Teachers (NETS·T)

All classroom teachers should be prepared to meet the following standards and performance indicators.

1. **Facilitate and Inspire Student Learning and Creativity**

   Teachers use their knowledge of subject matter, teaching and learning, and technology to facilitate experiences that advance student learning, creativity, and innovation in both face-to-face and virtual environments. Teachers:

   a. promote, support, and model creative and innovative thinking and inventiveness

   b. engage students in exploring real-world issues and solving authentic problems using digital tools and resources

   c. promote student reflection using collaborative tools to reveal and clarify students' conceptual understanding and thinking, planning, and creative processes

   d. model collaborative knowledge construction by engaging in learning with students, colleagues, and others in face-to-face and virtual environments

2. **Design and Develop Digital-Age Learning Experiences and Assessments**

   Teachers design, develop, and evaluate authentic learning experiences and assessments incorporating contemporary tools and resources to maximize content learning in context and to develop the knowledge, skills, and attitudes identified in the NETS·S. Teachers:

   a. design or adapt relevant learning experiences that incorporate digital tools and resources to promote student learning and creativity

   b. develop technology-enriched learning environments that enable all students to pursue their individual curiosities and become active participants in setting their own educational goals, managing their own learning, and assessing their own progress

   c. customize and personalize learning activities to address students' diverse learning styles, working strategies, and abilities using digital tools and resources

   d. provide students with multiple and varied formative and summative assessments aligned with content and technology standards and use resulting data to inform learning and teaching

3. **Model Digital-Age Work and Learning**

   Teachers exhibit knowledge, skills, and work processes representative of an innovative professional in a global and digital society. Teachers:

   a. demonstrate fluency in technology systems and the transfer of current knowledge to new technologies and situations

    b.   collaborate with students, peers, parents, and community members using digital tools and resources to support student success and innovation

    c.   communicate relevant information and ideas effectively to students, parents, and peers using a variety of digital-age media and formats

    d.   model and facilitate effective use of current and emerging digital tools to locate, analyze, evaluate, and use information resources to support research and learning

4. Promote and Model Digital Citizenship and Responsibility

Teachers understand local and global societal issues and responsibilities in an evolving digital culture and exhibit legal and ethical behavior in their professional practices. Teachers:

    a.   advocate, model, and teach safe, legal, and ethical use of digital information and technology, including respect for copyright, intellectual property, and the appropriate documentation of sources

    b.   address the diverse needs of all learners by using learner-centered strategies and providing equitable access to appropriate digital tools and resources

    c.   promote and model digital etiquette and responsible social interactions related to the use of technology and information

    d.   develop and model cultural understanding and global awareness by engaging with colleagues and students of other cultures using digital-age communication and collaboration tools

5. Engage in Professional Growth and Leadership

Teachers continuously improve their professional practice, model lifelong learning, and exhibit leadership in their school and professional community by promoting and demonstrating the effective use of digital tools and resources. Teachers:

    a.   participate in local and global learning communities to explore creative applications of technology to improve student learning

    b.   exhibit leadership by demonstrating a vision of technology infusion, participating in shared decision making and community building, and developing the leadership and technology skills of others

    c.   evaluate and reflect on current research and professional practice on a regular basis to make effective use of existing and emerging digital tools and resources in support of student learning

    d.   contribute to the effectiveness, vitality, and self-renewal of the teaching profession and of their school and community

ISTE's NETS for Administrators (NETS·A)

All school administrators should be prepared to meet the following standards and performance indicators.

1. Visionary Leadership

Educational Administrators inspire and lead development and implementation of a shared vision for comprehensive integration of technology to promote excellence and support transformation throughout the organization. Educational Administrators:

a. inspire and facilitate among all stakeholders a shared vision of purposeful change that maximizes use of digital-age resources to meet and exceed learning goals, support effective instructional practice, and maximize performance of district and school leaders

b. engage in an ongoing process to develop, implement, and communicate technology-infused strategic plans aligned with a shared vision

c. advocate on local, state, and national levels for policies, programs, and funding to support implementation of a technology-infused vision and strategic plan

2. Digital-Age Learning Culture

Educational Administrators create, promote, and sustain a dynamic, digital-age learning culture that provides a rigorous, relevant, and engaging education for all students. Educational Administrators:

a. ensure instructional innovation focused on continuous improvement of digital-age learning

b. model and promote the frequent and effective use of technology for learning

c. provide learner-centered environments equipped with technology and learning resources to meet the individual, diverse needs of all learners

d. ensure effective practice in the study of technology and its infusion across the curriculum

e. promote and participate in local, national, and global learning communities that stimulate innovation, creativity, and digital-age collaboration

3. Excellence in Professional Practice

Educational Administrators promote an environment of professional learning and innovation that empowers educators to enhance student learning through the infusion of contemporary technologies and digital resources. Educational Administrators:

a. allocate time, resources, and access to ensure ongoing professional growth in technology fluency and integration

b. facilitate and participate in learning communities that stimulate, nurture, and support administrators, faculty, and staff in the study and use of technology

c. promote and model effective communication and collaboration among stakeholders using digital-age tools

d. stay abreast of educational research and emerging trends regarding effective use of technology and encourage evaluation of new technologies for their potential to improve student learning

4. Systemic Improvement

Educational Administrators provide digital-age leadership and management to continuously improve the organization through the effective use of information and technology resources. Educational Administrators:

a. lead purposeful change to maximize the achievement of learning goals through the appropriate use of technology and media-rich resources

b. collaborate to establish metrics, collect and analyze data, interpret results, and share findings to improve staff performance and student learning

c. recruit and retain highly competent personnel who use technology creatively and proficiently to advance academic and operational goals

d. establish and leverage strategic partnerships to support systemic improvement

e. establish and maintain a robust infrastructure for technology including integrated, interoperable technology systems to support management, operations, teaching, and learning

5. Digital Citizenship

Educational Administrators model and facilitate understanding of social, ethical, and legal issues and responsibilities related to an evolving digital culture. Educational Administrators:

a. ensure equitable access to appropriate digital tools and resources to meet the needs of all learners

b. promote, model, and establish policies for safe, legal, and ethical use of digital information and technology

c. promote and model responsible social interactions related to the use of technology and information

d. model and facilitate the development of a shared cultural understanding and involvement in global issues through the use of contemporary communication and collaboration tools

Index